Peter Lynch

&

John Rothchild

Learn to Earn

A Beginner's
Guide
to the
Basics of
Investing
and
Business

A FIRESIDE BOOK

New York London Toronto Sydney Tokyo Singapore

FIRESIDE
Rockefeller Center
1230 Avenue of the Americas
New York, NY 10020

Manufactured in the United States of America

10 9 8 7 6 5 4 3 2 1

Library of Congress Cataloging-in-Publication Data
Lynch, Peter (Peter S.)
Learn to earn : a beginner's guide to the basics of investing and
business / Peter Lynch & John Rothchild.
p.   cm.
Includes index.
1. Investments—United States.   2. Corporations—United States—
Finance.   3. Capitalism.   I. Rothchild, John.   II. Title.
HG4910.L95   1996
658.15′2—dc20   95-47460
CIP

ISBN 0-684-81163-4

To the Lynch children
(Mary, Annie, Beth),
the Rothchild children
(Chauncey, Berns, Sascha),
and all beginning investors,
young and old.

Acknowledgments

The following people deserve special mention for the research and fact-checking help they provided on this book: Kathy Johnson, Charlene Niles, Deborah Pont, all courtesy of *Worth* magazine; Peggy Malaspina and her associates at Malaspina Communications: Lyn Hadden, Karen Perkuhn, Elizabeth Pendergast, and Susan Posner.

From Fidelity and its various resources: Robert Hill, Bart Grenier, Suzanne Connelly, Tim Burke, Evelyn Flynn, Shirley Guptill, Bob Beckwitt, Julian Lim, Debbie Clark, Jeffrey Todd, and Denise Russell. From the Securities Research Corporation: Donald Jones and his staff.

We'd also like to thank the staffs at the Wellesley Public Library and the Babson College Library; Joan Morrissey at St. Agnes School; David Berson at Fannie Mae; Nancy Smith, director of investor education at the Securities and Exchange Commission; our two agents, Doe Coover and Elizabeth Darhansoff; our editor, Bob Bender, and his assistant, Johanna Li.

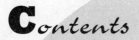

Contents

Preface

The junior high schools and high schools of America have forgotten to teach one of the most important courses of all. Investing. This is a glaring omission. History we teach, but not the part about the great march of capitalism and the role that companies have played in changing (and mostly improving) the way we live. Math we teach, but not the part about how simple arithmetic can be used to tell the story of a company and help us figure out whether it will succeed or fail in what it's trying to do and whether we might profit from owning shares of its stock.

Home economics we teach: how to sew, how to cook a turkey, even how to stick to a budget and balance a checkbook. What's often left out is how saving money from an early age is the key to future prosperity, how investing that money in stocks is the best move a person can make, next to owning a house, and how the earlier you start saving and investing in stocks, the better you'll do in the long run.

Patriotism we teach, but we talk more about armies and wars, politics and government, than we do about the millions of businesses, large and small, that are the key to our prosperity and our strength as a nation. Without investors to provide the money to start new companies that hire new workers, or to help older companies grow bigger, become more efficient, and pay higher wages, the world as we know it would collapse and there'd be no jobs for anybody and the United States would be out of luck.

In the past five years, a tremendous thing has happened in what used to be called the communist bloc, the countries behind the Iron Curtain. The citizens of those countries have risen up and overthrown their governments and sent their communist leaders packing, in the hope that someday they can improve their lot in life. Democracy is among the things they want, as are freedom of speech and freedom of worship, but up there with the Bill of Rights freedoms, they also want free enterprise. That includes the right to make things, sell things, and buy things in stores, the right to own a house, an apartment, a car, or a business, which until recently, perhaps half the world's population was not allowed to do.

The Russians and the Eastern Europeans marched, demonstrated, held strikes, organized, agitated, and fought as hard as they could to get the economic system that we have already. Many people went to jail for this cause, and many lost their lives. Yet in our own schools we don't teach the basics of how this economic system works, and what's good about it, and how you can take advantage of it by becoming an investor.

Investing is fun. It's interesting. Learning about it can be an enriching experience, in more ways than one. It can put you on the road to prosperity for the rest of your life, yet most people don't begin to get the hang of investing until they reach middle age, when their eyes start to go bad and their waistlines expand. Then they discover the advantages of owning stocks, and they wish they'd known about them earlier.

In our society, it's been the men who've handled most of the finances, and the women who've stood by and watched men botch things up. There's nothing about investing that a woman can't do as well as a man. Also, you don't get the knack for it through the chromosomes. So when you hear somebody say, "He's a natural-born investor," don't believe it. The natural-born investor is a myth.

The principles of finance are simple and easily grasped. Principle number one is that savings equals investment. Money that you keep in a piggy bank or a cookie jar doesn't count as an investment, but any time you put money in the bank, or buy a savings bond, or buy stock in a company, you're investing. Somebody else will take that money and use it to build new stores, new houses, or new factories, which creates jobs. More jobs means more paychecks for more workers. If those workers can manage to set aside some of their earnings to save and invest, the whole process begins all over again.

It's the same story for every family, every company, every country. Whether it's Belgium or Botswana, China or Chile, Mozambique or Mexico, General Motors or General Electric, your family or mine, those who save and invest for the future will be more prosperous in the future than those who run out and spend all the money they get their hands on. Why is the United States such a rich country? At one point, we had one of the highest savings rates in the world.

A lot of people must have told you by now that it's important to get a good education, so you can find a promising career that pays you a decent wage. But they may not have told you that in the long run, it's not just how much money you make that will determine your future prosperity. It's how much of that money you put to work by saving it and investing it.

The best time to get started investing is when you're young, as we'll discuss in more detail later. The more time you have to let your investments grow, the bigger the fortune you'll end up with. But this introduction to finance is not only for young people. It's for beginning investors of all ages who find stocks confusing and who haven't yet had the chance to learn the basics.

People are living much longer than they used to, which means they'll be paying bills for a lot longer than they used to. If a couple makes it to sixty-five, there's a good chance they'll make it to eighty-five, and if they make it to eighty-five, there's a decent chance one of them will reach ninety-five. In order to cover their living expenses they'll need extra money, and the surest way to get it is by investing.

It's not too late to start investing at age sixty-five. Today's sixty-five-year-olds might be looking at twenty-five more years during which their money can continue to grow, to give them the wherewithal to pay the twenty-five years' worth of extra bills.

When you're fifteen or twenty, it's hard to imagine the day will come when you'll turn sixty-five, but if you get in the habit of saving and investing, by then your money will have been working in your favor for fifty years. Fifty years of putting money away will produce astonishing results, even if you only put away a small amount at a time.

The more you invest the better off you'll be, and the nation will be better off as well, because your money will help create new businesses and more jobs.

INTRODUCTION

The Companies Around Us

When a group of people goes into business together, they usually form a company. Most business in the world is done by companies. The word "company" comes from a Latin word that means "companion."

The formal name for a company is "corporation." Corporation comes from "corpus," another Latin word, meaning "body," in this case, a body of people who join together to conduct business. "Corpse" also comes from "corpus," although this has nothing to do with the subject at hand, since corpses are unable to do business.

To form a corporation is easy. All it takes is paying a small fee and filing a few papers in the state in which you want to maintain a legal address. Delaware is the most popular choice, because the laws there are favorable to business, but thousands of new corporations are formed every year in every state. Whenever you see an "inc." attached to the end of the name of a business, it means that company has filed the papers to become a corporation. "Inc." is short for "incorporated."

In the eyes of the law, a corporation is a separate individual that can be punished for bad behavior, usually by the imposition of a fine. That's the main reason owners of a business go to the trouble of getting incorporated. If they do something wrong and they get sued, the corporation takes the rap and they get off the hook. Imagine if you borrowed your parents' car without permission and ran it into a tree, how much better you'd feel if you were incorporated.

Do you remember the *Exxon Valdez* disaster in Alaska, when an oil tanker ran aground and spilled 11 million gallons of oil into Prince William Sound? This created a huge mess that took months to clean up. The tanker belonged to Exxon, America's third-largest company. At the time, Exxon had hundreds of thousands of shareholders who were part owners of the business.

If Exxon hadn't been incorporated, all those people could have gotten sued individually, and lost their life savings on account of an oil spill that wasn't their fault. Even if Exxon were found innocent, they would have had to pay the legal bills to defend themselves—in this country you're innocent until proven guilty, but you pay the lawyers either way.

That's the beauty of the corporation. It can be sued, as can its managers and directors, but the owners—the shareholders—are protected. They can't be sued in the first place. In England, companies put the word "limited" after their names. This indicates that the liability of the owners is limited, just the way it is in U.S. companies. (If anybody ever asks you what the "limited" means, now you've got the answer.)

This is a crucial safeguard of our capitalist system, because if shareholders could be sued whenever a company made a mistake, people like you and me would be afraid to buy shares and become investors. Why would we want to run the risk of being held responsible for another big oil spill, or a rat hair in a hamburger, or the endless variety of mishaps that occur in business every day? Without limited liability, nobody would want to buy a single share of stock.

Private Companies and Public Companies

The vast majority of businesses in this country are private. They are owned by one person or a small group of people, and more often than not, the ownership is kept in the family. You can find examples of private companies up and down the block on every main street in every village and town, and scattered throughout the cities of America and the world. These are the barbershops, hair salons, shoe-repair outlets, bicycle shops, baseball-card stores, candy stores, junk stores, antique stores, second-hand stores, vegetable stands, bowling alleys, bars, jewelry stores, used-car lots, and local mom-and-pop restaurants. Most hospitals and universities are private as well.

What makes these businesses private is that the general public can't invest in them. If you spend the night at the Sleepy Holler motel, and you're impressed with the place and how it's run, you can't very well knock on the manager's door and demand to be made a partner. Unless you're related to the owners, or the owner has a son or daughter who wants to marry you, your chances of getting a share in this business are close to zero.

Look at the difference when you spend the night at a Hilton or a Marriott and you're impressed with those places. You don't have to knock on any doors, or marry anybody's son or daughter to become an owner. All you have to do is call a stockbroker and put in an order to buy shares. Hilton and Marriott sell their shares in the stock market. Any company that does this is called a public company.

(Although there are more private companies than public companies in America, the public companies are generally much bigger, which is why most people work for public companies.)

In a public company, you and your parents, your aunt Sally, or the neighbors down the block can all buy shares and become owners automatically. Once you've paid your money, you get a certificate, called a stock certificate, that proves you're one of the owners. This piece of paper has real value. You can sell it whenever you want.

A public company is the most democratic institution in the world, when it comes to who can be an owner. It's an example of true equal opportunity. It doesn't matter what color you are, what sex, what religion, what sign of the zodiac, or what nationality, or whether you have bunions, pimples, or bad breath.

Even if the chairman of the board of McDonald's holds a grudge against you, he can't stop you from becoming an owner of McDonald's. The shares are out there in the stock market, being sold five days a week, six-and-a-half hours a day, and whoever has the cash and pays the price can buy as many as he or she wants. What's true for McDonald's is also true for the thirteen thousand other public companies in the United States today—a list that continues to grow. Public companies are everywhere, and they surround you from morning to night. You can't get away from them.

What do Nike, Chrysler, General Motors, the Gap, the Boston Celtics, United Airlines, Staples, Wendy's, Coca-Cola, Harley-Davidson, Sunglass Hut, Marvel Comics, Kodak, Fuji, Wal-Mart, Rubbermaid, Time Warner, and Winnebago have in common? They're all public companies. You can play the alphabet game, A to Z, naming a public company for each letter.

Inside the house, down the street, around the school, and through the malls, you can't help running into a large crowd of them. Nearly everything you eat, wear, read, listen to, ride in, lie on, or gargle with is made by one. Perfume to penknives, hot tubs to hot dogs, nuts to nail polish are made by businesses that you can own.

The sheets on your bed might come from Westpoint Stevens; the clock radio from General Electric; the toilet, sink, and faucets from American Standard or Eljer; the toothpaste and shampoo from Procter & Gamble; the razors from Gillette; the lotions from the Body Shop; the toothbrushes from Colgate-Palmolive.

Put on your Fruit-of-the-Loom underwear, the skirts and slacks made by Hagar or Farah that you bought from the Gap or the Limited, sewn from fabric that came from Galey and Lord out of fibers produced by Du Pont Chemical. Lace up your Reeboks or the Keds you bought at the Foot Locker (a division of Woolworth), where you paid the bill with a Citibank VISA card. Already, you're involved with dozens of public companies, and you haven't gotten to the breakfast table.

There, you'll find the Cheerios supplied by General Mills; the

Pop Tarts and Eggo waffles supplied by Kelloggs; the Tropicana orange juice by Seagram, better known for whiskey than for fruit drinks; the Entenmann's brought to you by Philip Morris, which also produces Kraft cheese and Oscar Mayer hot dogs in addition to their Marlboros. Your toast may pop out of a toaster from Toastmaster, which has been in business since the 1920s and is still going strong.

The coffeepot, microwave, stove, and refrigerator are made by public companies, and the larger supermarkets where you or your parents buy the food are public as well.

Maybe you ride to school in a bus built by General Motors out of steel from Bethlehem Steel, with the windshield glass coming from PPG Industries, the tires from Goodyear, and the wheels made by Superior Industries from aluminum that Superior gets from Alcoa. The gas for the bus comes from Exxon, Texaco, or one of the many public oil companies. The bus is insured by Aetna. The bus itself may be owned by Laidlaw, a company that runs the bus system in many school districts.

The books in your book bag have likely been published by one of the publicly owned book companies, such as McGraw-Hill, Houghton Mifflin, or Simon & Schuster, the publishers of the book you're reading right now. Simon & Schuster is a division of Paramount, which until recently also owned Madison Square Garden, the New York Knicks basketball team, and the New York Rangers hockey team. In 1994, another public company, Viacom, swallowed Paramount in a takeover.

Takeovers happen all the time in business. On Wall Street, there are more raids and conquests than you'll see in any war movie made by Paramount; or by Universal Studios, a division of MCA that got taken over by the Japanese; or by MCA itself, which is now a part of Seagram.

Maybe you eat the school lunch that's cooked on an Amana Radar range made by Raytheon, the same company that makes the Patriot missile. Or maybe you drive off campus to the nearest publicly owned hamburger joints: McDonald's, Wendy's, or Burger King, which is a division of Grand Metropolitian, a British public company. Coke and Pepsi come from public companies, and Pepsi also owns Taco Bell, Pizza Hut, Frito-Lay, and Kentucky Fried Chicken, so Pepsi shareholders invest in all of these at once.

Hershey bars, Wrigley's gum, Tootsie Rolls, and most of the candy in vending machines are produced by public companies, except for Snickers candy, made by the Mars family.

When you get home in the afternoon and pick up the phone to call your boyfriend or girlfriend, you're using the services of at least one publicly traded phone company, and if it's a long-distance call, you're using three: the "Baby Bell" (NYNEX, PacTel, etc.) that serves your neighborhood; the long-distance carrier (Sprint, MCI, or the original "Ma Bell," AT&T) that carries the call out of town; and another "Baby Bell" at the other end of the line.

You can buy stock in any or all of these companies, as well as in the supporting cast of suppliers of cables and switches, companies that make and launch telecommunications satellites, and companies that manufacture the phones themselves.

Your TV set is made by a public company, most likely Japanese. If you've got cable, it's a good bet your cable company is public. Of the three major networks, CBS was recently taken over by Westinghouse, NBC is owned by General Electric, and ABC is merging with Disney. Westinghouse, General Electric, and Disney are all public companies, and so is Turner Broadcasting, which owns and operates CNN and has agreed to merge with Time Warner.

You can invest in *Jeopardy*, *Wheel of Fortune*, and *Oprah* by buying shares in King World, a public company that syndicates those three shows, among others. You can invest in *The Simpsons* or in *Cops* by buying shares in Rupert Murdoch's Newscorp. Newscorp owns Twentieth Century Fox Television—the Fox network—which in turn owns these two shows. Nickelodeon, *Nick at Night*, and MTV belong to Viacom, the parent company of Blockbuster Video.

Most of the products advertised on TV are made by public companies. Many of these ads are written and produced by public ad agencies such as the Interpublic Group.

It's easier to rattle off one thousand names of big-time companies that are public than it is to name ten that are still private. While there's no shortage of mom-and-pop businesses that are private, when you get to the major leagues, it's hard to find a company that doesn't sell shares to the public. As already mentioned, the Mars company, which makes Mars bars, Milky Way, and Snickers, is private; so is Levi Strauss, the blue jeans manufacturer. A few insurance giants—John Hancock, for instance—are mutual companies, but maybe not for long.

In almost every chain of stores or fast-food outlets you can think of, every major manufacturer, every company with a brand-name product, you can be an owner. It's not as expensive as you might imagine. In fact, for slightly more than the price of a one-day pass to the Magic Kingdom, you can become part owner of the entire Disney empire, and for the same price as twenty Big Macs plus fries, you can become an owner of McDonald's, along with a lot of big shots on Wall Street.

No matter how old you are or how many shares of stock you'll buy in your lifetime, it's always a thrill to walk into a McDonald's, a Toys R Us, or a Circuit City and watch the customers lining up to buy the merchandise, knowing that you've got a piece of the action and that some smidgeon of the profits will end up in your pocket. When you buy a VCR from Circuit City or rent a video from Blockbuster, if you're an owner of either of these companies, you're actually spending money for your own benefit.

This is an important part of our way of life that the Founding Fathers couldn't have dreamed up. From sea to shining sea, over 50 million men, women, and children have become part owners in thirteen thousand different public companies. Being a shareholder is the greatest method ever invented to allow masses of people to participate in the growth and prosperity of a country. It's a two-way street. When a company sells shares, it uses the money to open new stores, or build new factories, or upgrade its merchandise, so it can sell more products to more customers and increase its profits. And as the company gets bigger and more prosperous, its shares become more valuable, so the investors are rewarded for putting their money to such good use.

Meanwhile, a company that prospers can afford to give pay raises to its workers and move them up the line to bigger and more important jobs. It will also pay more taxes on its increased profits, so the government will have more money to spend on schools, roads, and other projects that benefit society. This whole beneficial chain of events begins when people like you invest in a company.

Investors are the first link in the capitalist chain. The more money you can manage to save, and the more shares you buy in companies, the better off you're likely to be, because if you pick your companies wisely and don't get impatient, your shares will be worth a lot more in the future than they were on the day you bought them.

ONE

A Short History of Capitalism

The Dawn of Capitalism

Capitalism happens when people make things and sell them for money. Or if they don't make things, they provide services for money. For much of human history, capitalism was an alien concept, because the bulk of the world's population never got their hands on money. Over thousands of years, the average person lived out his or her life without buying a single item.

People worked as serfs, slaves, or servants, for masters who owned the land and everything on it. In return, the workers were given free room in a hut and a tiny plot of ground where they could grow their own vegetables. But they didn't get a paycheck.

Nobody complained about working for zero pay, because there was no place to spend it. Once in a while, a pack of traveling salesmen would come through town and set up a market, but a market was an isolated event. The kings, queens, princes, princesses, dukes, earls, and so forth, who owned all the property— buildings, furniture, animals, ox carts, everything from gold jewelry to pots and pans—kept it in the family. It wouldn't have occurred to them to sell off a piece of land, even if they could make a big profit and have less grass to mow. There were no "for sale" signs in front of castles. The only ways to acquire real estate were to inherit it or to take it by force.

In many parts of the world, since the earliest days of Judaism and continuing with Christianity, business for profit was an X-rated activity, and lending money and charging interest could get you kicked out of the church or the synagogue and guarantee you an eternal spot in hell. Bankers had an unsavory reputation, and people had to sneak around and visit them on the sly. The idea of benefiting from a transaction, or getting ahead in life, was regarded as selfish, immoral, and counter to God's plan for an orderly universe. Today, everybody wants to improve his or her lot, but if you had lived in the Middle Ages and you said your goal was to "get ahead" or to "better yourself," your friends would have given you blank looks. The concept of getting ahead didn't exist.

If you want more details about what life was like before there were markets and before people worked for a paycheck and had the freedom to spend it, read the first chapter of Robert Heilbroner's classic book *The Worldly Philosophers*. It's a lot more fun than it sounds.

By the late 1700s, the world had opened up for business with brisk trade between nations, and markets were cropping up everywhere. Enough money was in circulation and enough people could buy things that merchants were making a nice living. This new merchant class of shopkeepers, peddlers, shippers, and traders was becoming richer and more powerful than princes and dukes with all their real estate and their armies. Bankers came out of the closet, to make loans.

Our Pioneer Investors

The history books give many reasons for America's great success—the favorable climate, the rich soil, the wide-open spaces, the Bill of Rights, the ingenious political system, the nonstop flow of hardworking immigrants, the oceans on each side that protect us from invaders. Backyard inventors, dreamers and schemers, banks, money, and investors also deserve a place on this list.

In the opening chapter of our story as a nation, we read about native Indians, French trappers, Spanish conquistadores, sailors who sailed in the wrong direction, soldiers of fortune, explorers in coonskin caps, and Pilgrims at the first Thanksgiving dinner. But behind the scenes, somebody had to pay the bills for the ships, the food, and all the expenses for these adventures. Most of this money came out of the pockets of English, Dutch, and French investors. Without them, the colonies never would have gotten colonized.

At the time Jamestown got started and the Pilgrims landed at Plymouth Rock, there were millions of acres of wilderness land along the eastern seaboard, but you couldn't just sail there, pick your spot, clear a space out of the forest, and start growing tobacco or trading with the Indians. You had to have permission from a king or a queen.

In those days, the kings and queens ran the whole show. If you wanted to go into business in the royal lands, which was most of the land on earth, you had to get a royal license, called a "charter of incorporation." These licenses were the forerunners of the modern corporation, and business people couldn't operate without a charter or a piece of somebody else's charter.

Religious groups such as the Quakers in Pennsylvania got charters. So did groups of merchants, such as the ones that founded Jamestown. And once you had the royal permit to settle the land and start a colony, then you had to look for the financing. That's where the earliest stock market comes into play.

As far back as 1602, Dutch people were buying shares in the United Dutch East India Company. This was the world's first popular stock, sold on the world's first popular stock exchange, which operated from a bridge over the Amstel River in Amsterdam. Crowds of eager investors gathered there, trying to get the attention of a stockbroker, and when their pushing and shoving got out of hand, police were called in to restore the peace. The Dutch spent millions of guilders (their version of the dollar) for the privilege of owning shares in United Dutch East India, which today, with so many companies known by their abbreviations, might well be called UDEI.

In any event, the Dutch company took these millions of guilders raised in the stock sale and used the money to outfit a few ships. These ships were sent off to India and points east to bring back the latest Far Eastern merchandise, which was the rage in Europe at the time.

While optimists paid higher and higher prices for the shares of United Dutch East India, figuring the company would make them a fortune, the pessimists bet against the stock through a clever maneuver called "shorting," which was invented in the 1600s and is still being used by the pessimists of today. In the case of United Dutch East India, the optimists turned out to be right, because the stock price doubled in the first years of trading, and the shareholders got a regular bonus, known as the dividend. The company managed to stay in business for two centuries, until it ran out of steam and was dissolved in 1799.

No doubt you've heard how Henry Hudson sailed his ship, the *Half Moon*, up the Hudson River in what is now New York, looking for a passage to India, thus repeating the navigational mistake made by Christopher Columbus. Have you ever wondered who paid for this wild goose chase? Columbus, we all know, got his financing from King Ferdinand and Queen Isabella of Spain, while Hudson got his from the aforementioned United Dutch East India Company.

Another Dutch enterprise, the Dutch West India Company, sent the first Europeans to settle on Manhattan Island. So when Peter Minuit made the most famous real estate deal in history, buying Manhattan for a small pile of trinkets worth sixty guilders (twenty-four dollars in our money), he was acting on behalf of the Dutch West India shareholders. Too bad for them the company didn't stay in business long enough to get the benefit from owning all that expensive downtown New York office space.

Seeing how the Dutch financed their New World adventures, the English followed their example. The Virginia Company of

London had exclusive rights to a huge area that extended from the Carolinas through present-day Virginia and up into part of today's New York State. That company footed the bill for the first expedition to Jamestown, where Pocahontas saved Captain John Smith from having his head bashed in by her angry relatives.

The settlers at Jamestown worked there but didn't own the place, a sticking point from the beginning. They were hired to clear the land, plant the crops, and build the houses, but all the property, the improvements, and the businesses belonged to the shareholders back in London. If Jamestown made a profit, the actual residents would never see a penny of it.

After seven years of nasty disputes and complaints from the settlers at Jamestown, the rules were changed so they could own their own private property. It turned out not to matter at the time, because the original colony went bankrupt. But there was a great lesson to be learned from Jamestown: A person who owns property and has a stake in the enterprise is likely to work harder and feel happier and do a better job than a person who doesn't.

The exclusive right to do business along the rest of the coastline from Maryland into Maine was awarded to yet another English company: the Virginia Company of Plymouth. The way the map was drawn in those days, most of New England was part of northern Virginia. When the Pilgrims landed at Plymouth Rock and stumbled onto shore, they were trespassing on property belonging to the Plymouth Company.

Every schoolchild learns how the Pilgrims risked their lives to find religious freedom, how they crossed the cruel ocean in a tiny ship, the *Mayflower*, how they suffered through cold New England winters, how they made friends with the Indians and got their squash and pumpkin recipes, but nothing about the remarkable story of how they got their money.

Let's back up for a minute to review this story. The Pilgrims had left England and taken up residence in the Netherlands, where the first stock market got its start—not that the Pilgrims cared about stocks. After several years in the Netherlands, the Pilgrims got fed up and decided to move. They had three possible destinations in mind: the Orinoco River in South America; a section of New York controlled by the Dutch; or a parcel of land offered them by the Virginia Company of London.

The one thing holding them back was a lack of cash. They needed supplies and a ship, and could afford neither. Without financial help, they would have been stuck in Europe forever, and we might never have heard of them. This is when Thomas Weston entered the picture.

Weston was a wealthy London hardware dealer, or iron-monger, as they were called in those days. He had access to property in New England and he had access to plenty of cash, and he and his pals thought the Pilgrims would make an excellent investment. So they made an offer they hoped the Pilgrims wouldn't refuse.

Weston's group, who nicknamed themselves "The Adven-turers" even though they weren't the ones going on the adventure, agreed to put up the money to send the Pilgrims to America. In return, the Pilgrims had to agree to work four days a week for seven straight years to make the colony profitable. At the end of seven years, the partnership would dissolve and both sides would split the profits, after which the Pilgrims would be free to go their own way.

The Pilgrims accepted these terms, because they lacked an alternative, and began packing their bags. Then at the last minute, Weston turned the tables on them and changed the contract. Now, instead of having to work four days a week for the good of the business, they were required to work six. This would give them no free time to plant a home garden, or mend their clothes, or practice their religion, other than on Sundays.

After arguing with Weston and getting nowhere, the Pilgrims decided to set sail without a signed agreement and without any travel money, because although Weston had paid for everything so far, he refused to advance them another cent. They had to sell some of the butter they'd made for the trip so they could pay the port charges and leave the harbor in the *Speedwell*, the ship they had outfitted in Holland.

The *Speedwell* leaked, so they were forced to return to port, suspecting all along that the captain and sailors were in cahoots with Weston and had deliberately sprung the leak. Most of them crowded into a second ship that was smaller and slower than the *Speedwell*—the *Mayflower*.

They were crammed into the *Mayflower*, on their way to their promised land in Virginia, when they drifted off course and overshot their destination. Realizing their mistake, they tried to turn south, but the rocks and shoals of Cape Cod blocked their passage. Rather than risk a shipwreck in these unfamiliar, rough waters, they dropped anchor in Provincetown harbor.

From there, they moved to Plymouth, where they built their shelters and planted their crops. With Weston having cut off the money flow, the Pilgrims needed a new source of cash. They worked out a new deal between another group of investors (headed by John Peirce) and the Plymouth Company, which owned the land.

The Pilgrims would get one hundred acres apiece to use as they pleased. Peirce would get one hundred acres per Pilgrim. On top of that, he and the other investors would get fifteen hundred acres apiece for paying the rest of the Pilgrims' moving expenses and for bankrolling the settlement.

Among their many other worries, how to survive the winter, how to get along with the natives, and so forth, the Pilgrims had to worry about how to pay back the two groups of investors, Peirce's and Weston's, who had put up considerable sums to carry them this far. As much as we like to think of the Pilgrims as focusing only on God, they had the same problems as the rest of us: bills.

After one year of the Plymouth colony's being in business, the *Mayflower* sailed back to England on a visit with an empty cargo hold: no furs, no gems, no crops, nothing the investors could sell. Plymouth was losing money and continued to lose money season after season, or as they say on Wall Street, quarter after quarter. This made the investors very upset, as investors always are when they get zero return on their money. Worse than that, they had to send more supplies back to the colony, so the costs were going up.

By 1622, Weston was fed up with Plymouth and supporting the high-cost Pilgrims with nothing to show for it, so he gave away his share of the business to his fellow "Adventurers." Meanwhile, John Peirce was sneaking around the other investors' backs, trying to get control of Plymouth for himself so he could become the "Lord Proprietor of Plymouth Plantation." He didn't get away with it.

For five years, Pilgrims and investors carried on their money dispute: the Pilgrims complaining about a lack of support and the investors complaining about a lack of profits. Then in 1627, the partnership was dissolved, with the exasperated investors selling the entire operation to the Pilgrims for the modest sum of eighteen hundred British pounds.

Since the Pilgrims didn't have eighteen hundred pounds, they had to buy the colony on the installment plan: two hundred pounds per year. This was the first "leveraged buyout" in American history, a forerunner of the famous RJR Nabisco deal of the 1980s that became the book and the movie *Barbarians at the Gate.* (In a leveraged buyout, a company is purchased with borrowed money by people who can't really afford it.) The Pilgrims' leveraged buyout was the first time in our history that workers took over the company business.

Now comes the most interesting part of the story. As soon as they had established themselves, the Pilgrims decided to live in a communistic way: They pooled their resources and no individual was allowed to own any private property. Governor William Bradford, the Pilgrim leader at the time, saw right away that the communist arrangement would fail. He realized that without private property, the people would have no incentive to work very hard. Why should they bother, when all the inhabitants of the colony got the same benefits (food, housing, and so forth) whether they worked or sat around doing nothing?

A few farsighted residents of the colony petitioned Governor Bradford to set things up so farmers and fishermen were allowed to own their own farms and boats and to make a profit from their efforts. In return, they supported the community by paying a tax on their profits. This free-enterprise system that Bradford put in place was basically the same as the one we have today.

Being independent did not solve the Pilgrims' money problems. In spite of their hard work, the debt of the colony increased from eighteen hundred pounds to six thousand. More Pilgrims were brought over from Holland to expand the fishing fleet. Their hope was to pay off part of the debt with the profits from fishing, but they never caught enough fish. For ten years, negotiations dragged on between the colony and its lenders, until the dispute was settled once and for all in 1642.

The Pilgrims helped build the social, political, religious, and economic foundation of modern America, but to the investors, they were nothing but a bust. Weston, Peirce, and friends were the big losers in this venture, and they were no dummies, either, which goes to show that investing is a tricky business, where the best-laid plans can often go awry. Or maybe they deserved what they got, for being so sneaky and underhanded, and for trying to renege on the original deal.

This is one instance in which the general population could be happy it didn't have a chance to buy shares: The Pilgrims were not a public company, the way the Dutch West and East India companies had been. But there were other opportunities for the European masses to get in on the New World bonanza, and with equally disastrous results. There was the ill-fated Mississippi Company and the South Sea Company, both of which appeared on the scene in the early 1700s, selling shares to tens of thousands of gullible customers in the stock markets of Paris and London.

The Mississippi Company was the pet project of a flashy wheeler-dealer named John Law, one of the most interesting characters of his century. Law left his native Scotland, after he'd killed a man in a duel over a failed business venture, and moved to France. He wangled an introduction to the king, Louis XV, who was underage and left the royal decisions to a regent, the Duke of Orleans.

Knowing a royal family was the only way to get ahead in those days, and Law convinced the regent that he, Law, could solve the problem of France's huge national debt.

Law's plan was for France to hire a printing press and print paper money, which it could use to pay off the debt. Paper money was a relatively new idea in the world, and the regent was very impressed. So impressed, in fact, that he gave the immigrant from Scotland complete control over the Royal Bank of France, along with the royal printing press.

Soon, Law's paper money was circulating everywhere. Almost overnight, he went from being a stranger in the country to being the king of French finance and the wealthiest inhabitant of Paris next to Louis XV himself.

With his popularity riding high in the opinion polls, or however they measured it in those days, Law announced his second big project: the Mississippi Company. Its purpose was to bring back fantastic treasures from the vicinity of the Mississippi River. The Mississippi flowed through Louisiana territory, first visited by French explorers (Colbert, Joliet, Marquette) and later claimed by the French. The French people back home thought Louisiana was another Mexico, rich in silver and gold deposits just waiting to be carried away. Law himself had never been to Mississippi, or anyplace else in the New World for that matter, but he did a convincing sales job to make the public believe that the fantastic stories they'd heard were true.

Like fans at a rock concert, hysterical Parisians rushed into the maze of narrow streets near Law's mansion. They had to apply to buy shares. Waving their new French money, they fell over themselves trying to get Law's representatives to accept their applications. The price of the shares rose and rose, until Law's company was worth more, on paper, than all the gold in circulation. And still the buyers kept coming.

There was hardly a person alive in France who didn't catch the Mississippi fever and dream of Mississippi gold that didn't really exist. They had no information whatsoever about Law's company, other than what Law himself said about it, and there was no *Wall Street Journal* or *Nightly Business News* to tell them that Law's scheme had no chance of success. In fact, whenever people questioned him or his company, they were shipped out of town, to distant prisons.

Whenever crowds of people bet their life savings on a hopeless proposition, it's called a "mania" or a "bubble." The pattern is always the same. Frantic investors pay ridiculous prices in order to get in on a spurious opportunity, and sooner or later, the prices come crashing down. After the Mississippi "bubble" burst, and people realized Law's company was a sham and Law himself was nothing more than a financial Wizard of Oz, investors tried to unload their shares and found no buyers. They lost their life savings, the French economy collapsed, and the banking system collapsed along with it. As quickly as Law had become a French hero, he became a French goat.

England had its own version of the Mississippi Company, the South Sea Company, founded in 1711. The organizers copied all their moves from Law. They promised to pay off England's huge military debt if the English monarch would grant them a monopoly on trade with countries in the "south seas"—particularly Mexico and Peru.

In 1720, the South Sea Company announced a new plan to lend the British government enough money to wipe out its entire national debt, military and otherwise, if the government would agree to pay 5 percent interest on the loan. At the same time, the company began to sell more shares of its stock. Half of London headed for Exchange Alley, the hometown stock market, in their horse-drawn carriages, determined to buy shares. This caused a nasty carriage jam, and the streets were blocked for weeks.

There was so much demand for these South Sea shares that the price tripled overnight, before the British Parliament had approved the debt deal. A British statesman even issued a warning: People should keep their money in their pockets. But during bubbles such as this one, nobody listens to a lone voice of reason.

When the word got out that the organizers of the South Sea Company had gotten very rich by selling shares, other companies were quickly created by people who also wanted to get rich. There was a company for every wild scheme you could think of: a perpetual motion machine, salt farms in the Holy Land, importing walnut trees from Virginia, drying malt in hot air, making lumber from sawdust, inventing a new kind of soap. One company refused to tell investors what it planned to do with their money. It described its purpose as follows: "carrying out an undertaking of great advantage, but nobody can know what it is."

Lords and laymen, merchants and menials, people from every profession and every rank in society got drawn into the London stock market expecting to strike it rich. When the bubble finally burst, the English suffered the same fate as the French. The price of South Sea shares took a nosedive, crowds of people lost their life savings, and the British financial system was on the brink of collapse.

One by one, the directors of the South Sea Company were brought to trial, had their estates confiscated, and were sent to prison, some in the infamous Tower of London. Sir Isaac Newton was caught in the bubble and lost a lot of money. "I can calculate the motions of heavenly bodies," he said, "but not the madness of people."

The South Sea fiasco gave the stock market such a bad name that Parliament passed a law making it illegal to buy or sell shares in any company, no matter what business it was in. The stock exchange was abolished and all trading, which back then was called "jobbing," was brought to a halt. The stockbroker went from being the most popular person in town to an outcast with a worse reputation than any pickpocket, highway robber, or prostitute.

This was a sad beginning for stocks, but matters have greatly improved since then, especially in recent decades.

Early Entrepreneurs

On our side of the Atlantic, residents of the colonies who had come here as part of somebody else's business began to go into business on their own.

Companies of many types were established in the early 1700s. Merchants who went into business for themselves, or with partners, soon discovered the advantages of forming corporations. Later on, after we got our independence, Americans took to the idea of incorporation far more readily than the Europeans had. None of the other major industrial nations—Great Britain, France, Germany, or Japan—produced as many corporations as we did.

In fact, a few of the companies that opened their doors nearly three hundred years ago are still operating today! This is an amazing feat, when you think of all the wars, panics, depressions, and other calamities the country has been subjected to. Generations have come and gone, products drifted in and out of fashion, cities burned, forests deforested, neighborhoods destroyed—hardly anything has lasted since the 1700s. But J.E. Rhoads & Sons has been around since 1702, when it manufactured buggy whips.

Rhoads & Sons would have disappeared long ago, if it hadn't been for its clever managers from the 1860s, who saw the railroads coming and realized there was no future in making buggy whips in a world without buggies. They retooled the factory to make conveyor belts.

The Dexter Company got its start as a gristmill in Windsor Locks, Connecticut, in 1767—two and a quarter centuries later, it's still in business, but not in the gristmill business. Like Rhoads, it was kept alive by quick-witted managers who knew how to change with the times. Milling was a dying industry, so Dexter got out of its mills and started to produce stationery. From stationery, it switched to tea bags, and from tea bags to glue. Today, it makes high-tech coatings and adhesives for airplanes.

A Baltimore firm, D. Landreth Seed, has survived since 1784—on vegetable seeds. It sold seeds to Thomas Jefferson at his Virginia estate, and more than two hundred years later, it's still selling seeds to Jefferson's estate. If a company makes a good product that's never out of date, it can stay in business forever.

Since none of these early companies was a public company,

people couldn't own shares in them. (Dexter went public on its 201st birthday, in 1968.) At the time of the Revolution there was not one home-grown public company in the country. The earliest to appear on the scene after the Revolution was a bank—the Bank of North America, founded in 1781. The Bank of New York (1784) was the first stock ever to trade on the New York Stock Exchange. It still trades there today.

The Bank of Boston followed New York's lead and sold shares, as did the Bank of the United States, whose main purpose in life was to figure out how to pay off the debts from the Revolutionary War.

In colonial America there had been no banks, because the British didn't allow them. We corrected this problem after the Revolution, but even so, there was a lot of fuss about the federal government sponsoring a bank. Some of the Founding Fathers, particularly Jefferson, distrusted bankers and their paper money.

Taking their cue from their European ancestors, our earliest shareholders paid too much for their bank stocks, and they knew very little about what they were buying. The bidding went higher and higher until it got to the level of ridiculous prices, and on Wall Street, whatever goes up that high must always come down. Bank stocks landed with a thud in the Crash of 1792, the first crash in Wall Street history. As soon as the dust settled, the New York State Legislature passed a law, similar to the laws passed earlier in London, making it a crime to traffic in stocks. Stock trading went underground.

This was a good lesson to investors in a young country, and it is a good lesson for young investors today. When you are an owner of a company, you only make money if the company succeeds. A lot of them don't. This is the risk of buying stocks: The company you own may turn out to be worthless. It is for taking this risk that people are rewarded so handsomely if they pick the right companies to invest in.

Investors were very happy to own shares in the company that built the bridge over the Charles River in Massachusetts. John Hancock was one of the founders. The sale of the Charles River

Bridge stock was held on the eleventh anniversary of Bunker Hill Day, in 1786. There was a parade across the bridge, complete with the firing of cannons, followed by a party at which eighty-three original investors were treated to a banquet. It was a joyous occasion, followed by many joyous years in which investors were paid a dividend.

These steady dividends came from the tolls collected from the people who used the bridge to get across the river. The customers of the bridge weren't nearly as happy as the investors in the bridge. Eventually, a second bridge, the Warren Bridge, was built across the Charles River to compete with the first. Once enough tolls were collected to pay off the costs of building this second bridge, the plan was to abolish the toll so people could cross the river for free. The owners of the original bridge objected to this plan, and filed a lawsuit that went all the way to the Supreme Court. They lost the case, and that was the end of their profitable monopoly.

Another successful company modeled along the lines of the Charles River Bridge was the Lancaster Turnpike in Pennsylvania. The Lancaster Turnpike sold shares (through a lottery, as it turns out) and also paid a nice dividend. Again, the money came from tolls collected along this sixty-mile road from Philadelphia to Lancaster. The customers of this road didn't like the tolls any more than the customers of the Charles River Bridge did, but they preferred paying them to driving their buggies through fields and woods.

Turnpike, bridge, and canal companies were the forerunners of the trolley, railroad, and subway companies that came along a bit later.

The Father of the Financial System

We all recognize George Washington as the father of our country, but Alexander Hamilton was the father of the financial system. That part gets lost in the history books, but without the financial system, the political system never would have worked. Hamilton deserves the credit for this. He's more famous for being a lousy shot and losing a duel to Aaron Burr, but he was also an astute economic planner and one of the founders of the Bank of New York.

Hamilton realized that the country couldn't get along without money, and to have money, it needed banks. It seems obvious today, but back then, banking was a controversial subject.

George Washington agreed with Hamilton about the banks, and even invested in one himself. Washington was a shareholder in the Bank of Alexandria, which opened near his home at Mount Vernon. But a lot of important people were opposed to Hamilton's ideas, and foremost among them was Thomas Jefferson. Jefferson was a gentleman farmer who believed there was virtue in tilling the soil and living off the land. He hated factories and the cities that grew up around the factories. To Jefferson, banks were the root of all evil, especially the government's bank.

As it turns out, Jefferson was no expert on personal finance. He ran through a large fortune and died virtually bankrupt in 1826. He was a big spender, particularly on gadgets and on books, and his library had more volumes than Harvard College, which had been in existence for more than one hundred years before Jefferson was born. He was a tinkerer, a bookworm, and a farmer at heart—the gentlemanly kind who left the farm work to others.

Jefferson wanted America to be a nation of pastures and wheat fields, where independent "yeoman" farmers could dominate local politics and have the strongest voice in public affairs. He rejected the European idea that government should be run by a ruling class of snooty aristocrats.

Never would Jefferson have imagined that the factories would lure millions of farm workers away from the farms and into the cities and the mill towns, or that factories would be their ticket to a better life, or that heavy industry with all its problems would provide Americans with the highest standard of living in the history of human beings. It couldn't have happened without the massive amounts of money that went into building the roads, canals, highways, bridges, factories—and where did most of this money come from? Jefferson's dreaded banks!

In spite of Jefferson's opposition, the first Bank of the United States got the congressional go-ahead in 1791 and managed to stay in business for twenty years, until 1811, when a new group of bank haters in Congress refused to renew the charter. The bank was shut down.

A second Bank of the United States was chartered in 1816, this time in Philadelphia, but it ran into trouble a few years later when Andrew Jackson was elected president. Jackson was a rough character who came from the wilds of Tennessee. They called him "Old Hickory," because he was tall like a tree (six feet one inch, which was very big for those days), he had a thick skin like a tree, and he grew up in a log cabin. In spite of his outdoorsy reputation, Jackson was sick most of the time and stayed indoors. Like Jefferson before him, Jackson believed that the states should have more power and the federal government less.

This second Bank of the United States was blamed for a nationwide financial panic in 1819, when a lot of businesses went bankrupt and people lost their life savings and their jobs. (This was the first of a long string of panics, which created havoc around the country.) Western farmers joined with eastern factory workers in waggling their fingers at the "monster bank" that they said was the culprit of the panic.

So when Jackson was elected president a decade after the panic, he listened to these people and took all the money out of the federally sponsored bank and shipped it off to be deposited in various state banks, and that was the end of the second Bank of the United States. From then on, the states controlled the banking business and gave out the charters. Soon, every John and Jane Doe with nothing better to do decided to start a bank.

Thousands of banks appeared on main streets and side streets in big towns and little towns, the way chicken restaurants are cropping up today. And since every one of these state banks could issue its own paper money, it was very confusing to do business, because from state to state it was hard to tell whose cash was worth what, and a lot of merchants wouldn't accept any of it. Traveling within the country then was very similar to traveling abroad today: You had to worry about changing money from place to place.

This is an area in which the United States and Europe have gone in different directions. Europe has always had a few banks with many branches, while we've always had a slew of different banks. By 1820, there were three hundred separate banks in the United States, as compared to a handful of banks in England. Today, there are over ten thousand banking institutions in the United States, if you add in all the savings and loans and the credit unions, while Great Britain has less than fifteen.

Many of our local banks were shoestring operations that lacked the necessary capital to tide them over in an economic crisis, and there was always a crisis waiting to happen. Half the banks that opened their doors between 1810 and 1820 had failed by 1825, and half the banks that opened between 1830 and 1840 had failed by 1845. When you put money into a bank, it wasn't insured the way it is today, so when a bank failed, people with savings accounts or checking accounts had no protection and lost all their money. There was no such thing as a safe deposit.

Banks were dangerous places to park cash, but that didn't stop Americans from putting their life savings into them. The banks would take these savings and lend the money to the bridge builders and the canal builders, the turnpike projects and the railroad projects that got America moving. When a bank loaned money to a railroad, or a bridge company, or a steel company, the money came from the savings accounts of the people who put money into the bank.

In other words, all this high energy, this excitement, this hustle and bustle that led to economic progress was financed out of the pockets of the man and woman on the street.

Whenever the government needed money for a project, it had four choices of where to get it: taxes, bank loans, selling lottery tickets, or selling bonds. (More about bonds on page 104.) Whenever a company needed money, it could borrow from a bank, sell bonds, or sell shares of stock. But in the first half of the nineteenth century, stocks were a company's last resort. The idea of selling shares to the public caught on very slowly.

The Father of Modern Economics

Markets were opening all over the place, and people were buying and selling at a furious pace, and to many people the whole situation was out of control. Never in history had masses of individuals been allowed to go their own way and work for their own benefit. There didn't seem to be any rhyme or reason to it.

This is where the economists came in. They were a new breed of thinker. For thousands of years, religious philosophers had tried to figure out how mankind could live according to God's wishes. They debated politics and the best form of government, and who the leaders should be. But it took economists to describe what happens when individuals have the freedom to seek their fortunes.

The first and the smartest early economist was a Scotsman named Adam Smith, a nerd of his day who lived at the time of the American Revolution. Smith avoided parties and picnics to stay at home thinking and writing, and he was so absorbed in his ideas that he got the reputation of being absent-minded. His great work was called *An Inquiry into the Nature and Causes of the Wealth of Nations*, which today goes by the shortened title, *The Wealth of Nations*.

The Wealth of Nations was published in 1776, the year America declared its independence, and it's a shame that Adam Smith didn't get more credit for writing it. He deserves a prime spot in history along with John Locke, Benjamin Franklin, Thomas Paine, and other revolutionary thinkers who argued that political freedom is the key to a just society where people can live in peace and harmony. The others didn't say much about how to pay the bills—but Smith did. He made the case for economic freedom.

Smith argued that when each person pursues his own line of work, the general population is far better off than it is when a king or a central planner runs the show and dictates who gets what. His point seems obvious today, but in 1776, it was a novel idea that millions of individuals making and selling whatever they pleased, and going off in all directions at once, could create an orderly society in which everybody had clothes, food, and a roof over their heads. What if ninety-nine out of one hundred people decided to make hats, and only one out of one hundred decided to grow vegetables? The country would be flooded with hats, and there would be nothing to eat. But this is where the Invisible Hand comes to the rescue.

There wasn't really an Invisible Hand, of course, but Smith imagined one working behind the scenes to insure that the right number of people grew vegetables, and the right number of people made hats. He was really talking about the way in which supply and demand kept goods and services in balance. For instance, if too many hat makers made too many hats, hats would pile up in the market, forcing the hat sellers to lower the price. Lower prices for hats would drive some hat makers out of the hat business and into a more profitable line of work, such as vegetable farming. Eventually, there would be just enough vegetable farmers and just enough hat makers to make the right amount of vegetables and hats.

In the real world, things don't work out quite as perfectly as that, but Smith understood the basics of how a free market works, and they still hold true today. Whenever there's a demand for a new product, such as computers, more and more companies get into the business, until there are so many computers for sale that the stores have to drop their prices. This competition is very good for you, me, and all the other consumers, because it forces the computer makers to improve their product and cut prices. That's why every few months, they come out with fantastic new models that cost less than the clunky old models. Without competition, they could keep selling the clunky old models and consumers could do nothing about it.

The Invisible Hand keeps the supply and demand of everything from bubblegum to bowling balls in balance. We don't need a king, a Congress, or a Department of Things to decide what the country should make, and how many of each item, and who should be allowed to do the manufacturing. The market sorts this out, automatically.

Smith also realized that wanting to get ahead is a positive impulse, and not the negative that religious leaders and public opinion makers had tried to stamp out for centuries. Self-interest, he noticed, isn't entirely selfish. It motivates people to get off their fannies and do the best they can at whatever job they undertake. It causes them to invent things, work overtime, put extra effort into the project at hand. Imagine what lousy carpenters, plumbers, doctors, lawyers, accountants, bankers, secretaries, professors, center fielders, and quarterbacks we'd have if people weren't allowed to profit from their talents, and success was never rewarded!

Smith said there was a "law of accumulation" that turned self-interest into a better life for everyone. When the owner of a business got richer, he or she would expand the business and hire more people, which would make everybody else richer, and some of them would start their own businesses, and so on. This is where capitalism created opportunities, unlike feudal agriculture, where a small number of big shots owned the land and kept it in the family, and if you were born a peasant, you would live penniless and die penniless, and your children and their children would be stuck in the same rut forever.

At the time Smith wrote his book, and throughout the century that followed, great thinkers were trying to find laws for everything. Scientists already had discovered physical laws, such as the law of gravity, the laws of planetary motion, and the laws for certain chemical reactions. People believed in an orderly universe, in which, if there were laws for how the planets move and how apples fall from the tree, there had to be laws for business, and laws for politics, and laws for how people react in different situations. Once you figured out the formula for how money gets passed around, for instance, you could predict exactly who would end up with how much.

It was one thing to say there was a law of supply and demand, or a law for how money travels, and quite another to find a formula that could nail it down. But economists kept trying, coming up with new theories to reduce the hustle and bustle of the marketplace to a single equation.

Our First Millionaires

According to the records, not a single millionaire existed in America in colonial times. Elias Hasket Derby of Salem, Massachusetts, a seafaring merchant who refused to get involved in the slave trade, was reputed to be the wealthiest person in the country. Today, his house belongs to the National Park Service and is open to the public. It's only a few hundred yards from the House of Seven Gables, the setting for Nathaniel Hawthorne's famous book. The fact that everybody knows Hawthorne and not Elias Hasket Derby tells you something about the relative importance of literature and finance in the schools.

Several hundred miles to the south, a Baltimore merchant, Robert Oliver, had also collected a sizeable fortune, but during and after the Revolution, the richest person in America was thought to be Robert Morris.

Morris formed a business syndicate that bought and sold ships. His ships sailed from the West Indies to Europe and back again, sending tobacco and foodstuffs in the European direction and bringing cloth and manufactured goods from them to us. He was chairman of a secret committee that supplied the revolutionary armies with coats, pants, shirts, and gunpowder, and his companies got the contracts to supply the army. Morris became superintendent of finance under the Articles of Confederation, and he was an avid supporter of Alexander Hamilton and of Hamilton's pet project, the first national bank.

Morris believed that only the better class of people should run the country. He argued for the superiority of gentlemen such as himself, for there was no doubt in his mind he was one. He was entirely opposed to Jefferson's idea that the small independent farmer was the backbone of the nation and should be given the right to vote.

Like many of the great wheeler-dealers who followed in his footsteps, Morris built his empire on money borrowed from the banks. He had many friends in high places, and since his biggest customer was the army, we could call him the original big defense contractor.

Also like some of our modern wheeler-dealers, including Donald Trump, Morris overextended himself and borrowed more money than he could pay back. There was a lull in the shipping business, his financial empire collapsed, and Morris declared bankruptcy.

In those days, declaring bankruptcy was a very serious thing to do, because owing money to people and not paying them back was a crime. Morris spent three years in a debtor's prison in Philadelphia, where one of his visitors was George Washington. From his jail cell, Morris organized a campaign to abolish this sort of penalty, and thanks to his efforts, we no longer lock people up when they can't pay their debts. If we still had debtor's prisons in the 1990s, they would be very crowded, because more than eight hundred thousand Americans file for personal bankruptcy every year. Most have gotten in too deep with their credit cards.

By 1815, there were a half-dozen millionaires in the country, and most made their profits on ships and trading. Number one among them was Stephen Girard of Philadelphia, who died in 1831 at the age of eighty-two, the richest person in America at that time.

Girard was born in France, the son of a ship captain. He went to sea as a teenager and later became an international trader and merchant. He came to America, invested in land, bank stocks, and government bonds, and managed to prosper in all these areas. Girard eventually started his own bank and joined a syndicate to do business with a younger wheeler-dealer named John Jacob Astor. More on him shortly.

At his death, Girard left an estate worth $6 million, a vast fortune at the time, even though today it would barely pay a year's salary for a top baseball player. The bulk of the money was donated to a college for male orphan children. Girard was a confirmed atheist who despised religion so much that under the terms of his will, no minister of any faith could set foot on the college property.

Girard's net worth was eclipsed by that of John Jacob Astor. Astor was a German immigrant who started out as a fur trader, then bought part interest in a ship that sailed back and forth to China—that's where the big fortunes were still being made, in ships and trading. From one ship, Astor expanded to two, three, four, and eventually he had a fleet of speedy vessels known as clippers. For an American to build a fleet of this kind was a major achievement, because it had to be done with borrowed money, and the American banks had a limited supply of money to lend, as compared, say, to the British banks.

During this period in history, money was backed by precious metals, so the amount of cash a bank could print depended on how much gold and silver it had in its vaults. In London, there was an ample supply, so the banks could roll the presses and create plenty of cash for their business tycoons to borrow. But the U.S. supplies of gold and silver were quite low, so the banks were often short on cash, and Astor and his fellow capitalists had trouble borrowing enough money to finance their grandiose projects.

When he realized he couldn't beat the competition, Astor turned away from international trade and concentrated on the U.S. market, where he did well enough, because in 1848, when he died at the age of eighty-four, he left behind an estate whose assets topped $20 million, roughly three times the estate of his old friend Girard.

Soon after Astor's funeral and all the articles that came out about his great wealth, people were furious to discover that his family inherited $19-plus million and only five hundred thousand dollars went to charity. This started a hot national debate: If you can't take it with you, who should get it? The public thought Astor should have left more to his fellowman in general, and less to his relatives, because capitalists were supposedly working for the benefit of society.

This debate still rages today. Everyone seems to agree that working hard and getting ahead is a good thing, but people are divided on the issue of what to do with the proceeds. These days, Astor couldn't possibly have given 95 percent of his wealth to his children, because the estate taxes would have taken 55 percent off the top as soon as he was laid to rest. The contemporary rich have a different sort of choice: They can leave their money to private charities and foundations, including colleges, hospitals, homeless shelters, AIDS research, and food banks, or they can do nothing and let the government take the biggest chunk of it.

A Slow Start for Stocks

By 1800, there were 295 corporations formed in the United States, but most of these remained in private hands so the general public couldn't own them. Corporations were very controversial. Their fans and supporters saw them as an important ally of democracy that could benefit the community at large. Their critics saw them as undemocratic, sneaky, and subversive organizations that only. cared about themselves.

It was a frustrating period for any investor in stocks. The states already had passed laws to limit the liability of shareholders if a company got sued, so people could invest without fear of losing more than the value of their shares. But not many people did invest. It was hard to find friends or neighbors to share in the enthusiasm and chat about their favorite public companies, the way investors do today whenever we get the chance.

There wasn't a business section of the newspaper, or a *Money* magazine, or books on how to pick stocks. In fact, there weren't many stocks to pick from: a dozen or so banks, a couple of insurance companies, a gas company or two, and that was it. In March 1815 the complete list was printed in the *New York Commercial Advertiser*, a popular paper of the day. There were twenty-four stocks, mostly banks. In 1818, there were twenty-nine stocks, and in 1830, thirty-one.

The earliest buying and selling was done under a large buttonwood tree on Wall Street, and after that, stocks were traded in small rented rooms or in coffeehouses. At one point, there was a fire in one of the rooms, and the traders moved into a hayloft and continued trading there.

The New York Stock Exchange (NYSE) wasn't what you'd call an exciting hangout. You could stand around and twiddle your thumbs waiting for a stock to be traded. Business was so slow that the traders started buying and selling at 11:30 and were done for the day by 1:30. It got so dull that on March 16, 1830, a prime candidate for the slowest trading day on record, only thirty-one shares changed hands. This was a far cry from the 338 million shares that changed hands on an average day in 1995.

The stock-trading business livened up a bit by 1835, when 121 companies were listed on the NYSE. The country was on the move with canals, turnpikes, and bridges. These fantastic improvements required money, and the money came from the sale of stocks and bonds. Bank stocks were no longer the hot items they had been a couple of decades before. The new hot item was railroad stocks and bonds. At one point, people were buying anything with the name "rail" in it, and not caring what prices they paid. They were also paying higher and higher prices for any piece of land near a railroad. If they didn't have the cash to buy the land, they could borrow it from the banks. Banks were lending huge sums on these real-estate deals, and large numbers of farmers were ignoring their crops and becoming real-estate tycoons.

This was a home-grown bubble, similar to London's South Sea bubble from long before, and in 1836 it burst. Stock prices and land prices came down as fast as they had gone up, as investors tried to cash out. The would-be tycoons who had borrowed money to buy the stocks and the land were stuck with debts they couldn't repay to the banks. The banks ran out of money, and people with savings accounts lost their savings when the banks closed their doors and went out of business. Soon, cash was in such short supply that nobody could afford to buy anything. The financial system was on the verge of collapse. This was the Panic of 1837.

The American economy (and the economies of most countries) lurched from euphoria to panic and back again. In the euphoric periods, when prices were rising and jobs were plentiful, speculators would spend their last paycheck, hock their jewelry, go into debt, do anything to buy stocks, or bonds, or land, and get in on the action. Then, in the panics, collapses, and depressions, the speculators got their comeuppance and people sobered up.

The stock market crashed in 1853 and again in 1857, when shares in the popular Erie Railroad fell from sixty-two dollars to eleven dollars. Still only a tiny percentage of the population owned stock—given the ups and downs in the market, perhaps this was for the best. The brunt of the losses was borne once again by the Europeans, who, not having learned an earlier lesson, were pumping money into U.S. investments. By the 1850s, nearly half of all U.S. shares were owned by foreigners, mostly British.

American Inventiveness

The American people were regarded as an uncouth rabble by the more refined Europeans, and they saw us as poorly educated, roughshod Yankee doodles, but what a surprise they got when all the great inventions began to pour out of American heads. American ingenuity was a response to our lack of manpower. In a huge country with a small population we needed to invent machines to do some of the work. Though clever inventors were dreaming up machines, this didn't mean the machines would be brought to life. It was capitalism—people willing to invest their money to manufacture the machines—that led to the golden age of American invention.

There was Fulton and his steamboat; George Cabot's mill; Francis Cabot Lowell's complete industrial factory; McCormick's giant harvesting machine, the reaper, that spared the farmers from back-breaking work. While serving as a tutor on a southern plantation, a Connecticut tinkerer named Eli Whitney invented the "gin" to remove seeds from cotton and single-handedly turned the South into a mecca for cotton production. McCormick's reaper, Samuel Colt's repeating pistol, and a new kind of padlock were the three American inventions that wowed the crowds at a famous exhibition of industrial machinery at the Crystal Palace in London in 1851. Europeans were amazed by American products, and just as amazed by our system of manufacturing that standardized the quality so each item that rolled out of the shop was exactly the same as the last.

Again, it took money to get these inventions off the drawing boards and into production. Some of it was borrowed from banks, but more and more was raised in the stock market, as shareholding grew in popularity at home and especially abroad. Foreigners bankrolled our fantastic progress by investing in our emerging market, and 150 years later, we are returning the favor by investing huge sums in the emerging markets of Asia, Africa, and Latin America.

On the farm, machines improved the life of the farmer, who up until the 1850s was still using the same primitive methods that had been used five thousand years earlier in Egypt. Farmers tilled the soil with plows pulled by animals, or with hand plows pulled by humans, and much of the stoop labor was done by slaves, who were victims of the system, the same as the slaves in ancient Mesopotamia.

Among the causes of slavery, primitive agriculture was a major culprit. Slavery was abolished when the bystanders came to their senses and raised enough of a ruckus to put a stop to this evil practice, but capitalism deserves some of the credit. It took investors and their money to build the factories that made the farm equipment (threshers, reapers, disk harrows, steel plows, grain elevators, and so forth) that changed agriculture forever. With new machines to do the backbreaking labor once reserved for slaves and serfs, there was no longer an economic benefit in forcing people into a life of servitude.

Several of the companies that made farm equipment one hundred years ago are still with us today: Deere, International Harvester (now called Navistar), and Caterpillar. While they were inventing and selling the machines that could hoe, plant, and harvest, other companies were inventing herbicides and fertilizers to kill the bugs and the weeds and enrich the soil. The combination of new equipment and new chemicals turned the American farm into the most efficient food bank on earth, capable of producing more wheat, corn, and so forth, per acre than any other country's farms in the history of agriculture.

True, ours was a fertile land, with hundreds of millions of acres of rich soil lying beneath the fruited plains, unlike the tired, leeched-out, pawed-over soil the farmers of Europe and Asia had worked mercilessly for centuries until it lost its fertility. Yet there's no denying that innovations and inventions kept our plains fruited, and made the American farm the envy of the world.

While a million Irish people lost their lives in potato famines, Chinese people starved because of rice shortages, and starvation was a fact of life for much of humanity, the United States produced and continues to produce more food than its citizens could eat.

Farm machinery changed the way farmers raised crops, but it didn't change the American diet, which was dreary and monotonous. Most families grew their own food. The basic menu was bread, potatoes, root vegetables, and dried fruits, livened up with the occasional slice of salted or smoked meat. People ate kidneys for breakfast. Kitchens lacked refrigerators, so fruits and vegetables could be eaten fresh only in the short stretches when the produce was "in season."

In the winter, you got cucumber salad, pickled cucumber salad, or no salad at all. If you didn't live near the water, you couldn't get fresh fish. Lemons were a luxury, and an orange was something you found once a year in your Christmas stocking, if you had a Christmas stocking. The tomato was an exotic Mexican export, widely distrusted because it was thought to be poisonous. Grapefruits were generally confined to Florida.

There were no refrigerated trucks or railcars to move vegetables from one place to another, and the canning industry had not yet developed vegetables that could be kept on a shelf. People did their own canning at home, in glass jars, whenever they could get the extra produce. Cattle, sheep, and pigs were walking rib steaks, lamb chops, and pork roasts, transported live from the farms to the cities so their meat could be preserved "on the hoof."

These days, we hear a lot of nostalgia about the "good old days" when life was "simpler" and more "natural," but the promoters of nostalgia might change their tune if they ever experienced what simple living was really about: sweat and backaches from dawn to dusk. Keeping a family fed, clothed, dry, and warm was a full-time job. Without our modern conveniences and products to help them along, women's work was never done, and neither was men's.

Most of the houses were handmade, and so were the clothes, the drapes, the furniture, and the soap. The average person might spend weeks without buying a product made by a company, public or private. It took hours to make the food, and hours to tend the gardens, and more hours to cut the firewood for the stoves. The smoke from stoves and fireplaces was a major pollutant, both in and around the houses where people spent most of their time. So much for the fresh air that everybody supposedly enjoyed in those days.

There was no TV, which might have been a blessing, because a lot of people had no time for TV. Today, we talk about "home entertainment," but in the old days, it really did come from inside the home: card games, puzzles, music making, storytelling, and jokes.

If this sort of entertainment was so wonderful, then why did so many people turn to the radio and later to the television?

Railroads and Commerce

The stock market continued to gain in popularity throughout the nineteenth century, thanks in part to Thomas Edison's first commercially successful invention, the tickertape machine. This was a printing device covered by a glass bowl that made it look like a bubblegum dispenser. Every time a stock was bought or sold, a record of the trade was sent via telegraph to tickertapes around the country and the world.

It came out on the tape, an endless roll of paper that showed the stock symbol, the price, the number of shares that changed hands. Anybody with access to a ticker could watch the tape and keep tabs on stock prices, up to the minute.

Before Edison invented this machine there was no way of telling what stocks were doing, unless you were standing on the floor of a stock exchange. But as soon as tickertapes were installed, investors could follow their favorite stocks right along with the insiders on Wall Street.

The American economy grew eightfold between the 1790s and the Civil War. This meant that the population was making eight times as many products, and buying and selling them at eight times the rate of the colonial inhabitants. We were well on our way to becoming the world's greatest industrial power. With the Civil War behind us and slavery abolished (although racial discrimination clearly was not abolished), the population expanded westward, and the skylines of the cities expanded upward, as everywhere in the country people were on the move.

By 1855, textile mills were popping up along the rivers in New England, and no fewer than forty-six cotton textile companies sold shares on the Boston stock exchange. When soldiers returned from the Civil War, where they'd gotten accustomed to wearing uniforms, they went out and bought a new kind of uniform, the ready-made suit. Soap and candles, leather and maple sugar, all traditional homemade products, could now be bought in stores. Trade barriers between one state and another were broken down so mass-produced goods could cross state lines.

Two railroad companies, the Union Pacific and the Central Pacific, were chosen to extend the lines across the country to the Pacific. Occasionally, a fight would break out among the Irish, German, or Chinese workers along the line, but together they put their muscle into laying the track and hammering the spikes.

Congress granted 170 million acres to various railroads in different parts of the country—this was the biggest gift of property in U.S. history, and a very controversial one. The railroads sold some of this land to farmers and used some of it as collateral for the huge loans they took out to pay the workers and buy the track, railroad cars, and other expensive equipment.

Several of today's railroad companies still own vast tracts of valuable acreage from the original government land grants. It's an incredible asset for them.

The railroads carried the freight, plus the passengers, and they brought crowds of new buyers into the stock market. In this second railroad boom, investors put $318 million of their own money into railroad stocks, and out came thirteen thousand miles of track. The federal government provided most of the land. It wasn't the cowboy and the six shooter that won the West as much as it was the railroads. Without this money and these breaks, who knows when the territory would have opened up?

Railroad stocks, how could they miss! was the rallying cry of investors from coast to coast. People saw the rail lines fanning out to the far corners of the nation, and the locomotives puffing along, and they were convinced that railroads were a can't-lose proposition.

A sizeable number of farmers were speculating in railroad stocks, in railroad land, and in the land companies created by the Homestead Act of 1862. Some of these railroad projects and land projects turned out to be fly-by-night schemes, as did many of the gold and silver mining ventures that came along behind the railroads.

Mark Twain is said to have once described a gold mine as a "hole in the ground owned by a liar," and more often than not, that liar was selling shares. Far more money was made by the people who sold shares in unproven mines than was made by all the prospectors who brought their pans and their picks to California. The victims of fly-by-night schemes had no federal or state regulators to protect them, and the laws that prohibit companies from putting out false or misleading information were yet to be written.

During the great era of the cowboy, which lasted only about twenty-five years, a slew of cattle-ranching stocks appeared on the stock exchanges. In the late 1860s, there were 38 million cows and 39 million people in the United States, or roughly one cow for every inhabitant. Cowboys made a big impression on the easterners who bought into this bull market.

By 1869, there were 145 different stocks sold on the New York Stock Exchange. Insurance companies had made their debut on Wall Street, along with the steel companies and the ironworks that grew into giants and dragged farmers off the land and lured immigrants from across the Atlantic into the factory towns.

The railroads had extended their track to all corners of the country, and there was heavy traffic on the canals of the Great Lakes where barges delivered iron and coal to be remade in the bellies of the steel mills, which poisoned the air with their toxic belch, but still the immigrants arrived by the boatload, looking for factory jobs.

They poured into New York harbor from Ireland, from continental Europe, from as far away as China, escaping potato famines, wars, secret police, injustice, intolerance, insecurity, upheavals of all kinds. They took low-paying jobs as garment workers, meat packers, welders, riveters, and grease monkeys, working long hours in unhealthy and often dangerous surroundings. They sought out these poor working and living conditions because however bad the situation was over here, it was better than the situation back home, where people were starving or were caught up in endless warfare. If life wasn't better over here, then why did so many make the trip?

They also realized that if they stayed home in Poland or Greece or wherever else, they had little hope of advancement, because in every country a small group of aristocratic families owned the farms, hoarded the money, and controlled the government. In America, they had hope, and more than hope, they had expectations. Wasn't this the land of opportunity? Workers saw the growing prosperity in the neighborhoods around them, and they expected to share in it—or if they couldn't, their children would and did.

The offspring of immigrant factory workers had a chance to go to college and become doctors, lawyers, executives, and even owners of the very companies where their parents and grandparents worked long hours for low pay.

By and large, the American worker of the late nineteenth century didn't blow the money on expensive vacations or champagne parties—at least most of them didn't. They put the money in banks, where the situation had become somewhat less chaotic than it had been when banking was run by the states. The endless varieties of currency that made shopping so confusing disappeared in the mid-1860s when a new federal banking system was established. From then on, we had one national currency, the U.S. dollar.

Americans stashed so much cash in the banks that from the Civil War to World War I they saved an amazing 18 percent of the country's total industrial output. Because the cash was used to build better factories and better roads to transport the goods from the factories, workers became more efficient. They could produce more goods for the same amount of work.

The supply of money increased forty times over, but there was hardly any inflation. These days, when a would-be emerging nation such as Russia prints more money, we see an immediate collapse in the value of the money, and prices go through the roof. But in the second half of the nineteenth century, when the United States was an emerging nation, prices held steady, even though the banks had begun printing money like crazy. The reason this printing of money didn't cause inflation was that our industrial output was growing right along with the money supply.

Another factor that may have contributed to the national prosperity is that our borders were effectively closed to many foreign-made goods by prohibitive tariffs. These days, we hear a lot about free trade and what a good thing it is, but during the heyday of the U.S. economy, when we had our fastest growth and our factories were running at full speed, foreign competitors had trouble entering our markets and our industries were somewhat protected from overseas competition.

The inventions kept coming out of the American mind: the telegraph, the telephone, the automobile, the vulcanized rubber tire. People were inventing better mousetraps, better everythings, a machine for every job that once had been done by human hands. In the 1880s, a bill was introduced in Congress to close the U.S. Patent Office, on the theory that every important invention had already been invented. How wrong that turned out to be!

There was a machine to roll cigarettes, made by a company called Bonsack and first used by a Carolina tobacco farmer named James Duke—the Duke of Duke University. There was a machine to make matches, a machine to make flour (Pillsbury got hold of that one), a machine to condense milk (the Borden milk company had the exclusive rights), a new method for making steel (the Bessemer process), and a machine for canning soup (first used at Campbell's). There was a machine to produce the floating Ivory soap that was created by mistake in a lab at Procter & Gamble.

Once new machines were invented, somebody had to invent more machines to make the new machines, plus parts and tools to repair them. Instead of machines putting people out of work, as many critics of the machine age had predicted, they actually created work. For every job lost to a hunk of metal, a couple of jobs were opened up. And with each advance in the sophistication of machines, the work got easier. Factory-made goods were cheaper to produce than handmade goods, and in many cases they were superior to handmade goods, or at least the quality was more consistent. Cheaper goods could be sold more cheaply to the customers, who got more and more for their money whenever an industry was mechanized.

The Growth of National Brands

When the twentieth century rolled around, there was a thriving snack-food industry, with all sorts of jellies, jams, biscuits, candies, and chewing gum being produced and distributed nationwide by companies that sold stock on the stock exchange. You could eat these things and invest in these things.

We'd come a long way from the dreary days when the only choices in snack foods were pilot bread, cold-water crackers, butter crackers, square soda crackers, and round sugar biscuits. These had been made by neighborhood bakeries and sold out of cracker barrels at the local general store.

The most famous cracker in the country was the Uneeda, a brand name as popular as Coca-Cola is today, made by the National Biscuit Company, otherwise known as Nabisco. Nabisco was the end result of decades of mergers in which many small family bakeries were consolidated into two regional bakeries: the American Biscuit Company in the Midwest and the New York Biscuit Company in the East. These two megabakeries joined forces to become Nabisco, which went public around the turn of the century by selling $30 million worth of stock. There were thirteen hundred original shareholders, including several celebrities, but anybody could have bought a share.

Under the clever leadership of Adolphus Green, Nabisco put an end to the cracker barrel as an American institution and put some fun into snack foods. It began to package the cookies and crackers to keep them crisp and dry and to protect them from being contaminated by dirty hands in the cracker barrel. While continuing to make the bland Uneeda biscuit, Nabisco produced a string of new products: Fig Newtons (named for Newton, Massachusetts), Premium Saltines, Barnum's Animal Crackers (1902), Lorna Doones and Oreo cookies (1912), and Ritz Crackers (1934).

The Oreo became the world's best-selling cookie, and it still is today. The Oreo has been around so long, we forget that it was produced in a Nabisco lab. Nabisco also acquired the rights to the first interesting snack for dogs, the Milk Bone.

There was Planter's peanuts, invented by a pushcart vendor named Amadeo Obici, who worked the streets of Wilkes-Barre, Pennsylvania, at the turn of the century. Obici decided one day to sprinkle his peanuts with salt. His salted peanuts were such a big hit that in 1906 Obici joined with a partner to form the Planter's Nut & Chocolate Company, later to become the Planter's Life Savers Company, which grew up to become a world-famous brand name, and a division of RJR Nabisco.

There was Heinz ketchup, concocted by a Pennsylvania pickle maker, Henry J. Heinz. Heinz, who was wiped out and went bankrupt in the Panic of 1873, went on to become the world's pickle king, sauce king, and popularizer of ketchup. He derived his formula from "ketsiap," an Oriental recipe whose main ingredient was pickled fish. Heinz left out the fish and added the tomato.

In colonial times and into the nineteenth century, Americans were convinced tomatoes were poisonous, even after a brave military man, Colonel Johnson, ate one on the steps of the county courthouse in Salem, New Jersey, to prove it wasn't fatal. But once Heinz put tomatoes in a bottle, people got into the habit of squirting ketchup on everything, a practice that has continued to this day. President Nixon squirted ketchup on his scrambled eggs.

Ketchup, mustard, olives, pickles, relish, everything you put on a hamburger was first mass-produced by Heinz. He had branch factories in six states, distribution centers and sales reps around the world, twenty-eight hundred full-time employees, plus twenty thousand farmers given contracts to grow the crops he put into his sauces.

While Heinz was busy making his ketchup and fifty-six other varieties of sauces, Sylvester Graham was inventing his famous cracker. A minister and lecturer for the Temperance Union, Graham spoke out against liquor, meat, mustard, and even Heinz's ketchup (which he said caused insanity) and in favor of cold showers, hard mattresses, fruits, raw vegetables, and whole wheat flour, which went into his new snack food. The way he saw it, the Graham cracker was no ordinary cracker. It was a cure for lust and a tamer of teenage hormones, which Graham thought were riled up by a diet of meats and fats. According to his theory, the teenager who ate Graham crackers was calmer and better behaved and could more easily concentrate on homework.

While Graham was on his cracker crusade, Dr. John Kellogg was also fighting teenage lust (he called it "dangerous desires") with cornflakes. A vegetarian and a health faddist who ran a famous sanitarium in Battle Creek, Michigan, Dr. Kellogg was experimenting with a bread recipe one day, trying to make a new kind of toast that was easier to chew than the popular "zwieback" that was so hard people chipped their teeth on it. He left the oven on too long and his experimental bread was reduced to flakes. Soon, Kellogg was convinced that a regular diet of these flakes could douse the flames of the hottest romance and keep the youth of America out of trouble.

Not too many people agreed with Kellogg, or for that matter, with Sylvester Graham, but that didn't stop the entire nation from falling in love with Graham's crackers and Kellogg's cereal.

Kellogg made the acquaintance of C. W. Post, a fast-talking promoter who was a patient at Kellogg's sanitarium. Post went there looking for a cure for his nervous exhaustion and ate his first bowl of Kellogg's flakes. He liked the cereal, but he hated the caramel coffee that Kellogg served at breakfast. So that he'd have something better to drink, Post invented Postum, a grain-based grog that tasted like coffee—at least Post thought so. Post set up a company to sell Postum on a grand scale, along with a couple of cereals he developed—Grape Nuts and Post Toasties.

There was Hershey and his candy bar—Milton Snaveley Hershey, to be exact, the owner of a tiny caramel store who went to the 1893 Chicago World's Fair and saw the demonstration of a German chocolate-making machine and ordered one for himself. Hershey used the machine to churn out chocolate-covered caramels, followed by the first mass-produced chocolate bar, followed by Hershey's Kisses in 1907 and the Hershey's Goodbar with peanuts in 1925. Hershey stock began trading on the New York Stock Exchange in 1927.

There was Jerome Smucker, who sold apple butter and apple cider made from trees planted by Johnny Appleseed in Ohio. In

1897, Smucker founded the J. M. Smucker Company, which a century later sells more jellies and jams than anybody else in the country.

At this point, a thousand trademarks were registered in the United States, and slogans and jingles had entered the American vocabulary, such as "absolutely pure," which came from the Royal Baking Company; "you press the button, we do the rest," from Kodak; "it floats," from Ivory soap; "the beer that made Milwaukee famous," from Schlitz; "all the news that's fit to print," from *The New York Times*; and "pink pills for pale people," from the ads for a vitamin concoction sold by a medicine man known as Dr. Williams.

The invention of all these products led to the creation of new stores where they could be sold. As late as the mid-1800s, the country had no supermarkets. Nobody had thought of a mass-market grocery until a couple of tea lovers, George Gilman and George Huntington Hartford, opened a tea shop in New York, near the site of today's World Trade Center, in 1859. It was a small business with a big-sounding name: the Great American Tea Company. Later, the name was changed so it sounded even bigger: the Great Atlantic and Pacific Tea Company.

One tea shop in New York led to five tea shops in New York, then tea shops out of state, and by that time Gilman and Hartford had put coffee, butter, and milk on the shelves. In 1912, they had a chain of four hundred stores, the first mass-market grocery, and by the late 1920s, they had fifteen thousand stores nationwide with $1 billion in annual sales. It would have been hard to find a serious shopper anywhere in the country who hadn't heard of the A&P.

Thanks to a growing number of chain stores and mail-order catalogues, people could buy mass-produced goods of reliable quality and at much lower prices than the prices charged by itinerant peddlers or local independent merchants. In small towns and on farms, the arrival of a package in the mail was an important event, especially if it came from Montgomery Ward (named for its founder, Aaron Montgomery Ward, who formed the first mail-order company in Chicago in 1872), or from Sears Roebuck and Company, which sent out its first catalogue in 1887.

At first, Sears only sold watches, but it quickly expanded into general merchandise. The story goes that a prospector in Nome, Alaska, sent Sears a prepaid order for one hundred rolls of toilet paper and enclosed cash in the envelope. Sears wrote back that it couldn't accept any order that didn't come from the catalogue. The customer replied, "If I had the catalogue, I wouldn't need the toilet paper."

As more merchandise was sent long-distance, the railroads had more freight to deliver, and the mail played a bigger role in people's lives. The mail was crucial to capitalism, because it was the most effective way to get mass-produced goods into the hands of the masses. Even then, the post office had a reputation for lousy service, and the producers of goods were upset about it. Speedy delivery was so important to business that Adolphus Green took time out from running Nabisco to spearhead a campaign to reform the post office.

The Industrial Era and the Robber Barons

Corporations had built the factories, the girders, the underpinnings of modern America. By the mid–nineteenth century, less than a quarter of the country's business was done by corporations, but moving toward the twentieth, companies were having an impact on every aspect of domestic life.

Mass production was the watchword of the day: The goods could roll from the factories into the railroad cars to be distributed across state lines, making regional markets out of what used to be neighborhood markets of small shops, with little variety in the merchandise. This expansion of markets was a revolutionary change in society, which affected people's daily lives as much as or more than the American Revolution itself. Whereas before 1820, two-thirds of the clothing worn in the United States was made at home by hand, by the end of the century most of it came from factories.

Company names and brand names such as Diamond, Pillsbury, Campbell, Heinz, Borden, Quaker Oats, Libby, and Procter
& Gamble became household words. Household products became celebrities, just as famous as well-known writers, painters,
entertainers, or politicians. By the 1880s, Ivory soap was recog-
nized from coast to coast. In 1884, George Eastman came up with
a way to mass-produce the film to make photographs, and ten
years later, taking pictures with Kodak film and Kodak cameras
had become a national pastime.

The machine age and mass production came along so fast that
people hardly had time to prepare for it. Property laws had to be
rewritten, new rules of commerce established, new business ar-
rangements entered into. A small group of people took advantage
of the situation and enriched themselves beyond the wildest
dreams of their contemporaries. These men amassed fortunes
that dwarfed the fortunes of the richest pharaohs, sultans, poten-
tates, kings, queens, conquistadores, and empire builders in all of
history. They were known as the robber barons, a term coined by
historian Matthew Josephson in the late 1920s.

The robber barons were not robbers in the traditional sense,
nor were they lawbreakers, although some of them bent the laws,
and even had the laws rewritten, for their own benefit. They were
high-rolling speculators, most of them raised in poverty, who
struggled, connived, and strong-armed their way to the top of
American industry. They stretched the envelope of money.

Among them were Jay Gould, the son of a poor farmer in
upstate New York, who by hook and by crook built a fabulous
railroad empire; Andrew Carnegie, the son of Scottish weavers,
who also owned railroads and became the nation's most powerful
iron magnate; Cornelius Vanderbilt, a roughneck on the docks of
New York, who built a fleet of steamships, controlled the shipping
industry and after that railroads, but in spite of his success and
his wealth, lived for many years in a small house with a ratty old
carpet; Daniel Drew, a cattle drover who was a master at manipu-
lating the stock market for his own benefit; J. P. Morgan, the
devoted churchgoer whose bank became so powerful he was

once asked to bail out the U.S. government; Jay Cooke, the eternally optimistic stock and bond dealer whose investment company was so big and powerful that when it collapsed, the country almost collapsed with it; "Diamond" Jim Fisk, a former pushcart peddler and circus fancier who wore loud clothes and rings on every fat finger; Russell Sage, a crafty stock speculator and railroad tycoon; Leland Stanford, who became governor of California and used his political clout to build the railroads there, enriching himself and later Stanford University, which took his name and his money.

Last but not least was John D. Rockefeller, son of a snake-oil salesman, and himself a devout Baptist, a combination that produced a shrewd and fearsome capitalist, who gathered all the oil companies into a giant monopoly that could raise prices at will and force all its rivals into submission. More on this later.

With one or two exceptions, the robber barons were conservative in their personal lives, often devoutly religious, and oddly frugal given the size of their bankrolls. Most of them built or owned railroads, and they were plotting constantly to take over each other's rail lines. They knew how to control the stock market to make the prices of railroad stocks zig and zag, and they made millions on the zigs.

Diamond Jim Fisk wasn't called "first in the pockets of his countrymen" for no reason, and Jay Gould was a champion at talking up his Erie Railroad stock, so people would pay much more than these shares were worth. It was because of Gould that the Erie was called the "Scarlet Woman of Wall Street"—a company with a ruined credit rating that paid no dividend to shareholders between 1873 and 1942.

When Jay Cooke closed the doors of his banking offices because his railroad investments had soured, he triggered the Panic of 1873, which brought down several brokerage houses and almost put Wall Street out of business.

While the population doubled from 1864 to the early 1900s, the rail network increased sevenfold, and every American was within earshot of a railroad whistle. A twenty-two-year-old veteran of

the Union forces, George Westinghouse, invented the air brake;
electric lights replaced the gas and kerosene lamps; and Pullman
came along with his manufactured railroad cars.

Even though the railroads were everywhere, people lost
money on the stocks. There was always a crisis or a scandal that
wiped out the small investors, while the robber barons managed
to rake in the profits. In 1877, one of the most successful among
them, Cornelius Vanderbilt, died in New York, leaving his entire
fortune, a whopping $100 million, to his son William Vanderbilt.

The elder Vanderbilt was considered the richest man in American when he died, and he made his pile on shipping and then on
railroads, particularly the New York Central. As often as he was
praised as a titan of commerce, he was cursed as an aristocratic
ingrate who gave nothing back to the people whose sweat had
built the railroads and created his fortune.

The public was outraged that he departed from life having left
nothing to the community. Vanderbilt himself believed he had
done enough good by creating the railroad, and his money was his
own business. His son William was more blunt about it. "The
public be damned," he once said.

In the emerging market of the United States, things didn't
happen in an orderly fashion. The same is true in many contemporary emerging markets. Every couple of decades, the economy
broke down, and people would panic and rush to the banks to
rescue their money, most of which had already been loaned out.
The banks couldn't possibly pay back all their depositors at once,
so they collapsed. Once the banks collapsed and entire commu-
nities were left without money, all sorts of businesses would fail,
and the financial system would go into the tank. The stock market
would crash, and so would the bond market, because the organizations that issued the bonds couldn't make the interest payments.

The Europeans were big losers in the Panic of 1873, just as
they had been in earlier such calamities. Because of our frequent
crashes and panics, the United States got the reputation of being
a nation of sharpies who couldn't be trusted in a business deal,
the same sort of thing that's recently been said about some of the

Chinese and Russian entrepreneurs. We were the deadbeats of yesteryear.

In the Panic of 1893 (the big ones seemed to come at twenty-year intervals) one-fourth of the railroad companies were forced into bankruptcy. There was a lesser panic in 1903. Panic or no panic, some great companies that got their start in this period are still great companies today, employing hundreds of thousands of workers and making money for the shareholders. Half the countries that appeared on the world maps of 1900 have disappeared, but Hershey's, Quaker Oats, Wrigley's, AT&T, Du Pont, the Bank of Boston, American Tobacco, U.S. Steel, and the various spinoffs of Standard Oil (Exxon, Chevron, Mobil, Amoco, and so forth) are going strong.

The Dreaded Monopolies

When the twentieth century rolled around, it was obvious that something was wrong with the way capitalism was going. It had started out as a free-for-all when anybody with a good idea had a chance to succeed. It was turning into a rigged game dominated by a few giant businesses. These were called monopolies.

You could make the case that monopolies are as big a threat to our way of life as any America ever faced, short of Adolf Hitler and communism. If you've played the game Monopoly, you understand the concept. The goal is to buy up all the properties so that people who land on them have no choice but to pay outrageous rents. A player who can do this ends up with all the money.

In the real world, a monopoly is exactly the same, but it doesn't just happen with real estate. It happens when there's one bigshot in an industry that controls everything and sets the prices. In a bakery monopoly, for instance, there's only one company making and selling cakes and cookies, so customers have to pay whatever the company wants to charge, or give up cakes and cookies. Whether it's bakeries, toy makers, or airlines, when a monopoly is formed, the customers have no choice. There's no other baker, toy maker, or airline they can go to, because all the competitors have either joined the monopoly or been driven out of business.

The trading companies you've already read about—the Virginia Company, the United Dutch East India Company, and so forth—were all monopolies. Their charters, granted by the kings of Europe, gave them the exclusive right to do business in huge expanses of territory in the New World. For a thousand miles along the coastline of America, these companies controlled farming, fishing, and trading with the Indians. Nobody could compete with them—without their permission.

The first person to understand that monopolies posed a threat to the future prosperity of the world was Adam Smith, the author of *The Wealth of Nations*. Smith realized that competition was the key to capitalism. As long as somebody else could come along and make a product better and cheaper, a company couldn't do a lousy job and expect to get away with it. Competition kept companies on their toes. They were forced to improve their products and keep their prices as low as possible, or they'd lose their customers to a rival.

By the middle of the nineteenth century, when the U.S. economy was booming along, there were many companies in every industry and the competition was fierce. The owners of the companies didn't necessarily like this situation, even if it was a good thing for society, as Adam Smith said. In fact, they thought competition was a menace. They were tired of having to fend off competitors by improving their products. They were looking for a chance to charge higher prices for things, prices customers would be forced to pay no matter what.

If they'd been allowed to, all the owners in a given industry, say bakeries, could have gotten together in a room somewhere and decided to charge the same high prices for their cookies and their cakes. They could have made deals to avoid competing with one another. They could have formed strategic alliances. In fact, price-fixing cartels were established in the United States in the 1870s and 1880s, but laws were passed to make cartels—or "pools," as they were called—illegal.

In the early 1880s, a clever lawyer named S. C. T. Dodd figured out how companies could get around the laws against cartels by forming trusts. A trust was an ancient method of putting a group of properties under the control of one manager. While working in the legal department at John D. Rockefeller's oil company, Dodd brought his idea to Rockefeller's attention. Why not put a bunch of oil companies together in a trust? That way, the owners could fix prices, make deals, and avoid having to compete—and it would all be completely legal.

Rockefeller immediately set out to organize a Dodd-style trust among his forty biggest competitors in the oil business. He invited them to participate, although they didn't have much choice. Any companies that refused the invitation, Rockefeller threatened to put out of business, by selling oil at such low prices they couldn't afford to compete with him.

His tactics were far from friendly, but they were effective. He and his forty cohorts, some of them reluctant, formed the Standard Oil Trust. Overnight, it became the largest and most powerful oil producer in the world, controlling most of the U.S. oil wells and 90 percent of the refineries. Rockefeller and his closest advisors were now dictators of oil, raising prices at will. Customers had no choice but to pay Rockefeller's high rates—otherwise, they'd get no oil.

The dictators also used their newfound muscle on the railroad companies, forcing them to lower their prices for transporting the oil. They didn't have much choice, either. Any railroad that refused to ship for less, Rockefeller could drive out of business. After all, if they didn't ship his oil, they didn't ship any oil, because more than 90 percent of the national output was refined by the trust.

Standard Oil extended its monopoly over every aspect of the business. From the wells to the refineries, Rockefeller was in charge. And once they'd heard of his success, the owners of other kinds of companies began to form trusts. There was a sugar trust, a whiskey trust, a cotton oil trust, a lead trust, and a tobacco trust created by James Duke and his rival tobacco farmers, who joined forces to become the American Tobacco Company.

There was a ham trust (Swift Brothers), a fruit trust (United Fruit), and a cookie-and-biscuit trust, (Nabisco). Companies that didn't form trusts could link themselves in a different way, by merging. Several companies could merge into what was called a conglomerate. Mergers produced International Harvester, Du Pont, Anaconda Copper, Diamond Match, and American Smelting and Refining now called ASARCO. The railroads got into the act, with several of the bigger ones involved in mergers and take-overs. Dozens of railroad lines were consolidated into a few big groups: the Vanderbilt roads, Pennsylvania roads, Hill roads, Harriman lines, Gould roads, and the Rock Island system. When railroads got into financial trouble, as they so often did, banker J. P. Morgan was there to reorganize them.

Morgan, a formidable presence on Wall Street in his vested suits and his top hat, took eight small steel companies and merged them in 1901 to form the giant U.S. Steel, the most powerful conglomeration to date and America's first billion-dollar enterprise.

One-third of all public companies in the United States disappeared into trusts and mergers between 1895 and 1904. In most major industries, trusts and conglomerates were raising prices at will. They were throwing their weight around in all areas of commerce.

The American people saw what was happening, competitors disappearing in one industry after another, the owners of trusts raking in the millions and building summer "cottages" as big as army barracks along the coast at Newport, Rhode Island. So the public turned against the trusts.

People realized that the giant companies would tighten their hold on the smaller companies, forcing them to join trusts or be driven out of business, and if this trend were allowed to continue, prices for everything would jump through the roof, and the wallets of the nation would be sucked dry. With a few insiders controlling both prices and wages, free-market capitalism would cease to exist.

This was one of the scariest periods in American history, and it is rarely discussed. Here we were, a 125-year-old country going

into a new decade after a tremendous spurt of growth and prosperity, and we were losing the economic freedom we had worked
so hard to gain, losing it to a bunch of trusts.

There were scandals everywhere: writer Upton Sinclair exposed meat-packing houses that sold tainted meat—this sort of
journalism was known as "muckraking." People joined unions
to fight for better pay and reverse the drop in wages imposed by
the trusts. Where trusts controlled the jobs, individual workers
had no leverage. They couldn't very well quit and find jobs
elsewhere—there was no elsewhere.

The unions, the newspapers, the courts, and some courageous
political leaders all had a hand in foiling the trusts and rescuing
the country from the greedy few. It if hadn't been for these trust
busters, we could have gotten ourselves into a situation in which
the average person in America was no better off than a Russian
peasant. Then we might have had a revolution like Russia's, and
what a tragedy that would have been.

Fortunately for everyone except the owners of the trusts, the
courts and the government fought hard against the trusts. In 1890,
Congress passed the Sherman Antitrust Act, but several big of-
fenders wiggled out of it by turning themselves into "holding
companies" and moving to New Jersey. New Jersey had passed its
own law making it easy for would-be trusts to organize as holding
companies and avoid the federal regulations. The giant U.S. Steel
was a holding company.

In 1904, the U.S. Supreme Court struck another blow—it
outlawed one of the biggest railroad trusts. Teddy Roosevelt was
president at the time. He revived the Sherman Act by bringing suit
against forty-four major trusts. A camper, hunter, and all-around
outdoorsman, Roosevelt was nicknamed "Rough Rider" after his
famous charge up Cuba's San Juan Hill in the Spanish-American
War. But far more important than winning that war was winning
the war against the trusts. He became the nation's "Trust Buster."
In 1914, Congress passed a second antitrust act, the Clayton Act.

Beginning with Standard Oil in 1911, many of the nation's
biggest trusts were broken up, and competition in the major

industries was restored. The government has been on the lookout ever since for companies that get too big and too powerful and threaten to monopolize an industry. Whenever that happens, the government can file an antitrust suit, and if it wins, the courts can force the company to divide itself into smaller companies that are independent from one another. That way, competition is restored.

At one point, Alcoa controlled the U.S. aluminum industry, until it was forced to break itself up. The same thing happened to AT&T, which was the only phone company of any consequence until Judge Harold Green, in a famous decision, forced AT&T to divide itself into eight parts, with Ma Bell, the parent company, keeping the long-distance business, and the seven Baby Bells getting the local business. Since that crucial ruling, dozens of other companies have come along to compete with Ma Bell and the Baby Bells, which is why phone calls are getting cheaper and cheaper every day. This is great for long-distance romance and keeps many couples in constant communication, so they won't have a breakup the way AT&T did.

The AT&T case is a good example of what's wrong with monopolies and why competition is in everyone's best interest. Before the AT&T breakup, the company employed 1 million people—one out of every one hundred American workers had a job with Ma Bell. Today, Ma Bell and the seven Baby Bells to-gether employ only six hundred thousand workers, while the volume of phone calls has more than tripled.

Competition has forced the phone companies to cut costs and become more efficient. They still have to comply with certain regu-lations, such as offering phone service to everyone in the region—otherwise, people who live in the boonies where it's expensive to string a phone line would never get a phone. But we can thank competition for the fact that more calls can be made with fewer workers, and we pay lower rates on our phone bills as a result.

Microsoft, as you probably know, is the world's largest soft-ware company. Recently, it announced a plan to take over an-other large software company, Intuit. The government objected to this plan, on the theory that a Microsoft-Intuit combination would create a software monopoly. After learning of the government's disapproval, Microsoft decided not to pursue Intuit. Nobody likes to fight the trust busters in Washington.

The one monopoly that has been allowed to survive with the government's blessing is major league baseball. Because it's the national pastime, Congress gave it an exemption from the antitrust laws. The players have complained bitterly about this, and after the recent baseball strike, Congress threatened to take away baseball's exemption. It hasn't happened yet, but someday it might.

Dow's Famous Average

In 1884, a journalist named Charles Henry Dow invented a way for fans of stocks to follow the overall stock market. He put together a list of eleven important stocks, and at the end of each trading session, he took the closing price for each one, added them up, and divided by eleven. This gave him an average, which he published in a news bulletin called the *Customer's Afternoon Letter*.

At first, Dow's average was nothing more than a curiosity, but eventually it gave him a place in history. It became known as the Dow Jones average (Jones being Dow's partner in the news business), which has been the financial yardstick for stocks for more than a century. Even today, 110 years later, when people ask "What is the market doing?" or "where did the market close?" they are talking about the Dow Jones average. When somebody says: "It's up thirty points," or "down fifty points," they are using Dow's number.

The original Dow Jones average included nine railroads, because the railroads were held in such high esteem on Wall Street, and people believed that the railroads would dominate American business forever. Twelve years later, Dow put together another average, the industrials, for the gritty businesses (oil and gas refiners, coal producers, smelters, and so forth) that turned raw materials into the fuel, steel, and rubber on which the entire economy depended. The earliest Dow industrials were dominant companies in their own right, big, powerful enterprises that were the Microsofts and the Wal-Marts of their day, but most of them have disappeared without a trace.

Who's ever heard of American Cotton Oil, Chicago Gas, Laclede Gas, National Lead, Tennessee Coal & Iron, or U.S. Rubber? All these companies made the Dow's original list of industrials. The only name you'd recognize is General Electric, which has kept its place on the list over the years.

This is an important lesson for investors. Business is like sports, in that the winning teams and successful organizations don't necessarily stay on top forever. As hard as it is to reach the top in business or in sports, it's even harder to stay there. The New York Yankees found that out after their dynasty came to an end in the 1970s. So did the Pittsburgh Steelers and the Boston Celtics. So did Tennessee Coal & Iron, Laclede Gas, and American Cotton Oil. General Electric is a rare example of a winner that manages to keep winning.

You can see how much America has changed by comparing the earliest Dow industrials to today's expanded list of thirty. McDonald's is on today's list—how industrial is a hamburger? Not very, unless you figure it takes a cast-iron stomach to digest one, but McDonald's is such an important company that it's been included. When Dow chose his original industrials, no restaurant company was big enough to have even crossed his mind. Coca-Cola is included in today's Dow. A company as far-reaching and as powerful as Coke belongs on the list. It's come a long way from the 1920s, when it was so small that most investors wouldn't have noticed it. Disney is in the Dow, but it didn't get started as a public company until 1940. When Clarence Dow invented the Dow, Walt Disney hadn't drawn the first Mickey Mouse.

The modern Dow is proof that America is no longer the gritty industrial giant that lives off the output from coal mines, iron-works, and steel mills. As factories and mills have faded into the background on Main Street and on Wall Street, the restaurants, banks, mass merchandisers, entertainment companies, and lately, the computer and software companies, have taken their place at the forefront.

Company Towns

The number of Americans who worked on farms was dropping fast. After 1920, most people lived in cities, because that's where companies did most of their business, and that's where the jobs were. Some companies even built their own towns so the workers would have a nice place to live. U.S. Steel created Gary, Indiana, and the Hershey Chocolate Company designed Hershey, Pennsylvania, from the ground up—not with gingerbread and gumdrop houses and lollipops for streetlights, the way Willy Wonka would have done it, but people liked it anyway. Hershey is still a nice place to live today, but several other company towns came to a bad end. One of the best examples was Pullman, Illinois, located on the rim of Chicago.

To live in Pullman, you had to be employed by the Pullman company that made passenger cars for the railroads. Nearly nine thousand Pullman employees and their families were lodged in identical houses, built around a park and a lake. Pullman was a model for environmental planning long before the word "environment" had entered the popular vocabulary. The lake served as a cooling basin for the factory power supply. Sewage from the town's toilets was used for fertilizer.

The schools were good, the landscaping was nice, the people were well taken care of, so Pullman was a happy town, until the train car business went sour and the company stopped making money. Pullman did what anybody does who stops making money. It cut back on expenses, including wages and benefits for the workers. The workers got mad and went on strike. The strike and the bitter feelings against the company destroyed the town. In the end, the company sold the houses and the rest of the buildings, and eventually the whole operation was shut down. Pullman went bankrupt.

There's a danger to having companies provide housing, education, medical care, and the other life-support systems that people depend on. As long as the company is doing well, it has no problem providing social services, but what if it falters? Then it has two choices. It can lay off workers and cut back on its spending to stop the flow of red ink, in which case the schools, hospitals, and parks may have to be shut down so the company can survive. Or it can keep all the services going and spend itself out of business and into bankruptcy.

Capitalism works best when a company that's losing money has a chance to try to turn things around, and if that doesn't happen, it can put itself out of its misery. That way, unproductive businesses can die, and the workers can go on to some other industry that's healthier. But when a company has a second role as the doctor, teacher, and caretaker for its workers, then it may have to stay in business just so its employees can continue to get all their benefits.

That's one of the reasons communism broke down and socialism has problems. Communist businesses weren't really businesses at all. They existed because the communist bosses, also known as central planners, decided they should exist. For instance, the Russian central planners liked the idea of building steel plants, and at one point, the Russians got very good at making steel. There were steel plants all over the place.

Meanwhile, there were very few factories that made shoes or clothes for the people. This created shortages and long lines at the shoe and clothing outlets. There was a huge potential market for consumer goods in Russia, and people would have been delighted to have more to eat and more to wear, but the planners didn't care. They built more steel plants. Maybe they thought millions of Russians would start wearing steel pants.

In a communist economy, all the resources—everything that's made, bought, or sold—are controlled by a small group of managers. In a capitalist economy, if there are too many steel plants, we'll have an oversupply of steel, the price will go down, the steel companies will lose money, people will stop buying steel stocks, and the banks will stop lending money to the steel companies.

The steel plants will be forced to cut back their production, and without money to expand, they'll stop expanding.

Consequently, the money that isn't invested in steel companies will be used elsewhere, to build shoe factories, jeans factories, malls, water slides, or housing developments— products that haven't saturated the market and are still in demand. Smith's Invisible Hand has never lost its touch.

Karl Marx

The most influential communist economic theories came out of the head of Karl Marx, a philosopher who was born in 1818. Marx was German, but he developed most of his ideas in London, where his wife and children were stuck in a cold apartment with little to eat. Even though his favorite subject was economics, he was a dunce at personal finance.

Marx tried to reduce capitalism to a formula, the way Newton did with gravity. His book *Das Kapital* became the Bible of communists everywhere, and outside the Bible, one could argue it was the most influential book ever written. It convinced Lenin and other influential Russians to set up a communist state after they won the Russian Revolution.

According to Marx, capitalism was doomed, because as business grew, and more and more people were harnessed to machines, the value of their labor was bound to decline. Workers of the world would be required to work longer and longer hours for less and less pay, until eventually they would get mad and burn down the factories and join the Communist party.

It's true that it was no fun to work in a factory at the time Marx was writing his book. Factories were dark, noisy, dirty, and dangerous. Women and children were forced to put in twelve to eighteen hours a day tending the machines, and they earned very little for their efforts. Some were herded into factories against their will, and many caught diseases there. The air was polluted from the smokestacks that blackened the sky with soot.

Marx saw all this and hated what he saw (even though his family was no better off than the average factory worker's), and he was determined to prove that the misery in the factories wouldn't last. But his theories were totally out of whack. Instead of people having to work harder and harder for less and less money, their hours got shorter and their paychecks got bigger, because factories installed updated equipment, which enabled each worker to produce more merchandise in the same amount of time.

With more efficient machinery, the workers' time became more valuable, not less, and the factories could afford to raise the workers' wages. These wages weren't always raised without a fight, but often enough, they were raised, and instead of the working class being doomed the way Marx said it was, the working conditions got cleaned up a bit, and the workers took home more cash. That's how prosperity came to the countries with the most factories—England, the United States, and those of Western Europe—while the rest of the world was stuck in a rut with a few land barons owning everything.

So much for Marx and his fancy equations. It was communism that was doomed, because the standard of living in communist countries continued to decline, while in capitalist countries, it continued to rise. It was the Russian and Eastern European workers who eventually overthrew the communist system, in favor of ours.

Before the Famous Crash of 1929

Just before the famous Crash of 1929, Wall Street was a busy place, especially for clerks, because most of the paperwork was done with primitive tools such as adding machines and typewriters. This work was very time-consuming, and the brokerage firms needed large warehouses to store the records.

The value of all the stock in all the companies that traded their shares on the New York Stock Exchange was $87 billion, a drop in the bucket compared to the $5.4 trillion that the NYSE shares are worth today. Exxon alone is worth more than $87 billion. It has more shareholders than any other public company.

In 1929, AT&T had the most shareholders. It was the biggest company in the world, but the railroads were still the biggest industry, followed by oil, and then steel. If you wanted a safe, secure investment you didn't have to worry about, you bought a railroad stock. They paid a nice, steady dividend, a role later taken over by the electric utilities.

Like AT&T, the railroads held up pretty well during the Crash, but they didn't do so well on the rebound. Few economists and fewer fortune-tellers would have predicted that in the long run, railroads would lose their leading role and shrink into the shadows of public life, and that their stocks would be mediocre investments for decades to come. Whether a stock is good or bad depends entirely on the time frame.

The auto industry that would contribute so much to the decline of the railroads had caught the attention of investors. Its development was typical of a new enterprise. At the outset, auto manufacturing was a mom-and-pop business, and cars were made in garages across the country. At the turn of the century, auto manufacturers were located in New England, the Middle Atlantic states, and the Midwest.

Along came Henry Ford, who put cars on the assembly line and mass-produced them, just as Duke had done with cigarettes and Heinz with pickles. He made a generic car of high quality with a low price, and the public loved it. They bought all the Model Ts that Ford could make, but they couldn't buy the stock, because Ford was private, owned by Ford, his family and friends, and nobody else. On the other hand, General Motors was a public company, and by 1929, it was a popular stock to own. So popular, in fact, that investors had made it the third largest, behind AT&T and U.S. Steel. While Ford was sticking with the Model T, GM made a variety of models to give customers a choice. In fact, GM roared past Ford, but Ford saw the light and added new models of its own. Lesser competitors in the industry were Chrysler, Hudson, and Nash.

By now, chain stores were familiar sights in cities and towns across America. The most prominent was Woolworth from Pennsylvania, founded in the nineteenth century and the earliest variety chain on record, followed by McCrory, Kress, and Kresge. A&P had its nationwide chain of supermarkets. The first shopping center, Country Club Plaza, was built near Kansas City, in 1922.

Many of today's biggest names in drugstores, candy stores, department stores, and grocery stores were small companies in 1929, insignificant when measured against such industrial giants as U.S. Steel, or such powerful railroads as the New York Central. The leading food companies of 1929 were United Fruit, National Dairy Products, and Borden. General Mills and Pillsbury Flour Mills were relative newcomers in the cereal and baking businesses. The total value of Coca-Cola's stock was $134 million; Wrigley's, $136 million; Gillette's, $226 million, and Procter & Gamble's, $345 million. To put this in perspective, in 1994 Coke made a profit of almost $7 million a day!

Sears was the dominant force in retailing, followed by its longtime rival, Montgomery Ward, which customers liked to call Monkey Ward. Woolworth had a nationwide network of its five-and-ten-cent stores, where everything sold for a dime or less.

Suburbs had begun to spring up around cities, but there were no malls in the suburbs, because the roads and highways hadn't been built to connect one suburb to another. Out of Boston, for instance, you could get from downtown to Brookline or to Natick on a train or a trolley car, but there was no way to get from Brookline to Natick. So if there had been a mall in Brookline, only the residents of Brookline could have reached it. Roads were lacking, and cars were in short supply.

People went shopping in the cities, in the downtown department stores, or in the towns and villages at the local mom-and-pop stores where the prices were high and the merchandise was limited, or if they lived far out in the boondocks, they shopped from the Ward catalogue or the Sears catalogue.

Today there's a store on every corner and a new mall at every other exit on the turnpike, so it's hard to imagine that a single retailer could win the hearts of shoppers the way Sears did. In remote areas of the country, Sears was much more than a mail-order catalogue. It was a source of excitement and a relief from boredom, and to its millions of devoted followers, Sears was nothing less than a commercial godsend. The governor of Georgia, Eugene Talmadge, in a campaign pitch to area farmers, once said: "Your only friends are Jesus Christ, Sears Roebuck, and Gene Talmadge."

Fast-growing small companies come out of nowhere to become the billion-dollar companies of tomorrow. It's happening in the 1990s, just as it happened in the 1920s and in every decade in between. Office equipment was no more than a cottage industry in 1929. The five biggest names in that business were Addressograph-Multigraph, Burroughs Adding Machine, International Business Machines, National Cash Register, and Remington Rand. The total value of each company ranged from $9 million to $65 million. Four out of the five (Addressograph-Multigraph was the exception) became corporate giants.

A lot of investors lost everything in the Crash of 1929, but the brokerage firms that sold them their stocks survived the calamity. A few lesser-known brokerage houses went bankrupt, but the majority stayed in business. In those days, people could buy stocks for 10 percent down, which is why the Crash wiped them out. They ended up owing much more money than they had invested in the first place. The brokerage houses had to collect on these debts, and they went after their customers' assets with a vengeance. Wall Street firms also bought stocks on borrowed money, but the banks that loaned it to them were sympathetic and gave them extra time to pay their bills. Individual investors weren't so lucky.

Fear of Crashing

No event in American history has worried more people over a longer stretch of time than the Crash of 1929. People who weren't even born in 1929 were worried about it. The children of people who weren't born in 1929 have worried about it as well.

The United States has managed to survive a Civil War, a Revolutionary War, two world wars, Korea, Vietnam, and many smaller deadly conflicts. We've survived the Chicago fire, the San Francisco earthquake and fire, the Los Angeles earthquake, plus numerous lesser earthquakes and dozens of major and minor hurricanes. We've survived typhoid epidemics, tuberculosis epidemics, the polio epidemic, droughts, floods, riots, work stoppages, and the St. Valentine's Day massacre. But we have not yet gotten over the 1929 stock market crash.

It's the most pernicious collective phobia on record, and it has kept millions of people from buying stocks and making a profit they could have used. The idea still lurks in the back of many brains that the stock market is headed for another crash that will wipe out everybody's life savings, and the suckers who put in their money will be roaming the streets, wearing old blankets, sleeping in homeless shelters, eating cold beans, and selling apples and pencils. That's what people said in the 1930s: "Uncle Joe is out selling apples and pencils." It was a major industry in those days.

Of course, there could be another crash. We had a big one in 1987, a smaller one in 1981–82, and another big one in 1973–74, but stocks bounced back, as they always do, eventually. Looking at the positive side, a crash is a unique opportunity to buy stocks cheap.

The major problem with crashes is how long it takes stocks to recover. The Dow Jones Industrial Average hit one thousand in 1972, and at one point ten years later it fell below eight hundred. Investors' patience was tested over this stretch, but not as sorely tested as it was after the Crash of 1929. Then, it took nearly twenty-five years for many stocks to recover. That's when people got tired of waiting and vowed never to buy a stock again.

But that slow recovery can't be blamed on the Crash itself. It had to do with the Great Depression. There was nothing really great about it, except the great amount of trouble it caused, but we call it that nonetheless. Sometimes we just call it the Depression, even though there had been many panics and depressions in the preceding century.

During the Great Depression, which lasted about ten years, money was scarce, and jobs were scarcer. Stores went out of business and the employees lost their jobs and their paychecks, which meant they couldn't buy anything, so more stores went out of business and their employees lost their paychecks. The economy was falling into a catatonic state. Companies couldn't earn a profit, and when that happened, the stock prices went down and stayed down.

Most historians will tell you the Depression wasn't caused by the Crash of 1929, although it often gets blamed as the cause. Only a tiny percentage of Americans owned stocks at the time, so the vast majority of people didn't lose a penny in the Crash. The Depression was brought about by a worldwide economic slowdown, coupled with the government's mishandling of the money supply and raising interest rates at the wrong time. Instead of putting more cash into circulation to perk up the economy, our government did just the opposite, pulling cash out of circulation. The economy came to a screeching halt.

Fortunately for posterity, the government learned from this mistake. Now when the economy slows, the government is quick to pump up the cash supply and lower the interest rates so there's more money around and it's less expensive to take out a loan. Cheaper loans encourage people to buy houses and make other expensive purchases and encourage businesses to expand. A good jolt of home buying and business expansion can shock the economy into action. It may take several drops in interest rates before the economy revives, but we've had nine slowdowns since World War II and in all nine cases, the economy has come back.

Before 1930, depressions and panics were a common occurrence, but since the Great One, we haven't had a single repeat. So in the last fifty years or so, the odds of a slowdown turning into a depression have been quite remote—in fact, they've been zero in nine chances. Nobody can be sure you'll never see a depression in your lifetime, but so far, in the past half-century, you would have gone broke betting on one.

Is it possible that we've found a permanent cure for economic depression, the way we have for polio? There are several reasons to think so. First, the government, through its Federal Reserve Bank system, stands ready to lower interest rates and pump money into the economy any time it begins to look sluggish and to jolt it back into action. Second, we've got millions of people on social security and pensions, with money to spend no matter what. Add in the 18 million employees of government at all levels, from federal to local, and you've got an army of spenders. As long as this huge group is throwing its money around, the economy can slow, but it can't come to a complete halt, the way it did in the 1930s.

Third, we've got deposit insurance at the banks and the savings and loans, so if the banks go bankrupt, people won't lose all their money. In the 1930s, when hundreds of banks shut their doors, their depositors lost everything. That in itself was enough to drive the country into a catatonic state.

The big change that underlies all these other changes is the government's rise to stardom. Today, it has the leading role in the economy, whereas in the 1930s it had only a supporting role, and before the 1900s, it was a bit player. When you hear people complain about big government that's ruining our lives, remember it's the same big government that runs the air traffic control and keeps the planes from colliding, and whose massive spending power keeps us from going into a second Great Depression.

If you buy the argument that we're not likely to suffer a relapse into depression, then you can be a little more relaxed about drops in the stock market. As long as the economy is alive and kicking, companies can make money. If companies are making money, their stocks won't go to zero. The majority will survive until the next period of prosperity, when stock prices will come back.

History doesn't have to repeat itself. When somebody tells you that it does, remind him or her that we haven't had a depression in more than a half-century. People who stay out of stocks to avoid a 1929-style tragedy are missing out on all the benefits of owning stocks, and that's a bigger tragedy.

Folk Tales from the Crash

A lot of hoodoo, folk tales, and nonsense have been passed along from generation to generation about the Crash of 1929. You may have heard the one about all the distraught investors committing suicide by jumping out of windows of tall buildings in New York. But according to a book called *1929: The Year of the Great Crash*, by William Klingaman, there was no increase in the national suicide rate in the weeks following the calamity on Wall Street; only a few people jumped from windows, and not necessarily because they lost money in stocks.

The vice-president of Earl Radio Corporation leaped to his death from the eleventh floor of the Hotel Shelton on Lexington Avenue, but that was in early October, a couple of weeks before the Crash. On October 24, a few days after the Crash, a crowd gathered around a construction project where a man was sitting on a girder. They thought he was a prominent investor about to do himself in, but he turned out to be a construction worker having his lunch.

British statesman Winston Churchill was staying at the Savoy Plaza Hotel, directly under a room where another man hurtled himself out a window fifteen stories to the ground and was dashed to pieces. This incident was counted as a stock market fatality, although there was no evidence it had anything to do with stocks. Most of the business types who committed suicide during this period shot themselves, stuck their heads into ovens, or chose other methods besides jumping out of windows without a bungee cord.

For instance, James Riordan of the County Trust Company bank put a bullet into his head; Harry Crew Crosby, a married man, died in an opium orgy with his girlfriend (this was publicized as a Wall Street scandal, because Crosby was the son of an investment banker at J. P. Morgan, but he was a writer and had nothing to do with the bank, nor did the bank have anything to do with him); the wife of a Long Island stockbroker shot herself in the heart (nobody knows why she didn't shoot him); an electric utility executive in Rochester, New York, gassed himself in his bathroom; a Philadelphia financier shot himself in his athletic club; a Providence, Rhode Island, investor dropped dead in his broker's office watching the tickertape; a Milwaukee investor turned a gun on himself and left a note that said: "My body should go to science, my soul to Andrew W. Mellon (the famous Pittsburgh tycoon) and sympathy to my creditors."

So where did we get the idea that victims of the Crash were throwing themselves off ledges in New York? The main source seems to be comedian Will Rogers. Soon after the Crash, Rogers said, "The situation has been reached in New York hotels where the clerk asks incoming guests, 'You wanna room for sleeping or for jumping?' And you have to stand in line to get a window to jump out of."

But Rogers was just trying to get a laugh. He could afford to make jokes, because he followed the advice of another famous Wall Street tycoon, Bernard Baruch. Baruch was smart enough to get out of stocks entirely before the market crashed, and Rogers did likewise. Other entertainers, such as Eddie Cantor and Groucho Marx, weren't so lucky.

The real victims of the Crash were the people who bought stocks with borrowed money, or "margin." In those days, you were allowed to invest with only 10 percent down. So if you had $10,000 you could borrow $90,000 and buy $100,000 worth of stocks. When the Crash cut the prices of your stocks in half, you were left with $50,000 worth of stocks and a $90,000 debt you couldn't pay back.

Good News in the Depression

Even the Great Depression wasn't equally depressing for everybody. Money was scarce and millions of people lost their jobs, so by and large, conditions were pretty bad. But for certain companies, and their employees and investors, business was OK.

The A&P grocery store company is a prime example. When everybody else was closing stores, the A&P was bucking the trend and opening new ones. It grew its sales and its earnings, because no matter how bad things got, people still had to buy groceries. The national income had fallen by half from 1928 to 1933, but whatever income they had left, people were spending on food.

Certain kinds of companies can ride out depressions and recessions and other periods when money is scarce. These are called consumer growth companies. They sell inexpensive items: beer, soft drinks, snacks, and so forth, or necessities, such as medicines that people can't live without. Chewing gum and candy companies, such as Wrigley's, can thrive on recessions, because as Mr. Wrigley himself once said: "The sadder they are, the more the people chew."

So it should have been no surprise that *Business Week* magazine reported in 1932 that A&P was in fine shape. But in business there's always a threat lurking around somewhere. The tricky part is, you never know exactly what the threat will be. This is one of the biggest mistakes investors make. They focus on what they think is the big threat, the one that everybody's talking about (global warming, nuclear warheads going off, the war in Bosnia, trade problems with Japan), while they ignore the little things that can make or break a company in which they've invested.

A&P had no problem coping with the Depression. It was the Piggly-Wiggly threat they had to worry about. A merchant in Memphis, Tennessee, had opened the original Piggly-Wiggly self-service store. Instead of asking the clerk behind the counter to pick items off the shelf, the Piggly-Wiggly shopper could roam the aisles and grab what she wanted (most shoppers were shes in those days) and bring it to the checkout line. This was new. Self-service meant that stores could operate with fewer clerks, and shoppers could be exposed to more items.

This was a dramatic moment for A&P. If the company's management had left well enough alone and ignored the challenge of Piggly-Wiggly, A&P would have gone the way of the dinosaurs. This is often the case with companies: Depressions they can handle, wars they can handle, the hole in the ozone layer doesn't bother them, but competition can do them in.

A company must quickly adapt to changes in the market, or it won't survive. A&P saw what it had to do and did it. It closed thousands of its small shops and opened a few supermarkets of its own.

In 1935, there were only ninety-six supermarkets in the entire country, and only twenty-four cities had one. But the Piggly-Wiggly idea was catching on fast, and by switching its strategy from small stores to big stores, A&P put itself in a position to take advantage of the boom in grocery stores that happened after World War II.

The American Revival

As horrible as it was for civilization in general, World War II brought the U.S. economy back to life. Soon after the GIs came home, the suburbs opened up in the countryside around the cities. People were buying cars, houses, refrigerators, washing machines, electrically powered vacuum cleaners, and other labor-saving devices at a rapid rate. What machines did for the farm in the nineteenth century, they did for the house in the twentieth.

With every new discovery, every time-saving appliance, every innovation and product that saved toil and trouble, there were traditionalists who sat back, scoffed, and bemoaned the passing of the simpler existence when meals were home-cooked, and motels were owned by moms and pops, and life was more natural, but they were swimming against a great tide of progress, because people knew a good thing when they saw it. Housewives preferred the vacuum cleaner to the simplicity of the broom, and the washing machine to the simplicity of the churn tub, and the processed foods to slaving over a hot stove. On the road, families looked forward to staying in the chain motel and eating at the chain restaurant, because there they knew what they were getting. Kids were excited to see a Howard Johnson's, a Holiday Inn, or a Golden Arch.

The postwar period was a busy one for public companies, with hundreds of new ones formed every year, but the vast majority of Americans avoided stocks. People remembered the Crash of 1929 and were determined not to risk their life savings in the market, at the very time shares of great companies were selling at bargain prices. The brave minority that bought stocks was well-rewarded.

Investor Protection

When you buy stocks, bonds, or mutual funds, you're taking enough of a risk already, without having to run the risk of being misled by false information or of being cheated. Investors deserve to be protected from fraud, hype, and shoddy merchandise, the same as customers in a retail store.

When you're buying a jacket, you want to know it's the kind of jacket the salesman says it is, that it's made out of the material listed on the label, and that you're paying a fair price. That's why the government has passed truth-in-advertising laws. When you're buying a stock, you need to know that the company is doing as well or as poorly as it claims to be doing, that its financial reports are reliable, and that in general you're getting what you pay for. That's why the government has passed strict rules for stockbrokers, traders, mutual funds, professional money managers, corporate executives, and companies themselves.

Prior to the Great Depression, many of these safeguards didn't exist. Companies weren't required to file detailed reports, and by not saying anything, they could hide their problems from investors. The so-called insiders—people who had advance notice of positive or negative developments in a company—could buy or sell shares before the news got out and make big profits from this "insider trading." Insider trading was frowned upon in theory, but a lot of insiders did it anyway.

Before the Crash of 1929, it was common practice for some of the robber barons and their cronies to run the price of a stock up and down for their own benefit. They knew how to manipulate the market in their favor, scaring the public into selling stocks at a low price, then luring them back to buy those same stocks at a ridiculously high price.

Few investors bothered to learn much about the companies they owned, because they realized that the gyrations in any stock had little or nothing to do with the fundamentals of a company. Instead, investors tried to figure out which way the smart money was betting—an impossible task, unless you were one of the insiders. Buying stocks in those days was like being in a poker game with the pros, where the pros could look at their cards, and you had to wear a blindfold. They should have put a warning label on the stock market: Invest at your own risk.

It was after the Crash that Congress held hearings on the various forms of Wall Street hanky-panky, and the government stepped in to put a stop to them. An agency known as the Securities and Exchange Commission (SEC) was established to lay down the law and punish the violators. The SEC has done such a good job that it is admired all over the world, where other stock markets may not be as fair and honest as ours is, and where small investors suffer as a result.

The situation on Wall Street is far from perfect, and you still hear about cases of insider trading, but these days, the perpetrators usually get caught and punished. It's against the law for employees of a company, from the top executives down to the mail clerks, to buy or sell shares when they know something's about to happen that will affect the price. Friends, relatives, bankers, lawyers, even people who overhear the inside information in the men's room or the ladies' room aren't allowed to profit from the tip. The SEC is very strict about this.

Let's say you're a vice-president of Boeing and you've just heard that China has agreed to buy five hundred new jumbo jets. Your first instinct is to rush to the phone and call your broker to put in an order to buy five thousand more shares of Boeing, but you can't. You can't even call your wife, husband, girlfriend, boyfriend, children, grandchildren, aunts, uncles, cousins, or racquetball partners to tell them to buy Boeing, because that would be insider trading and you'd be involving those people in a serious crime.

How do people get caught for something like this? The stock exchanges and the SEC have their own police forces and Sherlock Holmeses who watch the patterns of trading in a stock, and if there's an unusual amount of buying and selling, the alarm bells go off and the investigators jump into action to find out who's doing it. If they discover that the big buyers or sellers have any connection to the company or are related to people who do, they'll sniff around some more and collect enough evidence to file charges.

The SEC also supervises all the reports, statements, and other information that companies, brokerage houses, mutual funds, and so forth, release to the public. Every three months, a company has to release a short report on its progress, and once a year, it has to release a longer annual report. It has to tell the whole truth and nothing but the truth. Otherwise, the company can be fined and its officers or directors taken to court.

These officers and directors must also notify the SEC any time they buy or sell shares of the company's stock, and this information is available to the public. It's quite useful to know what these insiders are doing with their own investments, because they're involved with the company on a day-to-day basis. If several of them are selling their shares all at once, they can't be very optimistic about the company's prospects. On the other hand, if they're opening their wallets to buy more, they have to like what's going on.

The stock exchanges themselves are monitored by the SEC, and also by their own compliance departments. These people are the stock police. They watch the trading floor and the computers, looking for suspicious activity.

The Typical Shareholder

The NYSE does some checking every few years to find out who owns stocks and who doesn't. Since the 1950s, there's been a gradual increase in the number of people buying shares. This is a positive trend, because the more shareholders there are, the more the wealth gets spread around.

Twenty years after the Great Depression, the vast majority of Americans was afraid of stocks and kept their money in the bank, where they thought it was safe. You've heard the expression, "I'd rather be safe than sorry"? In this case, the money was safe and the people were sorry, because they missed the fabulous bull market in stocks during the 1950s. There were only 6.5 million shareholders in 1952, only 4.2 percent of the population, and 80 percent of those shares were in the hands of 1.6 percent of the population. All the gains went to a small group of people who weren't afraid of stocks and understood that the benefits far outweighed the risks.

In 1962 (the 1960s were another good decade for stocks), the number of shareholders had tripled, and 17 million Americans owned stocks. This was roughly 10 percent of the U.S. population. The more stock prices rose, the more people jumped on the bandwagon, and by 1970, there were 30 million shareholders in the country, 15 percent of the population.

No longer was the stock market the well-kept secret it had been in the 1950s. The record number of shareholders was good news in the long run, but the eager buyers had pushed prices to dangerously high levels, so by 1970, most stocks were fatally overpriced. By almost any measure, people were paying far too much for the companies they were buying. They lost their heads and fell in love with everything that was sold on a stock exchange.

This sort of craziness happens a few times in a century, and whenever it does, the market "corrects," the prices drop to more sensible levels, and the people who bought at the top are stunned and depressed. They can't believe they've lost so much money so quickly. Of course, they haven't really lost anything unless they sell their shares, but many investors do just that. They dump their entire portfolio in a panic. A stock they acquired for one hundred dollars when it was overpriced, they unload a few weeks later for seventy dollars or sixty dollars, at a bargain price. Their loss is the new buyers' gain, because the new buyers will make the money the sellers would have made if they'd held on to their investments and waited out the correction.

There were so many sellers during the brutal stock-market correction of the early 1970s that 5 million former shareholders, 3 percent of the population, exited the market en masse. It took five years for enough people to come back to stocks so that once again, the United States had 30 million shareholders.

By the mid-1980s, the ranks of shareholders had swollen to 47 million. One out of five Americans owned stocks, and 33 percent of those owners had invested through mutual funds. The market value of all stocks on the NYSE passed the $1 trillion mark.

By 1990, there were 51.4 million shareholders, an all-time record, and the number of people who invested through mutual funds had quadrupled in a decade. The average investor was no longer interested in picking his or her own stocks. The job was turned over to the professional fund managers at the nearly four thousand funds in existence at the time.

The typical shareholder in 1990 was a forty-five-year-old man or a forty-four-year-old woman. The man had a $46,400 annual income; the woman $39,400. He owned $13,500 worth of stocks, while she owned $7,200 worth. Lately, there's been a big jump in the number of young investors, with 3.7 million shareholders, or 7 percent of the total, under the age of twenty-one. This is a very positive development.

In 1995, the market value of all the stocks on the NYSE topped the $5 trillion mark, a long way from the $1.2 trillion these same stocks were worth in 1980. While investors large and small were working, playing, sleeping, and getting on with their lives, the money they put away in stocks had made them at least $4 trillion richer in a decade and a half. Talk about letting your money do the work!

TWO

The Basics of Investing

Invest Now: What Are You Waiting For?

Many people wait until they are in their thirties, forties, and fifties to start saving money. It dawns on them that they're not getting any younger, and soon enough they'll need extra cash for retirement so they can afford a cabin on the lake or a trip around the world. The trouble is, by the time they realize they ought to be investing, they've lost valuable years when stocks could have been working in their favor. Their money could have been piling up.

Instead, they spend what they have as if there's no tomorrow. Many of their expenses are unavoidable. They've got children to support, doctor bills, tuition bills, insurance bills, home repair bills, you name it. If there's nothing left over, there's not much they can do about it. But often enough, there is something left over, and still they don't invest it. They use it to pay the tab at fancy restaurants, or to make the down payment on the most expensive car in the showroom.

Before they know it, they're heading off into the sunset with nothing but a social security check in their pockets. They have to squeeze themselves into a tight budget at the very time they're supposed to be enjoying life, because you can't live it up on social security. It's hard enough just to survive on social security.

One of the best ways to avoid this fate is to begin saving money as early as possible, while you're living at home. When else are your expenses going to be this low? You have no children to feed—your parents are probably feeding you. If they don't make you pay rent, so much the better, because if you've got a job you can sink the proceeds into investments that will pay off in the future. The more you salt away now, while you're on the parental dole, the better off you'll be when you move away and your expenses shoot up.

Whether it's ten dollars a month, one hundred dollars a month, or five hundred dollars a month, save whatever amount you can afford, on a regular basis.

According to news reports, large numbers of twenty- and thirty-year-olds are migrating back to their parents' houses where they get a free roof over their heads and free use of the TVs, VCRs, gym equipment, and so forth. This trend is supposed to indicate that America has produced a new generation of freeloaders, who lack the gumption to go out into the world and make it on their own. There's a good side to this that we haven't heard much about, except in a recent headline in *The Wall Street Journal*: "Generation X Starts Saving for Retirement."

The gist of the story is that the freeloading twenty-somethings who belong to the so-called lost generation, or Generation X, have been quietly stashing away their loot. Apparently, there are more savers in this group than among their parents, the baby boomers who prefer buying things now to saving money for later. The Xers have realized that they can't count on social security to bail them out. They've watched their parents struggle to pay off credit-card debts, and they want to avoid repeating this mistake. They seek financial independence, and they're working toward it while they're still at home, with their parents picking up the tab.

This is a very positive development, and we can only hope that more teenagers will follow in the footsteps of the twenty-somethings and not fall into the familiar trap of buying an expensive car. Many kids can't wait to do this. As soon as they land that first steady job, they become slaves to the car payments.

It's cool to drive around in a flashy new Camaro instead of a used Ford Escort, but that kind of cool is very costly in the long run. What's the price of cool? Consider the following two cases: Joe Bigbelly and Sally Cartwheel.

Bigbelly gets a job as a clerk at Wal-Mart. He's living at home and saving every last dollar so he can make the $2,000 down payment on a $20,000 Camaro with the racing scoop on the hood. He takes out a car loan for the remaining $18,000. His parents have to sign for the loan, but Bigbelly is making the payments. It's a five-year loan at 11.67 percent interest, so he sends $400 to the finance company every month. He cringes the first time he seals the envelope, kissing $400 goodbye, but he forgets all about that when he's driving around in the Camaro and his friends are telling him what a cool car it is.

A few months later, there are scratches on the door and stains on the carpet and nobody is oohing and aahing when the Camaro pulls into the parking lot. It's just another car by now, but Bigbelly is stuck with the payments. To be able to afford the car and a date to ride in the car he works an extra night shift, which means he's too busy to get many dates.

At the end of five years, he's sick of the Camaro, which lost its cool a long time ago. He's finally paid off the car loan, which cost him an extra $6,000 in interest charges, so between the loan and the original purchase price, Bigbelly has invested $26,000 in this car, not including taxes and fees, insurance premiums, gas, oil, and maintenance.

At this point, the Camaro has dents and stains and the engine sounds a bit rough. If he sold the thing he could get maybe $5,000 for it. So what he's got to show for his $26,000 investment is a $5,000 car that he doesn't even like anymore.

Sally Cartwheel also lives at home and works the Wal-Mart checkout line a few feet away from Bigbelly, but she didn't buy a cool car. She took the $2,000 she'd saved up and bought a used Ford Escort. Since Sally paid cash, she didn't have car payments.

So instead of sending $400 a month to the finance company, she invested $400 a month in a mutual fund for stocks.

Five years later, when Bigbelly was mailing out his last car payment, the value of Cartwheel's mutual fund had doubled. Between the doubling of the fund itself and the steady stream of $400 contributions to the fund, Cartwheel has an asset of nearly $30,000. She also has the Escort, which gets her back and forth OK, and she never worries about the dents and stains because she never thought of her car as an investment. It's only transportation.

As we leave this economic morality tale, Cartwheel has enough money to make a down payment on her own house and move out of her parents' house, while Bigbelly continues to mooch. He's asked her out on a date, but she's taken a fancy to the real-estate agent who's showing her around.

Putting Your Money to Work

Money is a great friend, once you send it off to work. It puts extra cash in your pocket without your having to lift a finger. Let's say you deposit $500 in a savings account that pays 5 percent interest. A year later, you've got an extra $25 and you didn't have to mow a lawn or wash five cars to earn it. Your money earned it.

The $25 might not seem like much at first, but look what happens when you deposit $500 every year for ten years running, while the 5 percent interest is compounding and building up. At the end of the year after your tenth deposit, you've got $6,603.39—$5,000 of which you put in, plus the $1,603.39 that comes from the money that was made by the money.

If you invest $500 a year in stocks instead of putting it in the bank, the money gets a chance to do you an even bigger favor, while you're off someplace living your life. On average, you will double your money every seven or eight years if you leave it in stocks. A lot of smart investors have learned to take advantage of this. They realize that capital (money) is as important to their future as their own jobs (labor).

Warren Buffett, America's second-richest person at present

count, got there by saving money and later putting it into stocks. He started out the way a lot of kids do, delivering newspapers. He held on to every dollar he could, and at an early age he understood the future value of money. To him, a $400 TV set he saw in the store wasn't really a $400 purchase. He always thought about how much that $400 would be worth twenty years later, if he invested it instead of spending it. This sort of thinking kept him from wasting his money on items he didn't need.

If you start saving and investing early enough, you'll get to the point where your money is supporting you. It's like having a rich aunt or uncle who sends you all the cash you'll need for the rest of your life, and you never even have to send a thank-you note or visit them on their birthdays. This is what most people hope for, a chance to have financial independence where they're free to go places and do what they want, while their money stays home and goes to work. But it will never happen unless you get in the habit of saving and investing and putting aside a certain amount every month, at a young age.

The A-plus situation is when you're saving and investing a portion of your paycheck. The C-minus situation is when you're spending the whole thing. The F situation is where you're ringing up charges on your credit cards and running up a tab. When that happens you're paying interest to somebody else, usually a credit-card company. Instead of your money making money, the company's money is making money on you.

From Sears to Shell to the banks that sponsor credit cards, companies love it when you buy things with the card and don't pay the entire bill right away. They use their own money to pay your bill. It's a loan from them to you, although you might not see it that way. They charge you a high rate of interest on your unpaid balance. You may be paying them as much as 18 percent, which gives them a better return from your pocket than they could ever expect to get from the stock market. In other words, to a credit-card company, you're a better investment than a stock.

When you buy a $400 TV set on a credit card that charges 18 percent interest, it costs you an extra $72 a year for the loan. And if you pay the minimum amount every month and let this loan drag on, you end up spending $800 for the $400 TV set. Millions of credit-card users haven't figured this out, or there wouldn't be $340 billion of credit-card debts still owed to the banks in this country. It's estimated that in 1995, the total interest paid to banks on credit cards will reach $45 billion. Every year, people are shelling out this extra $45 billion, so they can buy things right away when they don't have the cash.

Instant gratification, it's called, and shoppers pay a high price for it. They read the ads and go into several different stores to find the best deal on a TV set to save themselves a few bucks, then they charge the TV set on a credit card, which may end up costing them an extra few hundred. They do this willingly, without even thinking about it.

In ancient times, forty-five years ago, before Diner's Club came out with the first credit card that could be used in multiple establishments, people actually waited until they had the cash in their hands before they went to the store to buy things. They saved up for their TV sets, appliances, furniture, vacations, and so forth. It might have taken them six months, nine months, a couple of years even, to raise the money to make a purchase, but they never had to pay interest.

Believe it or not, shopping in this primitive way, without instant gratification, was often enjoyable. While you saved up for a TV set, you could sit around the living room and talk about how much fun it would be to have one. Imagining the TV set, or the washing machine, or the new suit of clothes was entertaining in itself.

People felt great pride when they worked hard and made certain sacrifices in order to pay for something all at once. It made them nervous to owe money to the banks, and when they paid off their home mortgages, they had parties and invited all the neighbors to help them celebrate. It wasn't until the 1960s that Americans got into the habit of using credit cards, and it wasn't until the 1980s that average families were hocked to the limit on mortgages, car loans, home equity loans, and the unpaid balances on their cards.

This is the F situation that many households have gotten themselves into. Instead of their money making money in stocks or in the bank, the bank's money is making money on them. They're paying out hundreds, if not thousands of dollars a year on interest. It's OK to pay interest on a house or an apartment, which will increase in value, but not on cars, appliances, clothes, or TV sets, which are worth less and less as you use them.

Debt is saving in reverse. The more it builds up, the worse off you are. We see this in households across America, people struggling to make the payments, and in the government itself, which at the moment is hopelessly in debt to the tune of nearly $5 trillion. It now takes fifteen cents of every tax dollar just to pay the interest on this national debt, which is growing every day. It's been allowed to build up because the government spends more money than it takes in, and the rest it borrows from individuals, pension funds, banks, foreign governments—anybody who will make it a loan. We hear a lot of talk about balancing the budget and cutting the deficit, but every year we add another $100 billion, $200 billion, $300 billion in new debt on top of the old debt.

Let's imagine that last year you bought $1,000 worth of stuff and charged it to your credit card, and this year you buy another $900 worth of stuff and put it on that same card. Anywhere in the country but Washington, they'd say you just increased your debt by $900, because now you owe $1,900 on your credit card, whereas last year you owed $1,000. But in Washington, they don't look at it that way. They'd say you reduced your debt by $100, because you only added $900 in new charges to the card instead of the $1,000 you added last year.

That's how the government congratulates itself for cutting the deficit while the deficit continues to grow. This year, it adds, say, $200 billion to the debt and calls it a "reduction" because last year it added, say, $250 billion to the debt. Really, it's no reduction at all. It's another $200 billion, plus interest, that our children and our children's children will someday have to pay. The debt will continue to mount until the government stops using the credit card and spends only what it collects in taxes. Right now, it gets an F-minus and sets a great example for what the rest of us shouldn't do.

America was once a nation of savers. People of all income levels put aside as much money as they could, mostly in savings accounts at the local bank. They made money on this money as it grew with interest, so eventually they could use it for a down payment on a house, or to buy things, or to draw on in family emergencies. In the meantime, the bank could take people's savings and lend them out to home buyers, or home builders, or businesses of all kinds.

A country with a high savings rate can pay for roads, phone lines, factories, equipment, and all the latest innovations that help companies make better and cheaper products to sell to the world. An example is Japan. Japan was nearly ruined by World War II, but it managed to bounce back and become a great economic power. The Japanese started out making plastic toys and trinkets, and "made in Japan" was something to laugh at, but soon enough there was a Japanese car in one out of three American driveways and Japanese TV sets in two out of two American houses, and "made in Japan" meant high technology and high quality.

Japan was able to revamp its industries and rebuild its cities and towns because of the high savings rate. It's still a nation of savers today. The United States has a lot of catching up to do in this area, because we no longer save the way we once did. While we put aside 4 percent of our income every year, the people of Japan, Germany, China, India, Taiwan, and many other countries are saving 10 percent, 20 percent, or more. We lead the world in credit cards and in borrowing money to pay for things we want right away but can't quite afford.

Save as much as you can! You'll be helping yourself and helping the country.

The Pros and Cons of the Five Basic Investments

There are five basic ways to invest money: putting it in a saving account or something similar; buying collectibles; buying an apartment or a house; buying bonds; and buying stocks. Let's examine these one at a time.

1. Savings Accounts, Money-Market Funds, Treasury Bills, and Certificates of Deposit (CDs)

All of the above are known as short-term investments. They have some advantages. They pay you interest. You get your money back in a relatively short time. In savings accounts, Treasury bills, and CDs, your money is insured against losses, so you're guaranteed to get it back. (Money markets lack the guarantee, but the chances of losing money in a money market are remote.)

Short-term investments have one big disadvantage. They pay you a low rate of interest. Sometimes, the interest rate you get in a money-market account or a savings account can't even keep up with inflation. Looking at it that way, a savings account may be a losing proposition.

Inflation is a fancy way of saying that prices of things are going up. When gas goes from $1.10 a gallon to $1.40, or a movie ticket from $4.00 to $5.00, that's inflation. Another way to look at inflation is that the buying power of the dollar is going down.

In recent times, inflation has been running just below 3 percent, which means for every dollar you own, you're losing three cents every year. This adds up very quickly, and in ten years, at the present rate of inflation, all your dollars will have had thirty cents taken out of them.

The first goal of saving and investing is to keep ahead of inflation. Your money's on a treadmill that's constantly going backward. In recent years, you had to make 3 percent on your investments just to stay even.

As the chart on page 101 clearly indicates, money markets and savings accounts often don't pay enough interest to make up for the losses from inflation. And when you subtract the taxes you have to pay on the interest, money markets and savings accounts have been losers in at least ten years out of the twenty shown on the chart.

The Inflation Treadmill

Year	Money Market Fund Rates (%)	Passbook savings rates (%)	Inflation (%)
1975	6.4	5.25	9.1
1976	5.3	5.25	5.8
1977	5.0	4.9	6.5
1978	7.2	4.9	7.7
1979	11.1	5.1	11.3
1980	12.7	5.2	13.5
1981	16.8	5.2	10.4
1982	12.2	5.2	6.2
1983	8.6	5.5	3.2
1984	10.0	5.5	4.3
1985	7.7	5.5	3.6
1986	6.3	5.5	1.9
1987	6.1	5.3	3.7
1988	7.1	5.5	4.1
1989	8.9	6.1	4.8
1990	7.8	5.8	5.4
1991	5.7	4.3	4.2
1992	3.4	2.9	3.0
1993	2.7	2.5	2.8
1994	3.8	2.6	3.0

Sources: IBC's Money Fund Report, a service of IBC/Donoghue, Inc. U.S. Bureau of Labor Statistics; Federal Reserve.

That's the problem with leaving money in a bank or a savings and loan. The money is safe in the short run, because it's insured against loss, but in the long run, it's likely to lose ground against taxes and inflation. Here's a tip—when the inflation rate is higher than the interest rate you're getting from a CD, Treasury bill, money-market account, or savings account, you're investing in a lost cause.

Savings accounts are great places to park money so you can get at it quickly, whenever you need to pay bills. They are great places to store cash until you've got a big enough pile to invest elsewhere. But over long periods of time, they won't do you much good.

2. Collectibles

Collectibles can be anything from antique cars to stamps, old coins, baseball cards, or Barbie dolls. When you invest your money in such things, you are hoping to sell them at a profit in the future. There are two reasons this might happen: The things become more desirable as they get older, and people are willing to pay higher prices for them; and inflation robs cash of its buying power, which raises prices across the board.

The trouble with investing in things is they can get lost, stolen, warped, stained, ripped, or damaged by fire, water, wind, or in the case of antique furniture, termites. There is insurance for some of this, but insurance is expensive. Things in general lose value with wear and tear, although they also increase in value as they get older. That's the constant hope of collectors, that the age of the thing will raise its price more than the condition of the thing will lower it.

Collecting is a very specialized business, and successful collectors are experts not only in the items they collect, but also in the market and the prices. There's a lot to learn. Some of it you can pick up from books, and the rest you get the hard way, by experience.

Lesson one for all potential collectors, particularly young collectors, is that buying a new car is not an investment. The word "investment" showed up in a recent TV ad for a car, but if you see this ad, don't be swayed by it. Antique cars are investments, if they are kept in a garage and rarely driven, but new cars subjected to everyday use lose their value faster, even, than money does. Nothing will eat up your bankroll faster than a car will—unless it's a boat. Don't make the mistake that Bigbelly did.

3. Houses or Apartments

Buying a house or an apartment is the most profitable purchase most people ever make. A house has two big advantages over other types of investments. You can live in it while you wait for the price to go up, and you buy it on borrowed money. Let's review the math.

Houses have a habit of increasing in value at the same rate as inflation. On that score, you're breaking even. But you don't pay for the house all at once. Typically, you pay 20 percent up front (the down payment), and a bank lends you the other 80 percent (the mortgage). You pay interest on this mortgage for as long as it takes you to pay back the loan. That could be as long as fifteen or thirty years, depending on the deal you make with the bank.

Meanwhile, you're living in the house, and you won't get scared out of it by a bad housing market, the way you might get scared out of stocks when the stock market has a crash or a correction. As long as you stay there, the house increases in value, but you aren't paying any taxes on the gains. And once in your lifetime, the government gives you a tax break when you do sell the house.

If you buy a $100,000 house that increases in value by 3 percent a year, after the first year it will be worth $3,000 more than what you paid for it. At first glance, you'd say that's a 3 percent return, the same as you might get from a savings account. But here's the secret that makes a house such a great investment. Of the $100,000 it takes to buy the house, only $20,000 comes out of your pocket. So, at the end of year one, you've got a $3,000 profit on an investment of $20,000. Instead of a 3 percent return, the house is giving you a 15 percent return.

Along the way, of course, you have to pay the interest on the mortgage, but you get a tax break for that (unless the government decides to take away the tax break), and as you pay off the mortgage, you're increasing your investment in the house. This is a form of savings that people often don't think about.

Fifteen years up the road, if you've got a fifteen-year mortgage and you stay in the house that long, the mortgage is paid off, and the house you bought for $100,000 is worth $155,797, thanks to the annual 3 percent increase in the price.

Let's pick up where we left off with Joe Bigbelly and Sally Cartwheel. They've both moved up to assistant manager at Wal-

Mart, making identical salaries. Cartwheel is living in her own house, while Bigbelly's parents have kicked him out of theirs. He would have preferred to buy a house or an apartment on his own, but since he lacked a down payment, he had no choice but to rent an apartment.

Bigbelly's monthly rent is somewhat lower than Cartwheel's monthly mortgage payment, plus she has to buy home insurance, pay the lawn service, and make the occasional repair. So Bigbelly has more cash in his pocket at the outset. In theory, he could take this extra cash and invest it in the stock market and build up his assets for the future, but he doesn't. He spends it on stereo equipment, scuba gear, golf lessons, and so on.

A person who won't save money to buy an apartment or a house isn't likely to save money to invest in stocks. It's routine for families to make sacrifices so they can afford to own a house eventually, but when have you ever heard of a family making sacrifices so it could buy its first mutual fund?

By owning a house, Cartwheel already has gotten into the habit of saving and investing. As long as she's paying the mortgage, she's forced to invest in the house, and since she already invested in mutual funds to secure the down payment, there's a good chance she'll invest in mutual funds in the future, whenever she has money to spare.

In fifteen years, when her mortgage is paid off, Cartwheel will be living in a valuable asset, and her biggest monthly bill will have disappeared. Bigbelly will have nothing to show for all his rent payments, which will be much higher than they were when he first moved into the apartment. They will also be much higher than the final payment Sally Cartwheel had to make.

4. Bonds

You've probably heard newscasters talk about "the bond market," "the rally in bonds," or "the decline in bond prices across the board." Maybe you know people who own bonds. Maybe you've wondered, "What is a bond?"

A bond is a glorified IOU. It's printed on fancy paper with doodles around the border and artwork at the top, but its purpose is no
different from the purpose of the IOU that's scrawled on a napkin.
It's a record of the fact that you've loaned your money to somebody
else. It shows the amount of the loan and the deadline for paying it
back. It gives the interest rate that the borrower has to pay.

Even though it's called "buying a bond," when you purchase
one, you aren't really buying anything. You're simply making a
loan. The seller of the bond, also called the issuer, is borrowing
your money, and the bond itself is proof that the deal happened.

The biggest seller of bonds in the world is Uncle Sam. Whenever the U.S. government needs extra cash (which these days is
all the time), it prints up a new batch. That's what the $5 trillion
national debt is all about—it's owed to all the people who've
bought the government's bonds. Individuals and companies here
and abroad, even foreign governments, have loaned the $5 trillion
to Uncle Sam. They've got the IOUs in their safety deposit boxes
to prove it.

Eventually, these people have to be paid back—that's what
the deficit crisis is all about. In the meantime, the government has
to pay the interest on the $5 trillion worth of loans—Uncle Sam is
going broke trying to keep up with these payments. This is the
mess we've gotten ourselves into. The government owes so much
to so many that more than 15 percent of all the federal taxes goes
to paying the interest.

The type of bond that young people are most likely to get
involved in is the U.S. Savings Bond. Grandparents are famous for
giving savings bonds as gifts to their grandchildren. It's a round-
about way of putting money in their grandchildren's pockets.
Instead of handing them the money directly, the grandparents
lend it to the government, by purchasing the bond. Over the years,
the government pays back the money, plus interest—not to the
grandparents, but to the grandchildren.

The U.S. government is not the only seller of bonds, in spite of
its constant need for money. State and local governments also sell
bonds to raise cash. So do hospitals and airports, school districts

and sports stadiums, public agencies of all kinds, and thousands of companies. Bonds are in abundant supply. They're for sale in any stockbroker's office. You can buy them as easily as you can open a savings account or buy a share of stock.

Basically, a bond is quite similar to the CDs and the Treasury bills we've already talked about. You buy them for the interest you'll get, and you know in advance how much interest you'll be paid and how often, and when you'll get your original investment back. The main difference between bonds and CDs or Treasury bills is that with CDs and Treasuries, you get paid back sooner (the period varies from a few months to a couple of years), and with bonds you get paid back later (you might have to wait five years, ten years, or as long as thirty years).

The longer it takes for bonds to pay off, the greater the risk that inflation will eat up the value of your money before you get it back. That's why bonds pay a higher rate of interest than the short-term alternatives, such as CDs, savings accounts, or the money market. Investors demand to be rewarded for taking the greater risk.

All else being equal, a thirty-year bond pays more interest than a ten-year bond, which in turn pays more interest than a five-year bond, and so on. The buyers of bonds have to decide how far out they want to go, and whether the extra money they make in interest on, say, a thirty-year bond is worth the risk of having their money tied up for that long. These are difficult decisions.

At current count, more than $8 trillion worth of bonds of all varieties are owned by investors in the United States, making bonds a more popular investment than stocks. Meanwhile, investors also own more than $7 trillion worth of stocks traded on the major exchanges (and that doesn't count the ones traded in regional or pink-sheets exchanges), and there's a continuing debate over the merits of one versus the other. Both have their good points and their bad points. Stocks are riskier than bonds, and potentially far more rewarding. To understand why this is true, let's look at two choices: one where you buy McDonald's stock, and the other where you buy a McDonald's bond.

When you buy the stock, you're an owner of the company with all rights and privileges. McDonald's makes a bit of a fuss over you. They send you their reports, and they invite you to the annual meetings. They also pay you a bonus, in the form of a dividend. If they have a really good year at their sixteen thousand hamburger stands, they might raise the dividend, so you get an even bigger bonus. But even without the dividend, if McDonald's sells another zillion Big Macs and all goes well, the stock price will rise. You can sell your stock for more than you paid for it and make money that way.

Nevertheless, there are no guarantees that McDonald's will prosper, that you'll get a bonus, or that the stock price will rise. If it falls to less than what you paid for it, McDonald's won't reimburse you. They haven't promised anything, and they aren't obliged to pay you back. As an owner of the stock, you don't have a safety net. You must proceed at your own risk.

When you buy a McDonald's bond, or any bond, for that matter, it's a much different story. In that case, you're not an owner. You're a lender, giving McDonald's the use of your money for a fixed period of time.

McDonald's can have the greatest year in hamburger history, and if you're a bondholder, they won't even think about sending you a bonus. Companies are constantly raising the dividend on their stock to reward the stockholders, but you'll never hear of a company raising the interest rates on its bonds to reward the bondholders.

The worst part about being a bondholder is watching the stock go through the roof and knowing that you won't see a penny of the gain. McDonald's is a perfect example. Since the 1960s, the stock (adjusted for splits) has soared from $22.50 to $13,570 and investors have made 603 times their money, turning $100 into $60,300 or $1,000 into $603,000. The people who bought McDonald's bonds were hardly as fortunate. They collected interest payments along the way, but aside from that, they broke even.

If you buy a $10,000 ten-year bond and hold it for ten years, you get your money back plus interest, and nothing more.

Actually, you get back much less because of inflation. Let's say the bond is paying 8 percent a year, and the inflation rate over that ten-year period is 4 percent. Even though you've collected $8,000 in interest payments, you've lost almost $1,300 to inflation. Your original $10,000 investment is now worth $6,648 after ten years of 4 percent annual inflation. So the whole ten-year investment has left you with less than a 3 percent annual return, and that's before taxes. If you figure in the taxes, your return approaches zero.

The good thing about a bond is that even though you miss the gain when the stock goes up, you also miss the loss when the stock goes down. If McDonald's stock had gone from $13,570 to $22.50 instead of the other way around, stockholders would be crying and bondholders would be laughing, because McDonald's bonds aren't affected by the stock price. No matter what happens in the stock market, the company must repay its debts to the bondholders on the date when the loans terminate and the bonds "come due."

That's why a bond is less risky than a stock. There's a guarantee attached to it. When you buy a bond, you know in advance exactly how much you'll be getting in interest payments, and you won't lie awake nights worrying where the stock price is headed. Your investment is protected, at least more protected than when you buy a stock.

Still, there are three ways you can get hurt by a bond. The first danger occurs if you sell the bond before the due date, when the issuer of the bond must repay you in full. By selling early, you take your chances in the bond market, where the prices of bonds go up and down daily, the same as stocks. So, if you get out of a bond prematurely, you might get less than you paid for it.

The second danger occurs when the issuer of the bond goes bankrupt and can't pay you back. The chances of this happening depend on who is doing the issuing. The U.S. government, for example, will never go bankrupt—it can print more money whenever it wants. Therefore, the buyers of U.S. government bonds are repaid in full. It's an ironclad guarantee.

Other issuers of bonds, from hospitals to airports to corporations, can't always offer such a guarantee. If they go bankrupt, the owners of the bonds can lose a lot of money. Usually, they get something back, but not their entire investment. And sometimes, they lose the whole amount.

When an issuer of a bond fails to make the required payments, it's called a default. To avoid getting caught in one, smart bond buyers review the financial condition of the issuer of a bond before they consider buying it. Some bonds are insured, which is another way the payments can be guaranteed. Also, there are agencies that give safety ratings to bonds, so potential buyers know in advance which ones are risky and which aren't. A strong company such as McDonald's gets a high safety rating—the chances of McDonald's defaulting on a bond are close to zero. A weaker company that has trouble paying its bills will get a low rating. You've heard of junk bonds? These are the bonds that get the lowest ratings of all.

When you buy a junk bond, you're taking a bigger risk that you won't get your money back. That's why junk bonds pay a higher rate of interest than other bonds—the investors are rewarded for taking the extra risk.

Except with the junkiest of junk bonds, defaults are few and far between.

The biggest risk in owning a bond is risk number three: inflation. We've already seen how inflation can wreck an investment. With stocks, over the very long term, you can keep up with inflation and make a decent profit to boot. With bonds, you can't.

5. Stocks

Stocks are likely to be the best investment you'll ever make, outside of a house. You don't have to feed a stock, the way you do if you invest in horses or prize cats. It doesn't break down the way a car does, nor does it leak the way a house can. You don't have to keep it mowed, the way you do with real estate. You can lose a baseball card collection to fire, theft, or flood, but you can't lose a stock. The certificate that proves you own a stock might be stolen or burned up, but if that happens, the company will send you another one.

When you buy a bond, you're only making a loan, but when you invest in a stock, you're buying a piece of a company. If the company prospers, you share in the prosperity. If it pays a dividend, you'll receive it, and if it raises the dividend, you'll reap the benefit. Hundreds of successful companies have a habit of raising their dividends year after year. This is a bonus for owning stocks that makes them all the more valuable. They never raise the interest rate on a bond!

You can see from the chart below that stocks have outdone other investments going back as far as anybody can remember. Maybe they won't prove themselves in a week or a

Annual Rates of Return (%) of Selected Investments

	1945–1994	1984–1994	1989–1994
S&P 500*	11.9	14.4	8.7
Small Stocks	14.4	10.0	11.8
U.S. Treasury Bills	4.7	5.8	4.7
Inflation	4.4	3.6	3.5
U.S. Govt Bond	5.0	11.9	8.3
Intermediate Term Govt Bond	5.6	9.4	7.5
Corporate Bond	5.3	11.6	8.4
Residential Housing	N/A	4.3	2.9
Gold (from 1977)	6.4	0.7	0.1
Silver (from 1950)	4.6	(4.2)	(0.8)
Japanese Stocks (Tokyo Stock Exch, from 1973)	14.6	16.6	(4.2)
Foreign Bonds (J.P. Morgan Global Govt Bond)	N/A	N/A	9.1
Emerging Market Stocks (Morgan Stanley Emerging Market Fund)	N/A	N/A	22.7

* The Standard & Poor's 500 is a well-known index of 500 stocks that is often used as a barometer of the stock market in general.

Sources: Haver, Ibbotson Annual Yearbook, Datastream, The Economist
Created by: Equity Research Infocenter—JL

year, but they've always come through for the people who own them.

More than 50 million Americans have discovered the fun and profit in owning stocks. That's one out of five. These aren't all whizbangs who drive Rolls-Royces like the people you see on *Lifestyles of the Rich and Famous*. Most of these shareholders are regular folks with regular jobs: teachers, bus drivers, doctors, carpenters, students, your friends and relatives, the neighbors in the next apartment or down the block.

You don't have to be a millionaire, or even a thousandaire, to get started investing in stocks. Even if you have no money to invest, because you're out of a job or you're too young to have a job, or there's nothing left over after you pay the bills, you can make a game out of picking stocks. This can be excellent training at no risk.

People who train to be pilots are put into flight simulators, where they can learn from their mistakes without crashing a real plane. You can create your own investment simulator and learn from your mistakes without losing real money. A lot of investors who might have benefited from this sort of training had to learn the hard way, instead.

Friends or relatives may have warned you to stay away from stocks. They may have told you that if you buy a stock you're throwing your money away, because the stock market is no more reliable than a casino. They may even have the losses to prove it. The chart on page 110 refutes their argument. If stocks are such a gamble, why have they paid off so handsomely over so many decades?

When people consistently lose money in stocks, it's not the fault of the stocks. Stocks in general go up in value over time. In ninety-nine cases out of one hundred where investors are chronic losers, it's because they don't have a plan. They buy at a high price, then they get impatient or they panic, and they sell at a lower price during one of those inevitable periods when stocks are taking a dive. Their motto is "Buy high and sell low," but you don't have to follow it. Instead, you need a plan.

The rest of this book is devoted to understanding stocks and the companies that issue them. This is introductory material, which we hope will lay the groundwork for a lifetime of investing.

Invest for the Long Term

You don't have to be a math whiz to be a successful investor in stocks. You don't have to be an accountant, although learning the basics of accounting may help. You don't have to be a Phi Beta Kappa or a member of the National Honor Society or Mensa. If you can read and do fifth-grade arithmetic, you have the basic skills. The next thing you need is a plan.

The stock market is one place where being young gives you a big advantage over the old folks. Your parents or your grandparents may know more about stocks than you do—most likely, they've learned the hard way, by making mistakes. Surely, they've got more money to invest than you do, but you've got the most valuable asset of all—time.

The illustration on page 113 shows how time can do wonders for your pocketbook. The earlier you start investing, the better. In fact, a small amount of money invested early is worth more in the long run than a larger amount invested later.

Have you heard the old expression "Time is money"? It ought to be revised to "Time makes money." It's a winning combination. Let time and money do the work, while you sit back and await the results.

If you've decided to invest in stocks above all else, avoiding bonds, you've eliminated a major source of confusion, plus you've made the intelligent choice. When we say this, we're assuming you are a long-term investor who is determined to stick with stocks no matter what. People who need to pull their money out in one year, two years, or five years shouldn't invest in stocks in the first place. There's simply no telling what stock prices will do from one year to the next. When the stock market has one of its "corrections" and stocks lose money, the people who have to get their money out may be going home with a lot less than they put in.

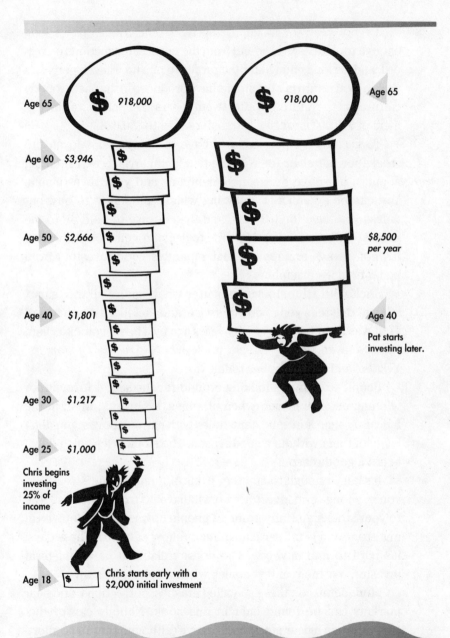

Age 65 — $918,000

Age 65 — $918,000

Age 60 — $3,946

Age 50 — $2,666

$8,500
per year

Age 40 — $1,801

Age 40

Pat starts
investing later.

Age 30 — $1,217

Age 25 — $1,000

Chris begins
investing
25% of
income

Age 18 — $ Chris starts early with a
$2,000 initial investment

Twenty years or longer is the right time frame. That's long enough for stocks to rebound from the nastiest corrections on record, and it's long enough for the profits to pile up. Eleven percent a year in total return is what stocks have produced in the past. Nobody can predict the future, but after twenty years at 11 percent, an investment of $10,000 is magically transformed into $80,623.

To get that 11 percent, you have to pledge your loyalty to stocks for better or for worse—this is a marriage we're talking about, a marriage between your money and your investments. You can be a genius at analyzing which companies to buy, but unless you have the patience and the courage to hold on to the shares, you're an odds-on favorite to become a mediocre investor. It's not always brainpower that separates good investors from bad; often, it's discipline.

Stick with your stocks no matter what, ignore all the "smart advice" that tells you to do otherwise, and "act like a dumb mule." That was the advice given fifty years ago by a former stockbroker, Fred Schwed, in his classic book *Where Are the Customers' Yachts?* and it still applies today.

People are always looking around for the secret formula for winning on Wall Street, when all along, it's staring them in the face: Buy shares in solid companies with earning power and don't let go of them without a good reason. The stock price going down is not a good reason.

It's easy enough to stand in front of a mirror and swear that you're a long-term investor who will have no trouble staying true to your stocks. Ask any group of people how many are long-term investors, and you'll see a unanimous show of hands. These days, it's hard to find anybody who doesn't claim to be a long-term investor, but the real test comes when stocks take a dive.

More details on these so-called crashes, corrections, and bear markets can be found later in this book. Nobody can predict exactly when a bear market will arrive (although there's no shortage of Wall Street types who claim to be skilled fortune-tellers in this regard). But when one does arrive, and the prices of nine out of ten stocks drop in unison, many investors naturally get scared.

They hear the TV newscasters using words like "disaster" and "calamity" to describe the situation, and they begin to worry that stock prices will hurtle toward zero and their investment will be wiped out. They decide to rescue what's left of their money by putting their stocks up for sale, even at a loss. They tell themselves that getting something back is better than getting nothing back.

It's at this point that large crowds of people suddenly become short-term investors, in spite of their claims about being long-term investors. They let their emotions get the better of them, and they forget the reason they bought stocks in the first place—to own shares in good companies. They go into a panic because stock prices are low, and instead of waiting for the prices to come back, they sell at these low prices. Nobody forces them to do this, but they volunteer to lose money.

Without realizing it, they've fallen into the trap of trying to time the market. If you told them they were "market timers" they'd deny it, but anybody who sells stocks because the market is up or down is a market timer for sure.

A market timer tries to predict the short-term zigs and zags in stock prices, hoping to get out with a quick profit. Few people can make money at this, and nobody has come up with a foolproof method. In fact, if anybody had figured out how to consistently predict the market, his name (or her name) would already appear at the top of the list of richest people in the world, ahead of Warren Buffett and Bill Gates.

Try to time the market and you invariably find yourself getting out of stocks at the moment they've hit bottom and are turning back up, and into stocks when they've gone up and are turning back down. People think this happens to them because they're unlucky. In fact, it happens to them because they're attempting the impossible. Nobody can outsmart the market.

People also think it's dangerous to be invested in stocks during crashes and corrections, but it's only dangerous if they sell. They forget the other kind of danger—not being invested in stocks on those few magical days when prices take a flying leap.

It's amazing how a few key days can make or break your entire investment plan. Here's a typical example. During a prosperous five-year stretch in the 1980s, stock prices gained 26.3 percent a year. Disciplined investors who stuck to the plan doubled their money and then some. But most of these gains occurred on forty days out of the 1,276 days the stock markets were open for business during those five years. If you were out of stocks on those forty key days, attempting to avoid the next correction, your 26.3 percent annual gain was reduced to 4.3 percent. A CD in a bank would have returned more than 4.3 percent, and at less risk.

So to get the most out of stocks, especially if you're young and time is on your side, your best bet is to invest money you can afford to set aside forever, then leave that money in stocks through thick and thin. You'll suffer through the bad times, but if you don't sell any shares, you'll never take a real loss. By being fully invested, you'll get the full benefit of those magical and unpredictable stretches when stocks make most of their gains.

Mutual Funds

At this point, we've come to two conclusions: First, you should invest in stocks, if at all possible, and second, you should hold on to these stocks as long as the companies behind them continue to do well. The next thing you have to decide is whether to pick your own stocks or let somebody else do it.

There's a lot to be said for taking the easy way out, especially if you are bored by numbers and couldn't care less what happens to Kodak's earnings, or whether Nike makes a better shoe than Reebok.

That's why mutual funds were invented—for people who want to own stocks but can't be bothered with the details. In a mutual fund, your only job is to send money, which gives you a certain number of shares in the fund. Your money is lumped together with a lot of other people's money (you never actually meet them but you know they are out there). The whole pile is handed over to the expert who manages the fund.

At least you hope there's an expert in charge, because you're counting on him or her to figure out which stocks to buy and when to buy them and sell them.

A mutual fund has another advantage, besides having a manager who does all the work. It invests in many companies at once. As soon as you sign up with a fund, you automatically become an owner of the dozens, even hundreds of companies the fund has already bought. Whether you invest fifty dollars or $50 million, you still own a piece of all the stocks in the fund. This is less risky than owning only one stock, which if you're a novice investor might be all you could afford.

A typical fund allows you to get started with as little as fifty or one hundred dollars, with the chance to buy more shares whenever extra cash comes into your possession. How much and how often you contribute is up to you. You can take the guesswork out of it by investing the same amount every month, three months, or six months. The interval isn't important, as long as you keep up the routine.

Can you see the wisdom in this sort of installment plan? Your worries about where the stock market is headed from one year to the next are over. In a correction or a bear market, the shares in your favorite fund will get cheaper, so you'll be buying more at low prices, and in a bull market you'll be buying more at high prices. Over time, the costs will even out and your profits will mount.

As an added attraction, many funds pay a cash bonus in the form of a dividend. It comes your way on a regular basis—four times a year, twice a year, or even twelve times a year. You can spend this money however you want—on movie tickets, compact disks, sunglasses—to reward yourself for investing in the fund. Or you can do yourself a bigger favor by using the dividend to buy more shares.

This is called the "reinvestment option," and once you've chosen it, your dividends are reinvested automatically. The more shares you own, the more you stand to gain from the future success of the fund, which is why your money will grow faster if you throw the dividends into the pot.

You can follow your fund's progress by looking it up in the newspaper, the same way you look up Disney or Wendy's. The price of a share in a fund goes up and down every day, and it moves more or less in lockstep with the prices of all the stocks in the fund's portfolio. That's why you want to invest in funds with managers who have the knack for picking the right stocks. You're rooting for the managers, because the better they do, the better you do.

Saying good-bye to a fund is easy. You can take your money out any time you want—either all of it or some of it—and the fund will send you a check immediately. But unless there's an emergency and you have a sudden need for quick cash, getting out of a fund should be the last thing on your mind. Your goal is to sell your shares for a much higher price than the price you paid to acquire them, and the longer you stick with the fund, the bigger your potential profit.

Along with the chance to share in the gains from a fund, you're also paying a share of the management fees and the fund's expenses. These fees and expenses are paid out of the fund's assets, and they generally cost investors between 0.5 percent and 2 percent annually, depending on the fund. That means when you own a mutual fund, you're starting out every year somewhere between 0.5 percent and 2 percent in the hole, and on top of that, the fund must pay a commission whenever it buys or sells a stock.

The managers are expected to do well in spite of the expenses, by being clever and picking the right stocks.

These professional stockpickers have an advantage over the millions of amateurs who do their own picking. It's a hobby for amateurs, but for the pros, it's a full-time job. They go to business school to learn how to study companies and decipher financial reports. They've got libraries, high-performance computers, and a research staff to back them up. If there's important news out of a company, they hear it right away.

On the other hand, professional stockpickers also have limitations that make it easy to compete with them. You and I could never beat a professional pool player at a game of billiards, and we couldn't do brain surgery better than a professional brain surgeon, but we have a decent chance of beating the pros on Wall Street.

They are part of the herd of fund managers that tends to graze in the same pastures of stocks. They feel comfortable buying the same stocks the other managers are buying, and they avoid wandering off into unfamiliar territory. So they miss the exciting prospects that can be found outside the boundaries of the herd.

In particular, they overlook the newer, inexperienced companies that often turn out to be star performers in business and the biggest winners in the stock market.

Fund History

The earliest mutual fund on record was started in 1822 by King William I of the Netherlands. The idea spread to Scotland, where the thrifty Scots took an immediate fancy to it. The Scots were regarded as a frugal lot, who frowned on frivolous purchases. They managed to save enormous quantities of money, which could be invested in the newly created funds.

Eventually, the inhabitants of the United States got wind of mutual funds, but they didn't catch on here until the end of the nineteenth century. In those days, mutual funds were called "stock trusts"—the earliest on record being the New York Stock Trust launched in 1889. The stock trusts evolved into "investment companies," which were popular in the 1920s.

The first homegrown mutual fund to describe itself that way was the Shaw-Loomis-Sayles fund. It appeared on the scene in November 1929, just weeks after the stock market crashed. This was bad timing by the organizers, because stock prices continued to drop until they finally hit bottom in 1932. By 1936, after the dust had settled, half the funds in the country (still called "investment companies") were out of business.

Investors learned an important lesson: When stocks go down in a heap, funds go down with them. It still applies today. The best fund manager on Wall Street can't protect you in a crash, whether it's the Crash of 1929, 1972–73, 1987, 1990, or a future Crash of 2000, 2010, or 2020. Whether you do the investing or a professional does it, there's no such thing as a crash-proof portfolio.

Eleven years after the Crash of 1929, Congress passed a key

piece of legislation, the Investment Company Act of 1940. This law, still on the books today, takes the mystery out of mutual funds. It requires that each fund describe itself in detail, so investors know exactly what they're getting and how much they have to pay to get it.

Every mutual fund registered in the United States (more than six thousand at present count) has to explain its overall strategy and tell you how risky that is. It has to explain how the money is invested. It has to reveal the contents of its portfolio, listing the biggest holdings by name and how many shares it owns in each.

It has to reveal the management fee, plus any extra fees levied by the management company. It has to report on its gains and losses in previous years, so everybody knows exactly how well or how poorly it has performed in the past.

Along with all these rules that force it to tell the whole truth and nothing but the truth, a fund must also follow strict rules on investing. It can't risk more than 5 percent of its customers' money on a single stock. This guards against its putting too many eggs in one basket.

Meanwhile, government watchdogs at the Securities and Exchange Commission (SEC) keep up a constant surveillance, so the funds that might otherwise be tempted to break the rules are held in check by the fear of getting caught. Overall, the fund industry does a good job policing itself, and it maintains a good relationship with the SEC's tough watchdogs.

Recently, with the support of the SEC, the various groups of funds have undertaken a worthy project. They are trying to eliminate the gobbledygook in their brochures and cut down on the legalese that often goes on for many pages, which few investors ever read. Much of this legalese is put there because the government requires it, but it ends up wasting time, confusing investors, and costing them money. The bill for printing all these pages is paid out of the assets of the fund.

The goal of this new campaign is to produce simpler and shorter explanations that people can understand without having to go to law school. The companies that run funds and the shareholders who invest in funds will both be better off if this campaign succeeds.

After the long period when the public avoided them, mutual funds came back into favor in the late 1960s, when they were sold in neighborhoods across the country by teachers, shopkeepers, clerks, you name it, working part-time on weekends and at night. This led to a poor result, because millions of investors got into funds just in time for the bear market of 1969–73, the worst since the Crash of 1929.

In this extended losing streak for stocks, the prices of some mutual funds dropped 75 percent—more proof that there's no safety in numbers when it comes to owning shares in a fund. Stunned by their losses, distraught investors made a mad dash for the exits, selling their shares for far less than they had paid, depositing the proceeds in savings accounts, and promising themselves to hang up the phone the next time they got a call from a fund salesman.

For nearly a decade thereafter, it was hard to get anybody to invest money in a stock mutual fund. High-quality funds were left sitting alone as if they had bad breath. Smart fund managers could find plenty of great stocks to buy, and at bargain prices, but without clients, they had no money to buy them with.

As the stock market revived in the 1980s, so did the mutual fund industry. It's been going gangbusters ever since, with 5,655 funds and counting, and more than thirteen hundred new funds created in the past two years alone. Every other day brings another fund: bond funds, money-market funds, and stock funds, to add to the more than twenty-one hundred stock funds that already exist. If this hectic birthrate keeps up much longer, we'll soon have more stock funds than stocks.

Buying Funds Now

It would take a whole book in itself to describe the different kinds of stock funds that are out there: the all-purpose funds, single-industry funds, multi-industry, small-company, large-company,

pure, hybrid, foreign, domestic, socially conscious, socially un-
conscious, growth, value, income, and growth-and-income funds.
It's gotten so complicated that there are funds of funds that
specialize in buying shares in other funds.

You could stay up day and night studying how to choose the
right fund, and you wouldn't get through half the information
that's been printed on the subject. If all these how-to books, pam-
phlets, and articles fell on top of you, it would take a rescue squad
several hours to pull you out. In fact, so much attention is devoted
to picking the right fund in any given year, it could begin to drive
people crazy. They'd be happier, more relaxed, and nicer to dogs
and children, plus they'd save on psychiatry bills if only they
would abandon the search for the absolutely perfect mutual fund.

At the risk of contributing further to the unhealthy fixation on
this quest, we present the following bits of advice:

1. You can buy mutual funds directly from the companies that
manage them, such as Dreyfus, Fidelity, and Scudder. You can
also buy them through a stockbroker, although a broker may not
be able to sell you the fund you want.

2. Brokers have to make a living, and they sometimes get a
bigger commission for selling the firm's own products. Convincing
you to buy one of the in-house mutual funds may be in their best
interest, but not necessarily in yours. Whenever a broker recom-
mends anything, always find out what's in it for the broker. Ask
him or her to provide information on the full range of what's
available. There might be a fund that's similar to the one the broker
is recommending but that has a better record overall.

3. If you're a long-term investor, ignore all the bond funds and
hybrid funds (those invest in a mixture of stocks and bonds) and
go for the pure stock funds. Stocks have outperformed bonds in
eight of the nine decades in this century (bonds ran a close
second in the 1980s, but stocks still did slightly better). In the first
half of the 1990s, stocks once again are way ahead of bonds. If
you're not 100 percent invested in stocks, you're shortchanging
yourself in the long run.

4. Picking the right fund isn't any easier than picking the right

auto mechanic, but with a fund, at least you've got the record of past performance to guide you. Unless you interview dozens of customers, there's no simple way of telling whether an auto mechanic is good, bad, or indifferent, but you can find out easily which of these ratings applies to a fund. It all boils down to the annual return. A fund that returned 18 percent a year over the past decade has done better than a similar fund with similar objectives that returned 14 percent. But before you invest in a fund on the strength of its record, make sure the manager who compiled the great record is still in charge.

5. Over time, it's been more profitable to invest in small companies than in large companies. The successful small companies of today will become the Wal-Marts, Home Depots, and Microsofts of tomorrow. It's no wonder then that funds that invest in small companies (the so-called small caps) have beaten out the "large cap" funds by a substantial margin. ("Cap" is short for "market capitalization"—the total number of shares issued by a company multiplied by the current share price.) A couple of Wal-Marts is all they need to outperform the competition. That one stock is up more than two-hundred-and-fifty-fold in twenty years.

Since small-cap stocks are generally more volatile than large-cap stocks, a small-cap fund will give you more extreme ups and downs than other types of funds. But if you have a strong stomach and can take the bumps and stay on the ride, you'll likely do better in small caps.

6. Why take a chance on a rookie fund, when you can invest in a veteran fund that's been around through several seasons and has turned in an all-star performance? A list of funds that have stayed on top over many years can be found in financial magazines such as *Barron's* and *Forbes*. Twice a year, *Barron's* publishes a complete roundup of funds, with the details provided by Lipper Analytical, a high-quality research company run by a prominent fund watcher, Michael Lipper. *The Wall Street Journal* publishes a similar roundup four times a year.

If you want more information about a particular fund, you can get it from Morningstar, a company that tracks thousands of funds and issues a monthly report. Morningstar ranks all these funds for safety, rates their performance, and tells who the manager is and what stocks are in the portfolio. It's the best one-stop source in existence today.

7. It doesn't pay to be a fund jumper. Some investors make a hobby of switching from one fund to another, hopping to the bandwagon of the latest hot performer. This is more trouble than it's worth. Studies have shown that top-ranked funds from one year rarely repeat their performance the next. Trying to catch the winner is a fool's errand in which you are likely to end up with a loser. You're better off picking a fund with an excellent long-term record and sticking with it.

8. In addition to taking the annual expenses out of the shareholders' assets, some funds charge an entry fee, called a load. These days, the average load is 3 to 4 percent. That means whenever you invest in a fund with a load, you lose 3 to 4 percent of your money right off the bat.

For all the funds that charge an entry fee, there are just as many that don't. These are the no-loads. As it turns out, the no-loads perform just as well, on average, as the funds with loads. This is one case where paying a cover charge doesn't necessarily get you into a classier joint.

The longer you stay in a fund, the less important the load becomes. After ten or fifteen years, if the fund does well, you'll forget you ever paid the 3 or 4 percent load to get into it.

The annual expenses deserve closer attention than the load, because those are taken out of the fund every year. Funds that keep their expenses to a minimum (less than 1 percent) have a built-in advantage over funds that run a bigger tab (2 percent or more). The manager of a high-cost fund is working at a disadvantage. Every year, he or she has to outperform the manager of a low-cost fund by 0.5 to 1.5 percent to produce the same results.

9. The vast majority of funds employ managers whose goal it is to beat the so-called market averages. That's why you're paying these managers—to pick stocks that do better than the average stock. But fund managers often fail to beat the averages—in

some years more than half the funds do worse. One of the reasons they do worse is that fees and expenses are subtracted from a fund's performance.

Some investors have given up trying to pick a fund that beats the averages, which has proven to be a difficult task. Instead, they choose a fund that is guaranteed to match the average, no matter what. This kind of fund is called an index fund. It doesn't need a manager. It runs on automatic pilot. It simply buys all the stocks in a particular index and holds on to them.

There is no fuss, no experts to pay, no management fees to speak of, no commissions for getting into and out of different stocks, and no decisions to make. For instance, an S&P 500 Index fund buys all five hundred stocks in the Standard & Poor's 500 stock index. This S&P 500 Index is a well-known market average, so when you invest in such a fund, you'll always get an average result, which based on recent performance will be a better result than you'd get in many of the managed funds.

Or, if you decide to invest in a "small cap" fund to take advantage of the big potential payoffs from small companies, you can buy a fund that tracks a small-stock index, such as the Russell 2,000. That way, your money will be spread out among the two thousand stocks in the Russell Index.

Another possibility is to put some of your money into an S&P 500 Index fund to get the gains from the larger companies, and the rest in a small-stock index fund to get the gains from the smaller companies. That way, you'll never have to read another article about how to pick a winning mutual fund, and you'll end up doing better than some of the people who study the situation very carefully, and then put themselves into funds that fail to beat the averages.

Picking Your Own Stocks

If you have the time and the inclination, you can embark on a thrilling lifetime adventure: picking your own stocks. This is a lot more work than investing in a mutual fund, but you can derive a great deal of satisfaction from picking your own stocks. Over time, perhaps you'll do better than most of the funds.

Not all your stocks will go up—no stockpicker in history has ever had a 100 percent success rate. Warren Buffett has made mistakes, and Peter Lynch could fill several notebooks with the stories of his. But a few big winners a decade is all you need. If you own ten stocks, and three of them are big winners, they will more than make up for the one or two losers and the six or seven stocks that have done just OK.

If you can manage to find a few triples in your lifetime—stocks that have increased threefold over what you paid for them—you'll never lack for spending money, no matter how many losers you pick along the way. And once you get the hang of how to follow a company's progress, you can put more money into the successful companies and reduce your stake in the flops.

You may not triple your money in a stock very often, but you only need a few triples in a lifetime to build up a sizeable fortune. Here's the math: if you start out with $10,000 and manage to triple it five times, you've got $2.4 million, and if you triple it ten times, you've got $590 million, and 13 times, you're the richest person in America.

Actually, there's nothing to keep you from investing in mutual funds and buying your own stocks as well. Many investors do both. Much of the advice in the mutual fund section—the advantages of starting early, of having a plan, of sticking to the plan and not worrying about crashes and corrections—also applies to the portfolio of stocks you pick on your own. Two problems confront you right away: How do I figure out which stocks to pick? Where do I get the money to buy them? Since it's dangerous to put money into stocks before you figure out how to pick them, you should put yourself through some practice drills before you risk your cash.

You'd be surprised how many people lose money by investing in stocks before they know the first thing about them! It happens all the time. A person goes through life with no experience in investing, then suddenly receives a lump-sum retirement benefit and throws it all into the stock market, blind, when he or she can't tell a dividend from a divot. There ought to be some formal training for this, the way they have drivers' ed in school. We don't put people on the highway without giving them a few lessons in the parking lot and teaching them the rules of the road.

If nobody else is going to train you, at least you can put yourself through training, trying out various strategies on paper, to begin to get a feel for the way different kinds of stock behave. Again, a young person has an advantage. You have the luxury of experimenting with imaginary investments, at least for a while, because you have many decades ahead of you. By the time you have the money to invest, you'll be fully prepared to do it for real.

You've heard of fantasy baseball, where you pick an imaginary team from the major-league rosters to see how your team's batting average, home run production, and so forth, measure up against the real teams, or against other fantasy teams? You can train for stocks with a fantasy portfolio. Take an imaginary bankroll—$100,000, perhaps, or $1 million if you're a big spender—and use it to buy shares in your favorite companies. If, for instance, your five favorite companies are Disney, Nike, Microsoft, Ben & Jerry's, and Pepsi, you can split $100,000 five ways and invest a mythical $20,000 in each. Choosing April 21, 1995, as your starting date, your fantasy investment lineup looks like this:

	Stock Prices 4/21/95	Number of Shares You Get for $20,000 (Rounded Off to Nearest Share)
Disney	54¾	365
Nike	73⅛	274
Pepsi	41¼	485
Ben & Jerry's	12⅝	1,584
Microsoft	75	267

Once you've chosen your stocks and written down the prices, you can track your gains and losses just as you would if you'd put in hard cash. You can compare your results to the results your parents are getting in their real investments (if they have any), or to the results of various mutual funds, or to other mythical portfolios your friends have made up.

Schools across the country have brought fantasy stockpicking into the classroom, with The Stock Market Game, sponsored and distributed by The Securities Industry Foundation for Economic Education. More than 600,000 students played the game during the 1994/1995 school year.

They divide into teams, and each team has to decide which stocks to buy with its mythical bankroll. The game takes about ten weeks from start to finish. Results are tallied, and the team whose stocks have gone up the most at the end of the period wins the game. The winning teams in each school compete with the winners from other schools in local, county, and regional or state competitions.

Playing The Stock Market Game can be fun as well as educational, as long as the players are taught the basics of investing and don't take the results too seriously. The problem with this sort of training is that over thirteen weeks, twenty-six weeks, or even a year, what happens to stock prices is largely a matter of luck. The practice sessions don't last long enough to give you a true test. A stock can be a loser in thirteen weeks, but a big winner in three years, or five years. Or it can be a winner in thirteen weeks but a loser down the road.

Stocks that do well in the long run belong to companies that do well in the long run. The key to successful investing is finding successful companies. To get the most out of your training sessions, you have to do more than follow the prices of the stocks. You have to learn as much as possible about the companies you've chosen and what makes them tick.

This brings us to the five basic methods people use to pick a stock. Here's the rundown on each, beginning with the most ridiculous and ending with the most enlightened.

1. *Darts.* The lowest form of stockpicking. You throw a dart at the stock page and wherever it lands, you buy that stock. Or you close your eyes and use your finger as the dart. Maybe you'll get lucky and your finger will hit on a stock that does well—but maybe you won't.

The best thing you can say about the dart method is that it doesn't take much work. If you're inclined to pick stocks at random, you'll be doing yourself a favor by avoiding the whole business and investing in mutual funds.

2. *Hot tips.* The second-lowest form of stockpicking, where somebody else tells you to buy a stock that's a cinch to go up. It could be your best friend, your English teacher, your uncle Harry, the plumber, the auto mechanic, or the gardener. Or maybe you overhear the tip on a bus. For some reason, overhearing a tip gets people more excited than if the tip was meant for them.

It's possible that Uncle Harry is directly involved with a certain company and knows what he's talking about. That sort of informed tip can be useful—a clue that's worth investigating further. But the dangerous kind of hot tip is based on nothing but hot air. Here's a typical example: "Home Shopping Network. The smart money is accumulating this stock. Buy right away, before it's too late. It looks like that sucker's going up."

People who won't buy a fifty-dollar toaster oven without checking several stores for the best price will throw thousands of dollars at a hot tip such as "Home Shopping Network." They do this because they can't stand to miss out on all the profit they'll "lose" if they ignore the tip and the Home Shopping stock quadruples. The truth is, if they don't buy Home Shopping and it quadruples, they haven't lost a penny.

People never lose money on stocks they don't own. They only lose money if they buy Home Shopping and it goes down and they sell it for less than they paid for it.

3. *Educated tips.* You get these from experts who appear on TV or are quoted in newspapers and magazines. There's a constant stream of educated tips flowing out of fund managers, investment advisors, and other Wall Street gurus. You're not the only person who's been let in on these educated tips. Millions of readers and listeners are hearing the same thing you are.

Nevertheless, if you can't resist acting on a tip, you might as well take a tip from an expert and ignore Uncle Harry's tip. There's a decent chance the expert has done enough homework to form an educated opinion, whereas Uncle Harry doesn't know what he's talking about, beyond "It looks like that sucker's going up."

The problem with expert tips is that when the expert changes his mind, you have no way of finding that out—unless he goes back on TV to inform the viewers and you happen to catch the show. Otherwise, you'll be holding on to the stock because you think the expert likes it, long after he's stopped liking it.

4. *The broker's buy list.* Stockbrokers of the "full-service" variety are never shy about giving their recommendations on what stocks you should buy. Often, these recommendations do not come from the broker's own head. They come from the analysts who work behind the scenes at the head office, usually in New York. These are well-trained Sherlocks whose job it is to snoop into the affairs of companies or groups of companies. They issue buy signals and sell signals based on the evidence they dredge up.

The brokerage firm collects the buy signals from its analysts and puts them on a buy list, which is sent out to all the brokers, including yours—if you have a broker. Usually, the buy list is divided into categories: stocks for conservative investors, stocks for aggressive investors, stocks that pay dividends, and so forth.

You can build an excellent portfolio by working with a broker to pick stocks from the buy list. That way, you can rely on the brokerage firm's research and still get to choose which of the "buys" you like best. This has one big advantage over relying on educated tips. If the brokerage firm changes its mind and moves one of your stocks from the buy list to the sell list, your broker will inform you of the fact. If he doesn't, then put the broker on *your* sell list.

5. *Doing your own research.* This is the highest form of stock-picking. You choose the stock because you like the company, and you like the company because you've studied it inside and out. Maybe you already did that with your five favorite companies in your fantasy portfolio, as in the example of Disney, Nike, Ben & Jerry's, Pepsi, and Microsoft shown on page 127.

The more you learn about investing in companies, the less you have to rely on other people's opinions, and the better you can evaluate other people's tips. You can decide for yourself what stocks to buy and when to buy them.

You'll need two kinds of information: the kind you get by keeping your eyes peeled and the kind you get by studying the numbers. The first kind, you can begin to gather every time you walk into a McDonald's, a Sunglass Hut International, or any other store that's owned by a publicly traded company. And if you work in the store, so much the better.

You can see for yourself whether the operation is efficient or sloppy, overstaffed or understaffed, well-organized or chaotic. You can gauge the morale of your fellow employees. You get a sense of whether management is reckless or careful with money.

If you're out front with the customers, you can size up the crowd. Are they lining up at the cash register, or does the place look empty? Are they happy with the merchandise, or do they complain a lot? These little details can tell you a great deal about the quality of the parent company itself. Have you ever seen a messy Gap or an empty McDonald's? The employees at any of the Gap outlets or the McDonald's franchises could have noticed long ago how fantastically successful these operations have been and invested their spare cash accordingly.

A store doesn't have to fall apart to lose customers. It will lose customers when another store comes along that offers better merchandise and better service, for the same prices or lower prices. Employees are among the first to know when a competitor is luring the clients away. There's nothing to stop them from investing in the competitor.

Even if you don't have a job in a publicly traded company, you can see what's going on from the customer angle. Every time you shop in a store, eat a hamburger, or buy new sunglasses, you're getting valuable input. By browsing around, you can see what's selling and what isn't. By watching your friends, you know which computers they're buying, which brand of soda they're drinking, which movies they're watching, whether

Reeboks are in or out. These are all important clues that can lead you to the right stocks.

You'd be surprised how many adults fail to follow up on such clues. Millions of people work in industries where they come in daily contact with potential investments and never take advantage of their front-row seat. Doctors know which drug companies make the best drugs, but they don't always buy the drug stocks. Bankers know which banks are the strongest and have the lowest expenses and make the smartest loans, but they don't necessarily buy the bank stocks. Store managers and the people who run malls have access to the monthly sales figures, so they know for sure which retailers are selling the most merchandise. But how many mall managers have enriched themselves by investing in specialty retail stocks?

Once you start looking at the world through a stockpicker's eyes, where everything is a potential investment, you begin to notice the companies that do business with the companies that got your attention in the first place. If you work in a hospital, you come into contact with companies that make sutures, surgical gowns, syringes, beds and bed pans, X-ray equipment, EKG machines; companies that help the hospital keep its costs down; companies that write the health insurance; companies that handle the billing. The grocery store is another hotbed of companies: dozens of them are represented in each aisle.

You also begin to notice when a competitor is doing a better job than the company that hired you. When people were lining up to buy Chrysler minivans, it wasn't just the Chrysler salesmen who realized Chrysler was on its way to making record profits. It was also the Buick salesmen down the block, who sat around their empty showroom and realized that a lot of Buick customers must have switched to Chrysler.

This brings us to the numbers. That a company makes a popular product doesn't mean you should automatically buy the stock. There's a lot more you have to know before you invest. You have to know if the company is spending its cash wisely or frittering it away. You have to know how much it owes to the banks. You have to know if the sales are growing, and how fast. You have to know how much money it earned in past years, and how much it can expect to earn in the future. You have to know if the stock is selling at a fair price, a bargain price, or too high a price.

You have to know if the company is paying a dividend, and if so, how much of a dividend, and how often it is raised. Earnings, sales, debt, dividends, the price of the stock: These are some of the key numbers stockpickers must follow.

People go to graduate school to learn how to read and interpret these numbers, so this is not a subject that can be covered in depth in a primer such as this one. The best we can do is to give you a glimpse at the basic elements of a company's finances, so you can begin to see how the numbers fit together. You'll find this information in Appendix Two: Reading the Numbers—How to Decipher a Balance Sheet, on page 251.

No investor can possibly hope to keep up with the more than thirteen thousand companies whose stocks are traded on the major exchanges in the U.S. markets today. That's why amateurs and pros alike are forced to cut down on their options by specializing in one kind of company or another. For instance, some investors buy stocks only in companies that have a habit of raising their dividends. Others look for companies whose earnings are growing by at least 20 percent a year.

You can specialize in a certain industry, such as electric utilities or restaurants or banks. You can specialize in small companies or large companies, new companies or old ones. You can specialize in companies that have fallen on hard times and are trying to make a comeback. (These are called "turnarounds.") There are hundreds of different ways to skin this cat.

Investing is not an exact science, and no matter how hard you study the numbers and how much you learn about a company's past performance, you can never be sure about its future performance. What will happen tomorrow is always a guess. Your job as an investor is to make educated guesses and not blind ones. Your job is to pick stocks and not pay too much for them, then to keep watching for good news or bad news coming out of the companies you own. You can use your knowledge to keep the risks to a minimum.

Owning Stocks for Real

You can play stock-market games from morning till night, but there's no substitute for the thrill of owning real shares. People remember their first shares the way they remember their first kiss. No matter how many dozens of companies you'll own in the future, you never get over the first.

At this point, if anything is holding you back, it has to be money. Young people have the time to invest, but they don't always have the cash. It's not just any cash that can safely be put into stocks; it's cash you can afford to live without for many years while it goes forth and multiplies. If you have a part-time job and can afford to invest a portion of your paycheck, so much the better. If not, perhaps you can drop some hints to family members around the holidays.

Here's where parents, grandparents, aunts, and uncles can play a leading role. The greatest source of investment capital for young people is relatives. When they ask what you want for your birthday, Christmas, Hanukkah, and so forth, tell them you want stocks. Let them know that if it comes down to a choice between owning a new pair of Nikes or owning a share of Nike, which costs about the same amount as the shoes, you'd rather have the share.

This is guaranteed to impress most adults. They'll be amazed by your foresight and your maturity, and your ratings will soar in the family popularity polls. If they own shares themselves, they can get you started by simply transferring one share, or many shares, over to you. The paperwork is no problem, and they don't have to pay a fee or a commission to do this. Thousands of young people in each generation are introduced to investing in this fashion, by older people giving them their first stocks. A steady stream of shares trickles down from grandparents to their grandchildren.

Many grandparents have gotten into the habit of giving savings bonds instead of stocks. If you have grandparents of this type, it's in your best interest to show them the chart on page 110, so they realize how much better off you'd be if they dispensed with the savings bonds and sent you shares of good companies at every opportunity.

While small numbers of shares are routinely handed down from parents or grandparents, it's been difficult for young people to buy small numbers of shares on their own. Until recently, in fact, young investors have been discouraged from buying the one share or few shares that would get them started investing. Two barriers stand in the way: First, most stock transactions are handled by brokers, and you can't open your own brokerage account until you're twenty-one years old, and second, most brokers charge minimum commissions, which range from $25 to $40. If you're buying one share of Pepsi for $47 and you have to pay the broker a $40 fee, the commission is almost as expensive as the share. No successful investor can afford to pay $87 for a $47 stock.

This sad state of affairs is changing, as companies have begun to sell small quantities of their own shares directly to the public, bypassing the brokers. After all, if McDonald's can sell you a hamburger, why shouldn't it be allowed to sell you its stock?

Already eighty companies have adopted a so-called direct investment program in which individuals can purchase a few shares and pay significantly lower commissions than the deepest discount broker, and in some cases, pay nothing at all. It's the best thing Wall Street has done for young people since the New York Stock Exchange invited the Beatles onto the floor in the 1960s. According to Jim Volpe, a vice-president at the First Chicago Trust Company and a spearhead of the direct investment campaign, at least 850 more companies have said they would be delighted to join the eighty that already are selling the shares directly to the public and the list is growing. (See Appendix One for the 900 number that offers access to this list.) The legal wrinkles are being ironed out.

You probably won't be able to buy just one share via direct investment, because most companies are requiring a minimum purchase of $250 to $1,000. Depending on which company you want to own, you'll have to save up your money until you've got the $250 or whatever it takes, but that's a minor drawback compared to the benefit of paying a significantly lower commission.

The best part is, once you've made your initial purchase, you can continue to buy shares directly from the company, whenever you want, and without paying a penny in commissions. And whenever the company pays a dividend, yours is automatically converted into more shares through the dividend reinvestment plan. In most cases, you're dealing directly with the company's transfer agent, without having to get involved with a stockbroker.

Keep an eye out for the news of this exciting new program, which will help put stocks into the hands of millions of investors who've been shut out of the market.

If you're still attached to the idea of buying one share at a time, there's a program that allows you to do it. But first your family has to join the National Association of Investors Corporation (NAIC). The NAIC is the support group for hundreds of investment clubs around the country. The address is 711 West Thirteen Mile Road, Madison Heights, MI, 48071, and the phone number is 1-810-583-6242.

As of January 1996 a membership costs thirty-five dollars a year. Individual club members or households pay fourteen dollars a year, which gives them an automatic subscription to a monthly magazine called *Better Investing* with all kinds of useful information that will help you become a better stockpicker. Most of this material is geared to experienced investors, but some of it is for beginners, and you can learn a lot from it. Aside from the magazine, you get the chance to buy one to ten shares in any one of 151 different companies, and you only have to pay a seven-dollar setup fee per transaction.

The buy-a-share program is designed for kids, although once again, you'll run into the "age of majority" problem. Depending on the laws in the state where you live, you have to be eighteen or twenty-one to make the purchase on your own. Otherwise, a parent or guardian can act on your behalf—you're going to need one or the other to sign up for the club membership, anyway.

The program works as follows. The NAIC provides you with the names of all 151 companies in which you can buy stock. You figure out which ones you want to purchase, and you look up the price per share of each. Then you send your buy list to the NAIC, along with a check for the current price of each stock you're buying, plus the seven-dollar fee per company, plus an extra $10 "fluctuation." For instance, if the current price of McDonald's is $40, you send $57.

Why the extra $10? If the stock price goes up between the day you send in your letter and the day your order is processed, the reserve will be used to cover the difference. In any event, the $10 won't be wasted. Whatever is left of it after you buy your first share will be used to buy a fraction of another share. So you'll end up with a share and a sixteenth, or a share and an eighth, or a share and a quarter.

At this point, the NAIC drops out of the relationship, and you deal directly with a representative (the transfer agent) of Wendy's, or McDonald's, or whatever company you just bought a share in. Since all the companies on the NAIC list have dividend reinvestment programs, you'll get additional fractions of shares whenever the company pays a dividend. You can also buy more shares whenever you want, paying a nominal fee, if any.

If you decide to sell your shares, you can either take them to a stockbroker (again, the high commissions might cause you to reject this option) or notify the company's agent (or agents) in writing. They will dispose of the shares on the next date they've scheduled for buying and selling, at whatever the price happens to be at that time. You won't know exactly what price you'll get until after the shares are sold.

As long as you've gone to the trouble of joining the NAIC, there's nothing to stop you from joining one of its investment clubs. There are NAIC-member clubs in cities, towns, villages, and schools across the country. Even some prisons have them.

Being in an investment club is like being on a team in the

Stock Market Game. The difference is, if you're in a club, you're investing real money. Most clubs meet once a month in a member's house—where the group hashes out the latest stockpicking ideas. Stocks are bought and sold on majority vote.

Each member agrees to invest a fixed amount every month. It could be fifty dollars, or one hundred dollars—whatever the majority decides. As it turns out, most people do better investing in a club than they do on their own. That's because the club gives them built-in discipline. They can't sell stocks in a panic, because cooler heads in the group will vote them down. They can't buy stocks without convincing the group that the stocks are worth buying. This forces them to do their homework. If somebody says, "I'm recommending Disney because I heard a hot tip in the cafeteria line," he'll be laughed out of the room.

To become a voting member of an investment club, you have to be at least eighteen, as we've already mentioned. But even if you're not eighteen, you can take part in meetings, recommend stocks, and add your opinion to every discussion. If a club member who's past the legal investing age is willing to act as your custodian, you can invest your own money through a custodial account.

Buying Shares on the Stock Exchange

If somebody asked you to name five institutions the country couldn't live without for a month or two, what would you say? The military? The police? Congress? The courts? Electric companies? The water department? Hospitals? Close your eyes for a minute and make your five choices, without looking at the next paragraph.

Did you include the stock market or the bond market in your list? Most people wouldn't. Wall Street doesn't immediately come to mind when we think about essential services that give us food, gas, lodging, and a dial tone, and keep the robbers from the door. But the truth is that the financial markets are very important to the well-being of the entire population, and not just the owners of bonds and stocks. The White House could give itself a month off and the world would go on, but without a stock market or a bond market, our whole economic system would seize up.

A company or a person that needed to sell stocks to raise cash would be out of luck, because without a market, there'd be no buyers. The government, $5 trillion in the red already, would have no way to sell bonds to cover its expenses, the way it normally does. It would be left with two choices, both bad. It could print tons of fresh cash, cheapening the value of the dollar and sending prices through the roof, or it could stop paying its bills, leaving millions of Americans without their main source of income. Companies would go bankrupt and banks would go bankrupt. Mobs of people would rush to the nearest branches to rescue their money, only to discover that the banks had run out. Stores would close, factories would close, and millions of people would be thrown out of work. You'd see them wandering the streets, searching the Dumpsters for half-eaten pizzas. Civilization as we know it would come to a quick end, and all because the markets shut down. So these markets are much more important than we give them credit for. We couldn't survive for long without them.

The Role of the Broker

Let's say you have the resources to buy enough shares so it makes sense to go the regular route—through a broker. If you're serious about investing, eventually you will reach this point. The broker is your conduit into the stock markets on which the fate of the world now depends.

Since there's no way you can walk into a stock market and buy and sell shares on your own, you have to work through a broker at a brokerage house. You've heard the names: Merrill Lynch, Smith Barney, Dean Witter, PaineWebber, Charles Schwab, and so forth. Schwab is a living person, and Witter a deceased one, but the rest of these names are composites. There was a Mr. Merrill and a Mr. Lynch, a Mr. Smith and a Mr. Barney, a Mr. Paine and a Mr. Webber, and so forth.

Brokerage houses such as these try to convey the impression they go back very far in history and are quite stable, when in fact they're always merging and changing their names. It's a very volatile business with many marriages of convenience, and casualties along the way.

All major brokerage houses handle stocks, bonds, and mutual funds, and they all have to abide by the same rules laid down by the government. But beyond that, they are quite different. The so-called full-service brokers, such as Merrill Lynch or Smith Barney, charge higher commissions than the "discount brokers," such as Schwab. Then there are the "deep-discount brokers," that offer fewer services.

The extra money you pay a full-service broker entitles you to the brokerage firm's advice. As a rule, discount brokers don't offer advice. They just buy and sell on your instructions.

Here you have another decision to make. Along with picking your first stock, you have to pick a broker. The best way to do this is to talk to several in your area—especially brokers who are recommended by your friends or relatives. If you don't like the first one you meet, there are plenty of others around. Some are very experienced and know a great deal about investing in stocks, while others have just come out of a short training course and know very little. Having a good relationship with a broker is part of the fun of investing.

Once you've settled on the brokerage house and the broker, the next step is opening an account. This brings us to another snag: Unless you're twenty-one, you can't have your own account. In most states, the investing age is the same as the drinking age. You can drive a car at sixteen, and join the Army at sixteen, but you're not allowed to do business with a broker until you've reached the "age of majority."

You can get around this "age of majority" problem by setting up an account with a parent or a guardian who can act as "custodian." This is like having a restricted driver's license, where you control the vehicle but there's an adult in the passenger's seat to cheer you on, or to yell when you veer off course.

Let's say you've opened the custodial account, signed the necessary papers, given the broker whatever amount of money you intend to invest, and told the broker you're interested in Disney. A good full-service broker will punch up Disney on the special computer that brokers have and read you the recent news about the company.

He or she will also give you the research reports on Disney prepared by the in-house expert, or analyst, who keeps tabs on the company. If they do their job right, analysts can be very valuable sources of information.

It's possible that the analyst doesn't like Disney at the moment, or thinks it's overpriced, or that low attendance at the theme parks will hurt the company. It's also possible that your broker will try to talk you out of Disney and into some other stock the brokerage house likes better.

But if you've done your homework and you still think Disney is a good buy, then you might as well stick to your guns and insist on buying it. After all, it's your money.

The next thing to consider is the price you want to pay for Disney. Again, you have a choice to make. You can buy a stock "at the market," which means you'll get whatever the price happens to be at the moment your order is sent to Wall Street. Or you can put in a "limit order" for a specific price and hope somebody will take you up on it. That's the chance you take with limit orders: You are waiting to buy at a certain price, which you may or may not get.

Let's say your broker has consulted on his computer and informed you that Disney is trading at fifty dollars a share. You decide to put in your bid "at the market." The broker transmits your order through the computer and into the New York Stock Exchange.

The New York Stock Exchange (NYSE) is the oldest and most prestigious stock exchange in the world, located just off Wall Street at 82 Broad Street, in a fancy building with Greek columns in front that reminds you of a courthouse or a post office. There are other stock exchanges, but the NYSE is where

Disney is "listed"—meaning that shares of Disney are always on sale there.

If you're in New York sometime and you've got nothing better to do, the NYSE is worth a visit. The tour begins in a room full of photos and display boxes where you can push buttons and learn the story of how the stock market got started under a tree in 1790. You'll hear about how the pioneer speculators and horse traders stood under this tree in the open air, buying and selling horses, wheat, sugar, you name it, in a noisy, nonstop auction. After the Revolutionary War was won by our side, these traders got the chance to auction off the IOUs issued by the government to pay for the war. This so-called scrip was the first financial commodity ever sold in a marketplace in the United States.

Long before that, a wall was built along Wall Street to keep invaders out, which is how the street got its name. The traders under the tree were a hardy bunch, but after a while they got tired of standing out in the rain and snow, so they moved indoors to the local coffeehouses, where at least they had a roof over their heads. As business picked up, they rented space in nearby basements and lofts until they found a long-term rental and stayed there. In 1864, they built the building that's been the home of the NYSE ever since. It's no more than a Frisbee toss from the spot where the original tree once stood.

After you've walked past the photos and the displays, and you've listened to a short spiel from a tour guide, you can head for the visitors' gallery, which is the most interesting part. You're looking down through a giant picture window, with a bird's-eye view of the trading floor one hundred feet below, where all the action takes place. The trading floor looks as long as a football field, and just as hectic and noisy as a stadium on game day.

The players on the stock exchange are dressed in sneakers and multicolored lab coats, which are their uniforms. Hundreds of them are scurrying around, waving their arms and shouting to get one another's attention, and the ones that aren't scurrying are standing in huddles at different spots on the floor, called posts. At each post, there's an overhead TV set, hung from a maze of girders and pipes that looks like exposed plumbing. It's around these monitors underneath the exposed plumbing that the shares of more than twenty-five hundred different companies are being bought and sold while you watch.

You can see the Disney post from your perch in the visitors' gallery, and if you took the elevator downstairs and managed to sneak past the security guards, you could be on the trading floor in no time, wading into the crowd to purchase a share of Disney in person. But it doesn't work that way. Your order has to come in through the brokerage house to the traders in the lab coats. They do the actual buying and selling, sometimes for themselves, but mostly for customers like you, who have sent in their orders from all over the world.

The basic routine at the post hasn't changed for decades. The best way to think of it is as a nonstop auction where the same item is continuously brought up for sale. In this case, the item is Disney stock.

Let's say a trader at the Disney post yells out "1,000 at $49⅞." That means one of his customers wants to sell 1,000 shares of Disney for $49⅞ apiece. If another trader at the post has a customer who wants to buy 1,000 shares at $49⅞, the two traders make a deal. But it doesn't always happen that way. It may be that nobody wants to pay that price at that particular moment. So the trader who's selling the Disney has to lower the price to $49¾ or perhaps to $49½, until he can attract a buyer.

Or it may be that there are buyers at $49⅞, but nobody wants to sell at that price. In that case, the buyers have to raise their bids to $50 or $50⅛, and so forth, until the bid gets high enough to attract a seller.

It goes on like this from 9:30 A.M. when the market opens to 4:00 P.M. when it closes, the prices of shares bobbing up and down from one minute to the next as the auction continues. A person called the "specialist" stands at the post in the middle of this commotion, listening to the bids and the offers, watching for the signals, matching the buyers with the sellers and keeping track of every deal.

At present, more than 1 million shares of Disney are bought

and sold on the NYSE every day, along with 338 million plus shares of stock in the other twenty-six hundred listed companies. You may wonder how the lone Disney specialist standing at the post could possibly handle this volume of business. The answer is, he can't.

Although most investors are not aware of it, 85 percent of the orders arrive at specialists' posts via computer. Computers are handling more transactions both on the stock exchanges and off the stock exchanges. The trading departments of the Wall Street investment houses use computers to make trades directly with other trading departments. When you look down on the trading floor from the visitors' gallery, you're seeing a colorful spectacle that is fast becoming obsolete.

With a good computer network, you don't need hundreds of people running around wearing out their sneakers and yelling themselves hoarse. All the bidding for stocks can take place on a screen, and most of it already does.

The NYSE has a special matchmaking system for small transactions such as yours. Your buy order for Disney is sent directly into the NYSE computer, where it is automatically matched with a sell order that comes in from somebody else.

Stock transactions are entirely anonymous. Unlike the deals you make at flea markets or garage sales, in a stock deal, you never come face-to-face with the other party. Maybe it's just as well, because then you don't have to sit there and listen to the seller of the Disney shares telling you why he's getting rid of them, the way you do when you buy a used car from a neighbor.

There could be many reasons why the other party to the transaction is selling the stock that you're buying. Maybe he needs the money to pay a college tuition bill, or to repaint the house, or to take a vacation. Maybe he doesn't like the latest Disney movies, and he's not as optimistic as you are about the future of the company. Or maybe he's found another stock he'd rather own. But whatever his motivation for selling, it shouldn't matter to you. If you've done your homework, you know why you're buying.

After the computer has made a match between you and a seller, the news of the sale will move across the electronic ticker-tape that runs across the bottom of your TV screen on the financial networks. Have you ever watched that continuous string of numbers? Every one is the record of an actual stock deal. For instance, "DIS 50, $50," means that 50 shares of Disney have just been sold at $50 apiece. So if you bought 50 shares at $50, the world would know about it, because your little "DIS 50, $50" would flash across on the TV screens and electronic display monitors in brokerage houses and investment companies from Boston to Beijing.

Andy Warhol, the famous painter of the Campbell's Soup can (another great public company!), once said that with all the media around us, every person would be famous for fifteen minutes. Warhol was only joking, but every stock trade of fifty shares or more gets its five seconds of international fame.

Other Places Stocks Are Traded

A hundred years ago, there were many stock exchanges in the United States besides the big two, the NYSE and the American. Milwaukee had one, and so did San Francisco, Philadelphia, Des Moines, and Dallas. A stock fan could spend vacations riding around the country visiting the action, the way a baseball fan sees games at different ballparks. But the smaller exchanges gradually lost their importance. Most have disappeared.

Today's big two are the NYSE and the NASDAQ, which is pronounced "nazzdack." NASDAQ stands for the National Association of Securities Dealers Automated Quotations System. You could stump a lot of people on this one—What does NASDAQ stand for?—because many professionals on Wall Street couldn't tell you. It's a mouthful, which is why you never hear anybody use the full name.

It used to be that companies that were too small to be listed on the regular stock exchanges sold their shares in neighborhood stock shops, where the deals were done across a counter.

A buyer in Detroit might pay 10 to 20 percent more for the same stock purchased the same day in San Antonio because there was no tickertape where people could track the latest prices. The over-the-counter market was a favorite with gamblers and wild speculators, but the average investor was smart to stay away from it.

The managers of the over-the-counter market were among the first to see how computers could revolutionize stock trading. They realized they didn't need a gigantic trading floor like the one at the NYSE. They didn't need a fancy building, or hundreds of traders in lab coats running around waving their arms. All they needed was a few computer terminals and enough people to sit in front of the terminals and make the trades on their screens. Presto, NASDAQ had its own electronic trading floor. Technically, it's not an exchange. It's a computer network.

When you want to buy shares of a company that trades on NASDAQ, say Microsoft, your broker sends your order into the NASDAQ computer system, where it shows up on the screen with all the other orders from people who want to buy or sell Microsoft. The NASDAQ "market maker" sits at a terminal in his or her own office, which could be anywhere in the country, and puts the transactions together.

Whereas a specialist at the NYSE has to stand at his post all day and may get cramps in his legs, the NASDAQ market maker can work from a easy chair. And whereas the NYSE specialist plays the role of matchmaker, the NASDAQ market maker puts himself in the middle of every stock trade. He buys the shares from the seller and turns right around and sells those shares to the buyer, at a slightly higher price. The difference is his profit, called the "spread."

In the twenty-five years since it was created, the NASDAQ system has grown very fast, and today it is the major rival of the NYSE and the second-busiest stock market in the country. Many tiny and obscure companies that got their start on the NASDAQ exchange in the 1970s and the 1980s—Microsoft, Apple

Computer, MCI, Intel, and so forth—have become corporate giants that employ thousands of workers, sell billions of dollars'
worth of products, and are famous around the world. They still
trade on NASDAQ.

Reading the Stock Pages

The day after you buy your shares of Disney, you will rush to the
newspaper and open it to the business pages to find out how
much it is worth. That's what shareholders do every morning. It's
their first important activity, after they've taken a shower,
brushed their teeth, put on their clothes, and poured themselves a
cup of coffee.

One way to tell who the investors are is by watching them read
the paper. Investors don't start with the comics, or sports, or Ann
Landers, the way other readers do. They head straight for the
business section, and run their finger down the columns of stocks
searching for yesterday's closing prices on the companies they
own.

Their mood can change in a second, depending on what they
see there. Maybe you've observed this in your own household.
You're sitting at the breakfast table and your father is scanning the
stock tables (usually, it's a father who does this, although more
and more women are taking an interest). If he gets a sour look on
his face and tells you for the umpteenth time not to leave the
bathroom light on because it wastes electricity, which wastes
money, you can be pretty sure he just found out his stocks went
down. On the other hand, if he starts humming "Hail to the Chief"
and offers to increase your allowance, or says he'll pay for the limo
to drive you to the prom, you can be pretty sure his stocks went up.

During business hours, when the stock exchanges are open
and shares are changing hands at a rapid rate, the prices rise and
fall minute by minute. But just before the closing bell rings at
4:00 P.M., and the trading stops, every stock has its last trade of the
day. It's the price of this last trade, called the closing price, that

gets quoted in the papers the next morning. That's what investors are looking for when they turn to the business section and scan those pages of numbers, arranged in lines that appear like this:

365-Day High-Low	Stock	Div	Yld %	P/E	Sales	High	Low	Last	Chg
62⅞ 37¾	DISNEY	.36	.06	23	11090	57¾	56¾	57⅝	+¼

A lot of information is packed into this tiny space. The name of the stock, DISNEY, appears in the second column from the left, under "Stock." In the first column, "365-Day High-Low," you see two numbers, 62⅞ and 37¾. These represent dollars, $62⅞ and $37¾. What you find out here is that $62⅞ is the highest price anybody has paid for a share of Disney in the last twelve months, and $37¾ is the lowest price. So there's a wide range of prices that people will pay for the same stock.

In fact, the average stock on the New York Stock Exchange moves up and down approximately 57 percent from its base price in any given year. More incredible than that, one in every three stocks traded on the NYSE moves up and down 50 to 100 percent from the base price each year, and about 8 percent of the stocks rise and fall 100 percent or more. A stock might start out the year selling for $12, rise to $16 during an optimistic stretch, and fall to $8 during a pessimistic stretch. That's a 100 percent move: from $16 to $8. Clearly, some investors pay a lot less than others for the same company in the same year.

You'll also notice that stock prices are quoted in fractions instead of the usual decimals, so $37.75 becomes $37¾. This old-fashioned numbering system dates back to the Spaniards, who divided their money into eighths—that's why parrots in the pirate movies are always squawking about "pieces of eight."

Wall Street has kept up the practice of doing its calculations in eighths, so instead of hearing that such-and-such a stock is "up ten cents today," you'll hear that it's up "an eighth of a point," and instead of "up twenty-five cents," it's up "a quarter of a point." A "point" is Wall-Streetese for "dollar."

In the four columns to the far right, "High," "Low," "Last," and "Chg" (Change), you get a recap of what happened in yesterday's trading. In this case, nothing much. The highest price anybody paid for Disney during this particular session was $57¾, and the lowest was $56¾, and the last sale of the day was made at $57⅝. That was the closing price that everybody was looking for in the newspaper. It was up $0.25 from the closing price of the day before, which is why +¼ appears in the "Chg" column.

Directly to the right of the word "Stock" is "Div," which stands for "dividend." Dividends are a company's way of rewarding the people who buy their stock. Some companies pay big dividends, some pay small dividends, and some pay no dividend at all. You'll learn more about dividends later.

The number shown here, .36, means "thirty-six cents." That's Disney's current annual dividend—you get thirty-six cents for each share you own.

In the column under the next heading, "Yld %" (Yield), you get more information about the dividend, so you can compare it, say, to the yield from a savings account or bond. Here, they've taken Disney's thirty-six-cent annual payout and divided it by the closing stock price ($57⅝). The result is 0.06 percent—the return you're getting on your money if you invest in Disney at the current price.

This .06 percent is a very low return, as compared to the 3 percent that savings accounts are paying these days. Disney is not a stock you'd buy just for the dividend.

To the right of "Yld," there's "P/E." "P/E" is an abbreviation for "price-earnings ratio." You get the p/e ratio by dividing the price of a stock by the company's annual earnings. But there's no need to do the math yourself, because the p/e can be found in the paper every day.

When people are considering whether to buy a particular company, the p/e helps them figure out if the stock is cheap or expensive. P/e ratios vary from industry to industry, and to some extent from company to company, so the simplest way to use this tool is to compare a company's current p/e ratio to the historical norm.

In today's market, the p/e of the average stock is about 16, and Disney's p/e of 23 makes it a bit expensive relative to the average stock. But since Disney's p/e ratio has moved from 12 to 40 over the past fifteen years, a p/e of 23 for Disney is not out of line, historically. It is more expensive than the average stock because the company has been a terrific performer.

Finally, there's "Sales": the number of shares that were bought and sold in yesterday's session at the stock exchange. You always multiply this number by 100, so the 11,090 tells us that 1.1 million shares of Disney changed hands. It's not crucial to know this, but it makes you realize that the stock market is a very busy place.

When you add the three major exchanges (NYSE, American, and NASDAQ) together, the volume of trading reaches a half billion shares a day.

Thanks to home computers and the electronic tickertape, people no longer have to wait for tomorrow's newspaper to check their stocks. During the day, they can watch the tape on TV, or call up the stock prices on their computers, or call an 800 number and get the prices that way. There's even a hand-held cellular receiver, connected to a satellite, that investors can carry anywhere—on a rafting trip, an ocean cruise, or a mountain-climbing expedition.

All this technology has a drawback: It can get you too worked up about the daily gyrations. Letting your emotions go up and down in sympathy with stocks can be a very exhausting form of exercise, and it doesn't do you any good. Whether Disney rises, falls, or goes sideways today, tomorrow, or next month isn't worth worrying about if you are a long-term investor.

The Perks of Ownership

Stocks are very democratic. They have no prejudices. They don't care who they belong to. Black or white, male or female, foreign or native, saint or sinner, it doesn't matter. It's not like a fancy country club, where before you can join you have to pass the membership committee. If you want to buy a share and become an owner of the public company of your choice, the company can't stop you. And once you've become a shareholder, they can never kick you out.

If you own just one share of Disney, you enjoy the same basic rights and privileges as the owner of a million shares. You'll be invited to attend the annual meeting, held at the original Disneyland in Anaheim, California, where you can sit next to Wall Street pros and listen to the top Disney executives explain their strategy. You'll get free coffee and doughnuts and the chance to cast

Here are some examples of the freebies, goodies, and so forth, shareholders of certain companies receive as a bonus for owning the stock.

COMPANY	PERKS
Ralston Purina	Discounts on lodging, ski rental at company's Keystone Resort in Colorado
Wrigley's	Each shareholder gets 20 free packs of gum every year
Disney	30 percent discount at theme parks and on merchandise if you join the Gold Card Program
Tandy	10 percent off at Radio Shack stores during Christmas holidays
3M	Free gift package including tape and Post-It note paper
Colgate-Palmolive	$15 in discount coupons
Supercuts	$3 off coupon on haircuts
Marriott	$10 off on weekends at some Marriott hotels

Source: *Free Lunch on Wall Street,* by Charles Carlson, McGraw-Hill, 1993

your vote on important matters, such as who will sit on Disney's board of directors.

These directors are not employees of Disney, nor do they answer to the bosses of the company. They make strategic decisions, and they keep tabs on what the bosses are doing. Ultimately, the company exists for the shareholders, and the directors are there to represent the shareholders' interests.

Public companies use a one-vote-one-share system in their elections, so if you own one share of Disney, your one vote isn't going to count for much against the million votes cast by people who own a million shares. Nevertheless, the company takes each vote quite seriously. It realizes that most shareholders can't interrupt their lives and travel to the annual meeting where important issues are decided, so it sends out absentee ballots. If you forget to fill yours out, they send you a reminder.

Any time you decide you don't like the management, its policies, or the direction the company is headed, you are always free to exercise the ultimate "no" vote and sell your shares.

Four times a year, you'll get the report card that tells you how the company is doing, how its sales are going, and how much money it has made or lost in the latest period. Once a year, the company sends out the annual report that sums up the year in great detail. Most of these annual reports are printed on fancy paper with several pages of photographs. It's easy to mistake them for an upscale magazine.

In the front, there's a personal message from the head of the company, recounting the year's events, but the real story is in the numbers. These run for several pages, and unless you are trained to read them, they will surely strike you as both confusing and dull. You can get the necessary training from a good accounting course. Once you do, these dull numbers can become very exciting, indeed. What could be more exciting than learning to decipher a code that could make you a prosperous investor for life?

Companies are required to send out all the reports. They can't say they forgot to write one, or that the dog ate it along with the homework. They can't cancel the annual meeting, or make up an excuse for not calling one. They can't hide the facts, no matter how unpleasant those facts may be. They must tell the whole story, good and bad, so every shareholder knows exactly what's happening. It's the law.

If there's a foul-up on the assembly line, or products aren't selling and the company is losing money, or the CEO runs off with the cash box, or somebody files a nasty lawsuit against it, the company must tell all.

In politics, it's common practice for elected officials and candidates alike to stretch the truth to bolster their point of view. When a politician distorts the facts, we say that's politics. But when a company distorts the facts, it's a scandal on Wall Street.

Companies that intentionally mislead their shareholders (this rarely happens) face severe penalties, and the perpetrators can be fined or sent to jail. Even if it's unintentional (a more common occurrence), a company that misleads shareholders is punished in the stock market. As soon as they realize it hasn't told them the whole truth, many big-time investors will sell their shares at once. This mass selling causes the stock price to drop. It's not unusual for share prices to fall by half in a single day after the news of the scandal gets out.

When a stock loses half its value overnight, that disturbs all the investors, including the corporate insiders, from the chief executive on down, who are likely to own large numbers of shares. That's why it's in their best interest to make sure the company sticks to the facts and doesn't exaggerate. They know the truth will come out sooner or later, because companies are watched by hundreds, if not thousands of shareholders. A baseball player can't brag about his .320 average when all the fans who read the box scores every day know he's hitting .220. It's the same on Wall Street. A company can't brag about its record-breaking earnings if the earnings aren't there—too many investors are paying close attention.

That Dirty Word—Profit

Companies are in business for one basic reason. No matter whether they are public or private, owned by a single shareholder or a million shareholders, the goal is the same. They want to make a profit.

Profit is the money that's left over after all the bills are paid. It can be divided among the owners of any business, whether it's General Electric, Pepsico, Marvel Comics, or the car wash you run on weekends in your driveway. You wouldn't want to stand out in the hot sun with a bucket and a soapy sponge if you didn't expect to come away with a profit. Maybe you enjoy washing cars because you can hose yourself down every once in a while and it keeps you cool in the summertime, but that doesn't mean you'd do it for free.

The same is true of people who own shares in companies. They're not doing it just for the fun of getting invited to the annual meeting, or getting a copy of the annual report sent to them in the mail. They're doing it because they expect the company in which they own shares to make a profit and to pass along some of that profit to them, sooner or later.

There's a mistaken idea still floating around that people who do things for profit are being greedy or underhanded, and they're trying to pull a fast one on the rest of society, because whenever one person makes a bundle, it's at the expense of everybody else.

A generation ago, there were more subscribers to this idea than there are today, but it's still lurking in the backs of more than a few minds. That one man's gain is another man's pain was the basic doctrine of communism, and it was also fashionable among socialists on college campuses and elsewhere, who never missed a chance to accuse capitalists of putting themselves first and everybody else last, and of getting rich on the sore backs of the wage earners.

Earlier we mentioned Adam Smith's book *The Wealth of Nations*, which is still popular two hundred years later. You might want to take a crack at it. As long as we have capitalism and the profit motive, Smith's Invisible Hand is there to guide the money to the places where it can do the most good.

Personal computers are a recent example of the Invisible Hand in action. When PCs were invented and people became attracted to them, a slew of new companies was formed, and investors lined up to buy shares and sink billions of dollars into the computer industry. The result was better and faster computers that could be manufactured more cheaply, and the fierce competition kept the costs down. The fierce competition also put a lot of companies out of business, but the ones that survived made the best products at the lowest prices.

It's not only in the animal world that we have survival of the fittest. It happens in the capitalist world as well. Profitable companies with good management are rewarded in the stock market, because when a company does well, the stock price goes up. This makes investors happy, including the managers and employees who own shares.

In a poorly managed company, the results are mediocre, and the stock price goes down, so bad management is punished. A decline in the stock price makes investors angry, and if they get angry enough, they can pressure the company to get rid of the bad managers and take other actions to restore the company's profitability.

When all is said and done, a highly profitable company can attract more investment capital than a less profitable company. With the extra money it gets, the highly profitable company is nourished and made stronger, and it has the resources to expand and grow. The less profitable company has trouble attracting capital, and it may wither and die for lack of financial nourishment.

The fittest survive and the weakest go out of business, so no more money is wasted on them. With the weakest out of the way, the money flows to those who can make better use of it.

All employees everywhere ought to be rooting for profit, because if the company they work for doesn't make one, they'll soon be out of a job. Profit is a sign of achievement. It means somebody has produced something of value that other people are willing to buy. The people who make the profit are motivated to repeat their success on a grander scale, which means more jobs and more profits for others.

If there is any truth to the charge that capitalists and investors are selfish and greedy, thinking only of fattening their own bankrolls, why is the wealthiest country in the world also the most charitable? Americans are found at the top of the money-giving chart, and individuals do most of the giving. In 1994, for instance, U.S. residents pulled $105 billion from their own pockets to help the homeless and the infirm, the jobless and the elderly, the hospitals and the churches, the museums and the schools, the veterans and United Way, Jerry's Kids and a host of other good causes.

Capitalism is not a zero-sum game. Except for a few crooks, the rich do not get that way by making other people poor. When the rich get richer, the poor get richer as well. If it were really true that the rich get richer at the expense of the poor, then since we're the richest country in the world, by now we surely would have created the most desperate class of poor people on earth. Instead, we've done just the opposite.

There is substantial poverty in America, but it doesn't come close to matching the poverty you'll see in parts of India, Latin America, Africa, Asia, or Eastern Europe where capitalism is just beginning to take hold. When companies succeed and become more profitable, it means more jobs and less poverty, the opposite of what the government has been telling us.

The Growth Factory

Every person who owns shares in a company wants it to grow. That doesn't mean it gets too big for its britches and has to move to a larger building, although moving to a larger building is a sign of growth. It means the profits are growing. The company will earn more money this year than last year, just as it earned more money last year than the year before that. When investors talk about "growth," they're not talking about size. They're talking about profitability, that is, earnings.

If you wash three cars for $6 each, and you spent $2 on a

plastic bottle of soap and $1 on a new sponge, you've earned $15—the $18 you got for doing the job minus $3 for the materials. Wash another five cars with the same soap and the same sponge, and you'll earn another $30, with no additional cost for the materials. Your earnings have just tripled. That's more cash in your pocket so you can buy CDs, movie tickets, new clothes, or more shares of stock.

A company doubling its earnings in twelve months can cause a wild celebration on Wall Street, because it's very rare for a business to grow that fast. Big, established companies are happy to see their earnings increase by 10 to 15 percent a year, and younger, more energetic companies may be able to increase theirs by 25 to 30 percent, but one way or the other, the name of the game is earnings. That's what the shareholders are looking for, and that's what makes the stocks go up.

Think of it this way. You've got a friend who's starting a rock group. The friend needs money for some music equipment. So he makes you the following offer. If you put up $1,000 for the high-powered amplifier, he'll give you 10 percent ownership in the band. The two of you sign a paper to this effect.

Before the band squawks its first squawk, it looks as if you've made a dumb deal. It cost you $1,000 for 10 percent ownership in a group whose only asset is the amplifier you paid for. At this point, you're getting a 10 percent stake in your own amplifier. But let's say the rock group is hired by a local club to play the Friday night dances at $200 a week. Now the band has a value that goes beyond the amplifier. It has earnings. Your 10 percent of the earnings will pay you $20 a week.

Then if the band makes a hit with the crowd and gets a raise to $400, the earnings double overnight, and all of a sudden you're getting $40 a week.

By this time, the piece of paper you've got is no longer worthless. You could probably sell it if you wanted to. But if you believe in this rock group, you'll hold on to your shares, because someday the band might cut a record and get on MTV and become the next Pearl Jam or Hootie and the Blowfish. If that happens, you'll be making thousands of dollars a week from the earnings, and your 10 percent stake will be worth far more than you could have dreamed at the time you provided the amplifier.

People who buy shares in Disney, or Reebok, or any other public company do it for the same reason you'd invest in a rock group. They're counting on Disney, Reebok, or whatever to increase their earnings, and they expect that a portion of these earnings will get back to them in the form of higher stock prices.

This simple point—that the price of a stock is directly related to a company's earning power—is often overlooked, even by sophisticated investors. The tickertape watchers begin to think stock prices have a life of their own. They track the ups and downs, the way a bird watcher might track a fluttering duck. They study the trading patterns, making charts of every zig and zag. They try to fathom what the "market" is doing, when they ought to be following the earnings of the companies whose stocks they own.

If earnings continue to rise, the stock price is destined to go up. Maybe it won't go up right away, but eventually it will rise. And if the earnings go down, it's a pretty safe bet the price of the stock will go down. Lower earnings make a company less valuable, just like the rock band that loses its audience and stops selling records.

This is the starting point for the successful stockpicker: Find companies that can grow their earnings over many years to come. It's not by accident that stocks in general rise in price an average of about 8 percent a year over the long term. That occurs because companies in general increase their earnings at 8 percent a year, on average, plus they pay 3 percent as a dividend.

Based on these assumptions, the odds are in your favor when you invest in a representative sample of companies. Some will do better than others, but in general, they'll increase earnings by 8 percent and pay you a dividend of 3 percent, and you'll arrive at your 11 percent annual gain.

By itself, the price of a stock doesn't tell you a thing about whether you're getting a good deal. You'll hear people say: "I'm avoiding IBM, because at $100 a share it's too expensive." It may be that they don't have $100 to spend on a share of IBM, but the fact that a share costs $100 has nothing to do with whether IBM is expensive. A $150,000 Lamborghini is out of most people's price range, but for a Lamborghini, it still might not be expensive. Likewise, a $100 share of IBM may be a bargain, or it may not be. It depends on IBM's earnings.

If IBM is earning $10 a share this year, then you're paying 10 times earnings when you buy a share for $100. That's a p/e ratio of 10, which in today's market is cheap. On the other hand, if IBM only earns $1 a share, then you're paying 100 times earnings when you buy that $100 share. That's a p/e ratio of 100, which is way too much to pay for IBM.

The p/e ratio is a complicated subject that merits further study, if you are serious about picking your own stocks. But while we're on the topic, here are some pointers about p/e's.

If you take a large group of companies, add their stock prices together, and divide by their earnings, you get an average p/e ratio. On Wall Street they do this with the Dow Jones Industrials, the S&P 500 stocks, and other such indexes. The result is known as the "market multiple" or "what the market is selling for."

The market multiple is a useful thing to be aware of, because it tells you how much investors are willing to pay for earnings at any given time. The market multiple goes up and down, but it tends to stay within the boundaries of 10 and 20. The stock market in mid-1995 had an average p/e ratio of about 16, which meant that stocks in general weren't cheap, but they weren't outrageously expensive, either.

In general, the faster a company can grow its earnings, the more investors will pay for those earnings. That's why aggressive young companies have p/e ratios of 20 or higher. People are expecting great things from these companies and are willing to pay a higher price to own the shares. Older, established companies have p/e ratios in the mid to low teens. Their stocks are cheaper relative to earnings, because established companies are expected to plod along and not do anything spectacular.

Some companies steadily increase their earnings—they are the growth companies. Others are erratic earners, the rags-to-riches types. They are the cyclicals—the autos, the steels, the heavy industries that do well only in certain economic climates. Their p/e ratios are lower than the p/e's of steady growers, because their performance is erratic. What they will earn from one year to the next depends on the condition of the economy, which is a hard thing to predict, as you'll see in Chapter Four.

That a company earns a lot of money doesn't necessarily mean the stockholders will benefit. The next big question is: What does the company plan to do with this money? Basically, it has four choices.

It can plow the money back into the business, in effect investing in itself. It uses this money to open more stores or build new factories and grow its earnings even faster than before. In the long run, this is highly beneficial to the stockholders. A fast-growing company can take every dollar and make a 20 percent return on it. That's far more than you or I could get by putting that dollar in the bank.

Or it can waste the money on corporate jets, teak-paneled offices, marble in the executive bathrooms, executive salaries that are double the going rate, or buying other companies and paying too much for them. Such unnecessary purchases are bad for stockholders and can ruin what otherwise would be a very good investment.

Or a company can buy back its own shares and take them off the market. Why would any company want to do such a thing? Because with fewer shares on the market, the remaining shares become more valuable. Share buybacks can be very good for the stockholders, especially if the company is buying its own shares at a cheap price.

Finally, the company can pay a dividend. A majority of companies do this. Dividends are not entirely a positive thing—a company that pays one is giving up the chance to invest that money in itself. Nevertheless, dividends are very beneficial to shareholders.

A dividend is a company's way of paying you to own the stock.

The money gets sent to you directly on a regular basis—it's the only one of our four options in which the company's profits go directly into your pocket. If you need income while you're holding on to the stock, the dividend does the trick. Or you can use the dividend to buy more shares.

Dividends also have a psychological benefit. In a bear market or a correction, no matter what happens to the price of the stock, you're still collecting the dividend. This gives you an extra reason not to sell in a panic.

Millions of investors buy dividend-paying stocks and nothing else. If you are interested in this kind of investing, you might want to get in touch with Moody's Investors Service, a Wall Street research firm. Among other things, Moody's compiles a list of companies that have raised their dividends for many years in a row. One company has been doing it for fifty years, and more than three hundred have been doing it for ten.

The list appears in Moody's *Handbook of Dividend Achievers*, along with a complete statistical rundown on each of the companies that have gotten into this dividend-raising habit. To order the latest copy of this book, call Moody's at 1-800-342-5647.

How to Catch a Twelve-Bagger

If you're going to invest in a stock, you have to know the story. This is where investors get themselves in trouble. They buy a stock without knowing the story, and they track the stock price, because that's the only detail they understand. When the price goes up, they think the company is in great shape, but when the price stalls or goes down, they get bored or they lose faith, so they sell their shares.

Confusing the price with the story is the biggest mistake an investor can make. It causes people to bail out of stocks during crashes and corrections, when the prices are at their lowest, which they think means that the companies they own must be in lousy shape. It causes them to miss the chance to buy more shares when the price is low, but the company is still in terrific shape.

The story tells you what's happening inside the company to produce profits in the future—or losses, if it's a tale of woe. It's not always easy to figure this out. Some stories are more complicated than others. Companies that have many different divisions are harder to follow than companies that make a single product. And even when the story is simple, it may not be conclusive.

But there are occasions when the picture is clear and the average investor is in a perfect position to see how exciting it is. These are the times when understanding a company can really pay off. Let's consider two examples from different periods: Nike in 1987, and Johnson & Johnson in 1994.

Nike is a simple business. It makes sneakers. Along with fast food and specialty retailers, this is the sort of company that anybody can follow. (See chart on page 164.) There are three key elements: First, is Nike selling more sneakers this year than last year? Second, is it making decent profit on the sneakers it sells? Third, will it sell more sneakers next year, and the years after that? In 1987, investors got some definite answers, which arrived in the quarterly reports and the annual report sent to every shareholder.

Since going public in 1980, Nike stock had been bouncing all over the place: jumping from $5 in 1984 to $10 in 1986, falling back to $5, rebounding to $10 in 1987. Looking at the scenery for this story, the prospects for sneakers couldn't have been brighter. Everybody was wearing them: toddlers, teenagers, even adults who hadn't worn sneakers since they were kids. There were different sneakers for tennis, jogging, basketball, you name it. It was obvious the demand for sneakers was growing, and Nike was a big supplier.

Yet the company had run into a rough stretch where its sales, earnings, and future sales were all declining. This was a very depressing turn of events, as shareholders found out when they received their first-quarter 1987 report. (As is the custom with many companies, Nike's year begins in June, so the first quarter of 1987 ends in August 1986.) If you owned Nike, you got the news in the mail in early October 1986. Sales were down 22 percent, earnings down 38 percent, and "futures" (future orders) down 39 percent. This was not a good time to buy more shares of Nike.

The second-quarter report was mailed out January 6, 1987. The results were just as bad as those in the first quarter, and the third quarter wasn't much better. Then lo and behold, in the fourth-quarter report, which arrived in late July 1987 along with the annual report, there was a positive note. Sales were still down, but only by 3 percent; earnings were still down; but future orders had turned up. This meant that stores around the world were buying more Nike sneakers. They wouldn't be doing that unless they thought they could sell more Nike sneakers.

By reading the annual report of that year, you would also have learned that in spite of its several quarters of declining earnings, Nike was still making a nice profit. That's because sneakers are a very low-cost business. It's not like the steel business, where you have to build and maintain expensive factories. In the sneaker business, all you need is a big room and a bunch of sewing machines and relatively inexpensive materials. Nike had plenty of cash on hand and was in excellent financial shape.

When you opened the first-quarter report of 1988, which arrived in late September 1987, you could hardly believe your eyes. Sales were up 10 percent, earnings up 68 percent, and future orders up 61 percent. This was proof that Nike was on a roll. In fact, the roll lasted for five more years: twenty straight quarters of higher sales and higher earnings.

In September 1987, you didn't know yet about the twenty straight quarters. You were happy the company had turned itself around, but you weren't rushing out to buy more stock. You were worried about the price, which had moved up sharply from $7 to $12.50.

So you awaited further developments, and this time you got lucky. Stock prices came tumbling down in the Crash of October 1987. Investors who confuse the stock price with the story were selling everything they owned, including their Nike shares. They heard commentators on the nightly news predict a worldwide collapse of the financial markets.

In the midst of this pandemonium, you kept your head, because you realized the Nike story was getting better. The Crash gave you a gift: the opportunity to buy more shares of Nike at a bargain price.

The stock dropped to $7 after the Crash and sat at that level for eight days, so you had plenty of time to call your broker. From there, it began a five-year climb to $90, while the story kept getting better. By the end of 1992, Nike shares were worth twelve times more than you'd paid for them in 1987. That's your twelve-bagger.

Even if you missed buying Nike for $7 a share after the Crash, you could have bought it three months, six months, or a year later as the quarterly reports you received in the mail continued to show good numbers. Instead of making twelve times your money, you would have made ten, or eight, or six times your money.

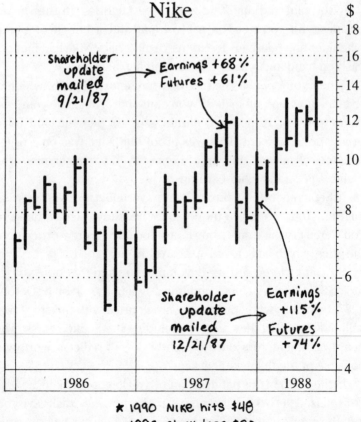

Nike $

Shareholder update mailed 9/21/87

Earnings +68%
Futures +61%

Shareholder update mailed 12/21/87

Earnings +115%
Futures +74%

1986　1987　1988

★ 1990 Nike hits $48
1992 stock tops $90

Nike—How to Catch a Twelve-Bagger

	Dates	Results	Stock Price
Q1 FY87	Q ends August 31, 1986 Shareholder update mailed September 30, 1986	Sales −22% Earnings −38% Futures −39%	9/30/86—$5.50 Range for 3 months following end of Q— $5.25–$7.87
Q2 FY87	Q ends November 30, 1986 Shareholder update mailed January 6, 1987	Sales −22% Earnings −47% Futures −35%	1/6/87—$5.88 Range for 3 months following end of Q— $5.75–$7.50
Q3 FY87	Q ends February 28, 1987 Shareholder update mailed March 25, 1987	Sales −23% Earnings −60% Futures −19%	3/25/87—$9.25 Range for 3 months following end of Q— $7.00–$9.50
Q4 FY87	Q ends May 31, 1987 Shareholder update mailed July 21, 1987	Sales −3% Earnings −16% Futures +6%	7/21/87—$9.38 Range for 3 months following end of Q— $8.12–$11.25
Q1 FY88	Q ends August 31, 1987 Shareholder update mailed September 21, 1987	Sales +10% Earnings +68% Futures +61%	9/21/87—$11.13 Range for 3 months following end of Q— $7.00–$12.50
Q2 FY88	Q ends November 30, 1987 Shareholder update mailed December 21, 1987	Sales +28% Earnings +115% Futures +74%	12/21/87—$9.88 Range for 3 months following end of Q— $7.50–$11.50

Johnson & Johnson

A more recent example of a clear-cut story that any investor could follow is Johnson & Johnson. Peter Lynch was on to this one, not that it took any particular genius to figure it out. If you had seen the 1993 annual report, you would have arrived at the same conclusion: Invest in this company.

The 1993 annual report was mailed out on March 10, 1994. The first thing you noticed on the inside cover was the fate of the stock over the past couple of years. It had been dropping steadily from about $57 at the end of 1991. At the time the report arrived, the stock had fallen to $39⅝.

For such a great company to have produced such a lousy stock in a rising market, you suspected that something had to be wrong. You scanned the annual report for the bad news, but everywhere you looked, there was good news, much of it summarized on page forty-two. The earnings had gone up steadily for ten years in a row and had quadrupled during that period. The sales had risen steadily as well.

The company also mentioned it had raised the dividend ten years in a row, but neglected to mention a more incredible fact: It had raised the dividend for thirty-two years in a row. Perhaps Johnson & Johnson was trying to be modest.

Also on page forty-two, you learned that the company had become more productive in recent years. In 1983, Johnson & Johnson, with 77,400 employees, manufactured and sold $6 billion worth of products, while in 1993, with 81,600 employees, it manufactured and sold $14 billion worth of products. That's more than twice as much manufacturing and selling, with only 4,200 additional employees. From 1989 to 1993, the sales increased from $9.7 billion to $14 billion and the number of employees dropped.

This told you that Johnson & Johnson was getting to be highly efficient and adept at cutting costs. The company's workers were using their time more effectively. They were producing more value for the company, for the shareholders (although you couldn't see it in the stock price), and for themselves. Many of the workers owned shares, and even if they didn't, when sales went up, and profits went up, they got raises.

On pages twenty-five and forty-two, you found out that Johnson & Johnson had been buying back its own shares: 3 million shares in 1993, 110 million shares in a decade. It spent billions of dollars in this effort. When a company takes its own shares off the market in this fashion, the investors are likely to benefit. Fewer shares means higher earnings per share, which leads to a higher stock price. Looking at Johnson & Johnson's stock price, you wouldn't think there'd been a buyback.

The balance sheet on page twenty-nine of Johnson & Johnson's annual report showed that the company had over $900 million in cash and marketable securities, and the company was worth $5.5 billion—its "total equity." It owed $1.5 billion in long-term debt, a modest amount for a company with $5.5 billion in equity. With this much financial clout, Johnson & Johnson is no threat to go out of business.

By this time, you're wondering what the flaw in this story is. Could it be that Johnson & Johnson hadn't prepared itself for the future? The headline on the cover of the annual report suggested otherwise. Right there in big letters it said, "Growth Through New Products." The text gave the details: 34 percent of the company's 1993 sales came from products introduced to the market in the last five years.

On page forty-two, you discover that Johnson & Johnson spent more than $1 billion on research and development in 1993—8 percent of sales. The R&D budget had more than doubled in ten years. Obviously, the company was doing what the headline said: growing new products. It hadn't been caught napping.

To put this story into a larger context, you compared the price of the stock to the earnings. The company was expected to earn $3.10 in 1994, and $3.60 in 1995, giving it a price/earnings ratio of 12 and 11, respectively. Future earnings are always hard to predict, but Johnson & Johnson had had very predictable results in the past. So, if these estimates turned out to be correct, the stock was cheap.

At the time, the average stock was selling for sixteen times its estimated 1995 earnings. Johnson & Johnson was selling for eleven times its estimated 1995 earnings. And Johnson & Johnson was far better than your average company. It was a terrific company, doing everything right: earnings up, sales up, prospects bright. Despite all this, the stock already had dropped to to $39⅝, and it dropped further, to nearly $36, in the weeks after the report arrived.

As hard as it was to believe, you reached the inescapable conclusion: There was nothing wrong with Johnson & Johnson to cause the stock price to go down. The company wasn't the problem, the "health-care scare" was the problem. In 1993, Congress was debating various health-care-reform proposals, including the ones advanced by the Clinton administration. Investors worried that health-care companies would suffer if the Clinton proposals became law. So they dumped Johnson & Johnson along with the rest of their health-care stocks. The entire industry took a beating in this period.

Some of this concern would have been justified if the Clintons had had their way, but even then Johnson & Johnson would have been affected less than a typical health-care company. On page forty-one of the annual report, you learned that over 50 percent of Johnson & Johnson's profits came from its international business— the Clinton proposals couldn't have affected that. Then on page twenty-six you found out that 20 percent of the company's profits came from shampoo, Band-Aids, and other consumer items that had nothing to do with pharmaceuticals, which the Clintons had targeted for reform. Either way you sliced it, Johnson & Johnson had a limited exposure to the threat that people were worried about.

It didn't take more than twenty minutes to read that annual report and decide that Johnson & Johnson at $39⅝ was one of the bargains of the decade. Johnson & Johnson is not a complicated story. You didn't have to be a full-time professional investor or a graduate of the Harvard Business School to figure it out.

This was an easy call: The stock was down, while the fundamentals of the company were improving. As in the case of Nike, you didn't have to rush to buy shares. Peter Lynch recommended Johnson & Johnson in an article in *USA Today* at the end of 1993, when the stock was selling for $44⅞. In the spring of 1994 on *Wall Street Week* with Louis Rukeyser he recommended it again. By then, the stock was $7 cheaper at $37.

The fact that it had dropped $7 didn't bother Lynch at all. The latest quarterly report told him that sales and earnings were on the rise, so the story was getting better. It was a perfect chance to buy more shares at the lower price.

Lynch publicly recommended Johnson & Johnson once again in midsummer 1994. The stock had rebounded to $44, but it was still cheap on earnings. By October, 1995, it had risen above $80. The price had doubled in eighteen months.

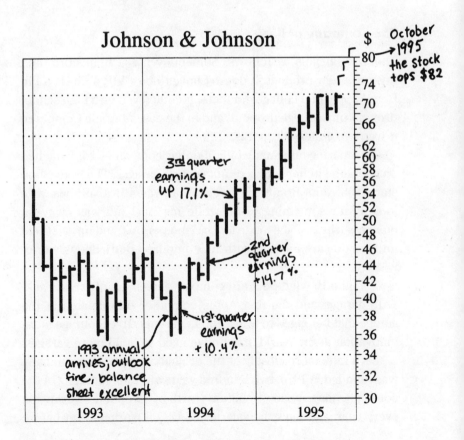

Johnson & Johnson

THREE

The Lives of a Company

The Company at Birth

The story begins as follows. Somebody has a brainstorm and invents a new product. It doesn't have to be a VIP, a Ph.D., a Phi Beta Kappa, or a college graduate. It could even be a high-school dropout or a college dropout, and in the case of Apple Computer, it was two college dropouts.

It's amazing how many billion-dollar companies got launched on people's kitchen tables or out of their garages. The Body Shop started in Anita Roddick's garage. She was a British housewife looking for something to do while her husband was away on business trips. So she made lotions and potions, and turned them into a skin-care empire, with nine hundred Body Shops worldwide.

The first Hewlett-Packard computer came out of David Packard's garage, and the first Apple computer was created in the garage that belonged to Steve Jobs's parents. To encourage more innovation in the world, maybe we need to build more garages.

Let's look more closely at the origins of Apple. The company was founded in 1976, two hundred years after the founding of the country. Today, it sells $5 billion worth of computers worldwide every year, and pays the salaries of 11,300 workers. But before

1976, Apple didn't exist, except as a gleam in the eyes of two California boys.

One was Jobs, and the other was his buddy Steve Wozniak. Jobs was twenty-one at the time; Wozniak, twenty-six. That both were college dropouts gives them something in common with Ben Cohen, the Ben of Ben & Jerry's ice cream. All three left school early, started a company from scratch, and become multimillionaires before they were thirty-five.

That doesn't mean you should drop out of school and wait for something wonderful to happen. These three people knew how to read, write, and count, and the two Steves had already learned a great deal about computers. They didn't leave school so they could sleep late and goof off the rest of the day. They fiddled around with transistors, wires, and printed circuits.

Wozniak was one of the original "hackers"—pesky computer whizzes who experimented with homemade equipment and learned how to break security codes and invade databases and create havoc in government agencies and corporate offices. On a more constructive note, he thought about designing a simple computer that could be used at home by people who had never handled one, and who were so confused by the whole business that they couldn't tell a disk drive from a disc jockey. That was 99.9 percent of the population.

So Wozniak and Jobs set up shop in the Jobs's family garage, took some generic computer parts and put them together in a plastic box, and called it the Apple I. Both of them got very excited about what they'd produced. They decided to sell everything they owned—which amounted to one old van and two calculators—and sink the proceeds into the business.

They raised thirteen hundred dollars of their own money, which at 1976 prices helped finance the production of fifty more Apples. Then they sold those fifty and used that money to develop an improved model and sold several hundred copies of that.

In this first stage, the source of the bright idea is paying the bills out of his own pocket. When the cash runs out, he hocks the family jewels, sells the second car, gets a home equity loan from the bank—whatever it takes to move the project along.

The risk of losing their house, prized possessions, and life savings is a risk that many backyard inventors are ready to take in order to launch a fledgling enterprise. These are people with grit and gumption, willing to wander into uncharted territory just like the pioneers of old. In starting a new business, they choose excitement over the security of a regular paycheck. It's not enough that they invest all their money in the project. They must also work long hours and invest most of their time.

If they're lucky and they don't hit any snags or run out of money too quickly, they'll be able to make a sample or a scale model of the gizmo they've invented, or pay a consultant to write a detailed plan for the business they're hoping to get into. At this point, they move to the exciting stage when even more money is required. They pitch the project to an "angel."

The angel could be a rich uncle, a distant cousin, or a friend with big bucks and a willingness to invest in a longshot. It's not out of charity that angels put up the money. They do it because they are convinced the new idea has a fighting chance to succeed. And in return for their capital, they ask for a share of the business—often a rather large share.

Already you can see that the person who has the great idea can't hope to succeed by being selfish and keeping 100 percent ownership for him- or herself. As the project moves beyond the scale-model stage or the planning stage, more money will have to be raised from new investors with bigger bankrolls. These are the venture capitalists.

Venture capitalists usually enter the picture when the gizmo is in production, and a sales force has been hired to sell it. They reduce their risk by waiting until the new company is established and the idea has already proven itself to some extent. These people have a keen eye for detail, and they review every aspect of the company's brief history looking for flaws. They want to know if the management knows what it's about, and whether it has the ability to turn the operation from small-time into big-time.

In return for financial aid, the venture capitalists also demand a piece of the action. Now our young company has three groups of owners: the original inventor who put up the first batch of money; the angels who put up the second batch; and the venture capitalists who put up the third. By this time, the original inventor may own less than 50 percent of the business, because the bigger the pie gets, the more people with their fingers in it.

Let's check in again on the progress of the two Steves at Apple. Sensing they had a popular product on their hands, they brought in a retired electronics engineer who was also a marketing expert. His name was Mike Markkula. Markkula had worked for two giants in the computer industry: Intel and Fairchild Semiconductor. He was old enough to be the father of the two inventors.

Markkula could have dismissed the pair as the rank amateurs they were, but he knew a good thing when he saw it. Not only did he agree to write their business plan, he bought a one-third share of the company for $250,000—making him Apple's original angel.

People who are good at inventing things are not necessarily good at promotion, advertising, finance, or personnel management—any one of which can make or break a young enterprise. Realizing the two Steves needed more help than even he could give them, Markkula recruited Mike Scott, an experienced corporate executive, to be Apple's president.

The company also hired Regis McKenna, a veteran copywriter from one of the best advertising firms in the area, who designed the Apple logo. With these new associates taking care of marketing and promotion, the two Steves were free to concentrate on improving the product.

Apple was the first personal computer to offer color graphics, and the first to use a TV monitor as a screen. Wozniak installed a disk drive to replace the cassette tapes that were used to store data in those days. By June 1977, they'd sold $1 million worth of Apples, and by the end of 1978, when they introduced the Apple II, Apple was one of the fastest-growing companies in the United States.

As sales continued to climb, the two Steves kept themselves busy in the Apple lab (no more garages for them!) designing more Apples. Meanwhile, in 1979, they raised more money: Wozniak sold some of his stock to financier Fayez Sarofim, and a group of venture capitalists organized by the L. F. Rothschild company invested $7.2 million.

The company had produced its fourth new model by the time it went public in December 1980. This is typical—Apple waited until it had proven itself and the Apples were flying off the shelves before going public.

Going Public

It's in this stage that the stock market comes into play. By now, the company has refined its gizmo and taken the kinks out of it and is preparing for a full-scale expansion. Or, if the original idea was a new kind of store, the first store has already proven itself, and the company is already planning a second store, and a third, and so on. This sort of ambitious campaign requires more money than the angels and venture capitalists have kicked in so far, and the best place to get it is from you and me.

It's a momentous decision to take a company public, not unlike the decision of a private person to run for public office. Once you do either, you open yourself up to reporters sticking their noses into your business and government agencies following your every move. The life of a politician is no longer his or her own, and neither is the life of a company that goes from private to public.

Companies take this step and put up with the hassles of living in a fishbowl, because going public is their best chance to raise enough money to reach their full potential.

A company has two important birthdays—the day it incorporates and the day it goes public. This blessed event is called the "initial public offering." Each year, hundreds of stocks are born in this fashion, with an assist from the investment-banking firms that oversee the delivery.

The bankers' part of the job, selling the shares to interested parties, is called the underwriting. These bankers go out on a "road show," where they try to convince would-be investors to buy the stock. These would-be investors are given a document (the "prospectus") that explains everything about the company, including all the reasons why they shouldn't buy the stock. These warnings are printed in large red letters so people can't say they didn't see them. On Wall Street, the warning labels are called "red herrings."

In the prospectus, the bankers must also estimate the price at which the first shares will be sold. Usually, they pick a range, say, from twelve dollars to sixteen dollars, with the final price determined by what sort of reception they get on the road show.

The bankers publicize an underwriter by putting in the papers an ad called a tombstone. The so-called lead bank on the deal gets its name in a prominent spot on the tombstone. You'd be surprised at the squabbling and jostling that goes on behind the scenes among banks that compete to get the credit for being the lead bank. A sample tombstone is shown on page 176.

Whereas a human life comes to an end with an undertaker and a tombstone, a company's public life begins with an underwriter and a tombstone. This is one of the curiosities in the financial lingo of Wall Street.

In a peculiar twist of fate, the small investor (this term, "small investor," is used to describe the size of the portfolio and not the size of the person) rarely gets the chance to buy shares in small, newborn companies at the initial offering price. These initial shares are usually reserved for "big" investors, such as fund managers who have millions, and even billions of dollars to work with.

The 4.6-million-share offering for Apple Computer was sold out within an hour, and mutual-fund managers were scrambling to get their hands on as many shares as they could. As usual, amateur investors were shut out of the deal, especially in Massachusetts. Many states have "blue-sky" laws to protect the public

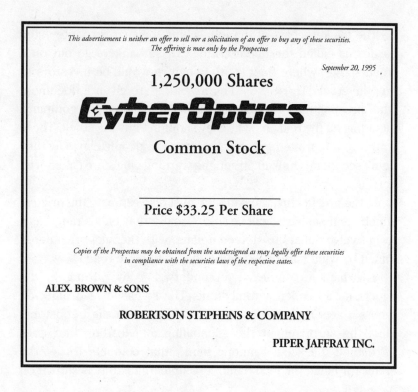

from fraudulent promotions, and the Massachusetts regulators put Apple in that category. They couldn't have been more wrong.

In any event, once an offering is completed, the proceeds are divided. A small chunk of the money goes to the underwriters—the investment banks that organized the road show and put together the deal. Another chunk goes to the founders of the company, plus the angels and the venture capitalists, who use the offering to sell some of their shares. The rest of the money is returned to the company itself. This is the capital it uses to expand the business.

At this point, the company has a new set of owners—the investors who bought shares in the offering. It's their money that pays the underwriters, enriches the founders, and helps the company to expand. Now comes the moment everybody has been waiting for: The shares begin to trade on the stock exchange.

Apple made its debut on the NASDAQ over-the-counter market in December 1980. Now, anybody could buy the stock, including all the small investors who were shut out of the initial offering. What often happens is that the newly issued stock may rise for a few days, weeks, or months, but after that, the excitement tends to wear off, and the price comes down. This is a great time for small investors to pounce on a bargain. After twelve months of trading, Apple shares had dropped from the twenty-two-dollar offering price to fourteen dollars.

It doesn't always happen this way, but it happens often enough that small investors get the last laugh on the big shots who bought the original shares.

The founders don't have to sell their entire stake in the company in the public offering. Normally, they sell only a part of their stake. That's how Jobs, Wozniak, and Markkula cashed in. They kept most of their shares of Apple, which after the first day of trading on the open market gave them each a net worth of more than $100 million. For Jobs and Wozniak, it was not a bad return on an initial investment of thirteen hundred dollars, made just four years earlier. (Markkula bought in at $250,000—not a bad investment for him, either.)

Only in the capitalist system can backyard inventors and school dropouts start companies that employ thousands of people and pay taxes and make the world a better place to live. The citizens of communist countries never had that chance.

The only time a company benefits from its own stock is in a public offering. When you buy a used Chrysler minivan, it doesn't do Chrysler any good, and when you buy a share of Chrysler on the stock exchange, that doesn't do Chrysler any good, either. Millions of shares of Chrysler trade back and forth every week on the stock exchange, and Chrysler doesn't benefit in the least. These shares are being bought and sold by private owners, just like the people who sell each other used cars and minivans. The money passes directly from one private owner to another.

Only when you buy a new Chrysler does the company get something out of it. Likewise, only when a company issues new shares does it get something out of its stock. It may issue new shares only once in its lifetime, in the initial public offering, or it may have subsequent offerings called "secondaries."

The Company When It's Young

The young company is full of energy, bright ideas, and hope for the future. It is long on expectations and short on experience. It has the cash that was raised in the offering, so chances are it doesn't have to worry about paying its bills at this point. It expects to be earning a living before the original cash runs out, but there's no guarantee of that.

In its formative years, a company's survival is far from assured. A lot of bad things can happen. It may have a great idea for a product but spend all its money before the product is manufactured and shipped to the stores. Or maybe the great idea turns out not to have been so great after all. Or maybe the company gets sued by people who say they had the great idea first, and the company stole it. If the jury agrees with the plaintiffs, the company could be forced to pay millions of dollars it doesn't have. Or maybe the great idea becomes a great product that fails a government test and can't be sold in this country. Or maybe another company comes along with an even greater product that does the job better, or cheaper, or both.

In industries where the competition is fierce, companies knock each other off all the time. Electronics is a good example. Some genius in a lab in Singapore invents a better relay switch, and six months later it's on the market, leaving the other manufacturers with obsolete relay switches that nobody wants.

It's easy to see why one-half of all new businesses are dissolved within five years, and why the most bankruptcies happen in competitive industries.

Because of the variety of calamities that can befall a company in the high-risk juvenile phase of its life, the people who own the shares have to protect their investment by paying close attention to the company's progress. You can't afford to buy any stock and then go to sleep and forget about it, but young companies, especially, must be followed every step of the way. They are often in the precarious position where one false step can put them into bankruptcy and out of business. It's especially important to assess their financial strength—the biggest problem with young companies is that they run out of cash.

When people go on vacation, they tend to take twice as many clothes as they're going to need, and half as much money. Young companies make the same mistake about money: They start out with too little.

Now for the good part: Starting from scratch, a young company can grow very fast. It's small and it's restless, and it has plenty of room to expand in all directions. That's the key reason young companies on the move can outdistance the middle-aged companies that have had their growth spurt and are past their prime.

The Company in Middle Age

Companies that manage to reach middle age are more stable than young companies. They've made a name for themselves and they've learned from their mistakes. They have a good business going, or they wouldn't have gotten this far. They've got a proven record of reliability. Chances are they've got money in the bank and they've developed a good relationship with the bankers, which comes in handy if they need to borrow more.

In other words, they've settled into a comfortable routine. They're still growing, but not as fast as before. They have to struggle to stay in shape, just as the rest of us do when we reach middle age. If they allow themselves to relax too much, leaner and meaner competitors will come along to challenge them.

A company can have a midlife crisis, the same as a person. Whatever it's been doing doesn't seem to be working anymore. It abandons the old routines and thrashes around looking for a new identity. This sort of crisis happens all the time. It happened to Apple.

In late 1980, just after Apple went public, it came out with a lemon: the Apple III. Production was halted while the problems were ironed out, but by then it was too late. Consumers had lost faith in Apple III. They lost faith in the whole company.

There's nothing more important to a business than its reputation. A restaurant can be one hundred years old and have a wall full of awards, but all it takes is one case of food poisoning or a new chef who botches the orders, and a century's worth of success goes out the window. So to recover from its Apple III fiasco, Apple had to act fast. Heads rolled in the front office, where several executives were demoted.

The company developed new software programs, opened offices in Europe, installed hard disks in some of its computers. On the plus side, Apple reached $1 billion in annual sales in 1982, but on the minus side, it was losing business to IBM, its chief rival. IBM was cutting into Apple's territory: personal computers.

Instead of concentrating on what it knew best, Apple tried to fight back by cutting in on IBM's territory: business computers. It created the Lisa, a snazzy machine that came with a new gadget: the mouse. But in spite of the mouse, the Lisa didn't sell. Apple's earnings took a tumble, and so did the stock price—down 50 percent in a year.

Apple was less than ten years old, but it was having a full-blown midlife crisis. Investors were dismayed, and the company's management was feeling the heat. Employees got the jitters and looked for other jobs. Mike Markkula, Apple's president, resigned. John Sculley, former president of Pepsi-Co, was brought in for the rescue attempt. Sculley was no computer expert, but he knew marketing. Marketing is what Apple needed.

Apple was split into two divisions, Lisa and Macintosh. There was spirited rivalry between the two. The Macintosh had a mouse like the Lisa and was similar in other respects, but it cost much less and was easier to use. Soon, the company abandoned the Lisa and put all its resources into the Macintosh. It bought TV ads and made an incredible offer: Take one home and try it out for twenty-four hours, for free.

The orders poured in and Apple sold seventy thousand Macintoshes in three months. The company was back on track with this great new product. There was still turmoil in the office, and Jobs had a falling out with Sculley.

This is another interesting aspect of corporate democracy: Once the shares are in public hands, the founder of the company doesn't necessarily get what he wants.

Sculley changed a few things around and solved a few more problems, and the Macintosh ended up doing what the Lisa was supposed to do: It caught on with the business crowd. New software made it easy to link one Macintosh to another in a network of computers. By 1988, more than a million Macintoshes had been sold.

A company's midlife crisis puts investors in a quandary. If the stock has already dropped in price, investors have to decide whether to sell it and avoid even bigger losses or hold on to it and hope that the company can launch a comeback. In hindsight, it's easy to see that Apple recovered, but at the time of the crisis, the recovery was far from assured.

The Company When It's Old

Companies that are twenty, thirty, fifty years old have put their best years behind them. You can't blame them for getting tired. They've done it all and seen it all, and there's hardly a place they can go that they haven't already been.

Take Woolworth. It's been around for more than one hundred years—several generations of Americans grew up shopping at Woolworth's. At one point, there was a Woolworth's outlet in every city and town in America. That's when the company ran out of room to grow.

Recently, Woolworth has suffered a couple of unprofitable years. It can still make a profit, but it will never be the spectacular performer it was when it was younger. Old companies that were great earners in the past can't be expected to keep up the momentum. A few of them have—Wrigley's, Coca-Cola, Emerson Electric, and McDonald's come to mind. But these are exceptions.

U.S. Steel, General Motors, and IBM are three prime examples of former champions whose most exciting days are behind them—although IBM and GM are having a rebound. U.S. Steel was once an incredible hulk, the first billion-dollar company on earth. Railroads needed steel, cars needed steel, skyscrapers needed steel, and U.S. Steel provided 60 percent of it. At the turn of this century, no company dominated its industry the way U.S. Steel dominated steel, and no stock was as popular as U.S. Steel stock. It was the most actively traded issue on Wall Street.

When a magazine wanted to illustrate America's power and glory, it ran a picture of a steel mill, with the fire in the furnaces and the liquid metal pouring like hot lava into the waiting molds. We were a nation of factories then, and a good deal of our wealth and power came from the mill towns of the East and the Midwest.

The steel business was a fantastic business to be in, and U.S. Steel prospered through both world wars and six different presidents. The stock hit an all-time high of $108⅞ in August 1959.

This was the beginning of the electronic age and the end of the industrial age and the glory of steel, and it would have been the perfect time for investors to sell their U.S. Steel shares and buy shares in IBM. But you had to be a very farsighted and unsentimental investor to realize this. After all, U.S. Steel was classed as a blue chip, Wall Street's term of endearment for prestigious companies that are expected to excel forever. Hardly anyone would have predicted that in 1995, U.S. Steel stock would be selling for less than it sold for in 1959.

To put this decline in perspective, the Dow Jones Industrial Average was bumping up against the five hundred level in 1959, and it's gone up more than four thousand points since. So while stocks in the Dow have increased in value more than eight times over, U.S. Steel has gone downhill. Loyal shareholders have died and gone to heaven waiting for U.S. Steel to reclaim its lost glory.

There's a lesson here that may save you some grief in the future. No matter how powerful it may be today, a company won't stay on top forever. Being called a "blue-chip" or a "world-class operation" can't save a company whose time is past, any more than Great Britain was saved by having the word "Great" in its name.

Long after Great Britain had lost its empire, the British people continued to think of their country as stronger and mightier than it really was, the same as the shareholders of U.S. Steel.

International Harvester, the dominant force in farm equipment for an entire half-century, peaked in 1966 and never came back, even though it tried to change its luck by changing its name to Navistar. Johns-Manville, once number one in insulation and building supplies, topped out in 1971. The Aluminum Company of America, better known as Alcoa, a Wall Street darling of the 1950s when the country was discovering aluminum foil, aluminum siding, and aluminum boats, rose to $23 a share in 1957 (adjusted for splits), a price it didn't see again until the 1980s.

General Motors, the dominant car company in the world and the bluest of the automotive blue chips, reached a peak in October 1965 that it wouldn't see again for nearly thirty years. Today, GM is still the largest company in the United States, and first in total sales, but it's far from the most profitable. Sometime in the 1960s, its reflexes began to slow.

The Germans came ashore with their Volkswagens and their BMWs, and the Japanese invaded with their Toyotas and Hondas. The attack was aimed directly at Detroit, and GM was slow to react. A younger, more aggressive GM might have risen to this challenge more quickly, but the older GM was set in its ways.

It continued to make big cars when it could see that small foreign cars were selling like crazy. Before it could build new models that could compete with the overseas models, it had to overhaul its outmoded factories. This cost billions of dollars, and by the time the overhaul was complete, and small cars were rolling off the GM assembly lines, the public had switched back to bigger cars.

For three decades the largest industrial company in the United States has not been largely profitable. Yet if you had predicted this result in 1965, when GM was riding the crest of its fame and fortune, nobody would have believed you. People would sooner have believed that Elvis was lip-synching.

Then there's IBM, which had reached middle age in the late 1960s, about the time GM was in decline. Since the early 1950s, IBM was a spectacular performer and a great stock to own. It was a top brand name and a symbol of quality—the IBM logo was getting to be as famous as the Coke bottle. The company won awards for how well it was managed, and other companies studied IBM to learn how they should run their operations. As late as the 1980s, it was celebrated in a best-selling book, *In Search of Excellence*.

The stock was recommended by stockbrokers everywhere as the bluest of the blue chips. To mutual-fund managers, IBM was a "must" investment. You had to be a maverick not to own IBM.

But the same thing happened to IBM that happened to GM. Investors were so impressed with its past performance that they did not notice what was going on in the present. People stopped buying the big mainframe computers that were the core of IBM's business. The mainframe market wasn't growing anymore. IBM's personal-computer line was attacked from all sides by competitors who made a less-expensive product. IBM's earnings sank, and as you probably can guess by now, so did the stock price.

By now you might be wondering what's the point of investing in a stodgy old company such as IBM, GM, or U.S. Steel? There are several reasons you might do this. First, big companies are less risky, in that they generally are in no danger of going out of business. Second, they are likely to pay a dividend. Third, they have valuable assets that might be sold off at a profit.

These corporate codgers have been everywhere and seen it all, and they've picked up all sorts of valuable property along the way. In fact, studying an old company and delving into its finances can be as exciting as rummaging through the attic of a rich and elderly aunt. You never know what amazing stuff you'll find stuck in a dark corner.

Whether it's land, buildings, equipment, the stocks and bonds they keep in the bank, or the smaller companies they've acquired along the way, old companies have a substantial "break-up value." Shareholders act like the relatives of that aged rich aunt, waiting around to find out who will get what.

There's always the chance an old company can turn itself around, as Xerox and American Express have been doing in the past couple of years.

On the other hand, when an old company falters or stumbles as badly as these companies did, it may take twenty or thirty years before it can get itself back on track. Patience is a virtue, but it's not well rewarded when you own stock in a company that's past its prime.

The Corporate Soap Opera

There are a lot of goings-on between companies. Watching them can be a great soap opera. If they aren't getting married (called a "merger"), then they're getting divorced (called a "divestiture" or the "spinoff of one of our divisions"). On top of that, there are "takeovers," where one company is swallowed up by another. When the company that's about to be swallowed doesn't put up a fight, we call it a "friendly takeover." When it objects to being swallowed and makes a struggle and tries to squirm out of it, we call it a "hostile takeover."

This isn't as bad as it sounds, because in the world of finance, taking over a company is generally considered acceptable behavior. It comes with the territory, because when a company goes public, it no longer controls who the owners will be. It may try to protect itself from being taken over, but few companies are takeover-proof. And since they have the right to do it to somebody else, they can't get too mad when somebody else tries to do it to them.

In either kind of takeover, friendly or hostile, the company that gets swallowed loses its independence and becomes a division of the company that's doing the swallowing. A good example of this is Kraft. Kraft was once an independent cheesemaker with its own stock that anyone could buy. It was owned by individuals, mutual funds, and pension funds alike. Then along came Philip Morris.

The directors of Philip Morris decided it was unwise for them to sell cigarettes and nothing else. So they started taking over companies that made other kinds of products, such as cheese and beer. A long time ago, they bought the Miller Brewing Company. They also acquired Wisconsin Tissue, 7 UP, and General Foods. In 1982, they bought Entenmann's and got into the doughnut business, and in 1988, they took over Kraft.

The way a takeover happens is that the acquiring company buys all the shares from the thousands of different owners of the company being acquired, in this case, Kraft. Generally, the acquiring company, in this case, Philip Morris, makes a "tender offer" at a fixed price. As soon as Philip Morris gets its hands on 51 percent of the Kraft shares, the deal is all but done. It has majority control, and from then on, it's easy to convince the owners of the other 49 percent of Kraft to sell their shares as well.

Friendly takeovers are short and sweet. If a company isn't doing well on its own, its shareholders will welcome the change in management. In most instances, they are delighted to sell their shares, because the acquiring company offers a price that is generally much higher than the going rate for the shares on the stock market. The stock price of a target company may double or even triple overnight when the deal is announced.

A hostile takeover can turn into a knock-down, drag-out battle in the courts, as well as a bidding war, if two or more companies are fighting over the same target. These battles have been known to last for months. Once in a while, a flea swallows an elephant, but usually it's the other way around, and the company doing the swallowing is bigger than the company getting swallowed.

Usually, when a big company starts looking around for an acquisition, it's got more cash in the bank than it knows what to do with. It could send this extra cash to the shareholders as a special dividend or a bonus, but the people who run companies will tell you that mailing out bonus checks isn't nearly as exciting as plotting a takeover and using the extra cash to finance it.

Whatever kind of business they're planning to take over, they're convinced they can manage it better and more profitably than the current leadership can. So these deals aren't only about money. They're also about egos.

The most successful mergers and takeovers are those in which the parties involved are in the same line of work, or at least have something in common. In romance, we call this "seeking a compatible partner." In business, we call it "synergy."

Georgia Pacific, a lumbering giant, once took over two smaller lumber companies, Puget Sound Pulp & Timber Co. and Hudson Pulp & Paper, thereby expanding its operations. This was the classic "synergy" because all three were in the tree business. They benefited from moving in together under the same roof for the same reason that couples benefit from getting married: Two, or in this case, three, can live more cheaply than one.

Another example of classic "synergy" is Hershey's acquisition of H. B. Reese Candies, which took place in the 1960s. This was a strategic alliance between a famous peanut-butter cup and a famous chocolate bar, and both have lived happily ever since.

Pepsi-Co has done well with its multiple takeovers of Kentucky Fried Chicken, Taco Bell, and Pizza Hut, among other brand names. There's a definite synergy between fast food and soft drinks. Pepsi's fast-food restaurants sell a lot of Pepsis along with their tacos, chicken, and pizza.

With Philip Morris, it's a little harder to detect the synergy between cigarettes, cheese, beer, doughnuts, and toilet paper, until you realize that Philip Morris has been buying great brand names that consumers recognize.

There's an ironic synergy in Heinz's acquisitions of Star Kist tuna, Ore-Ida potatoes, and Weight Watchers. One part of the company is selling groceries, while the other part is selling diets. People laughed about the Weight Watchers, but Heinz understood how to make a brand name out of it and sell the product in stores. It's been a bonanza.

Sara Lee, once known as the Kitchens of Sara Lee, went on a takeover binge and captured Booth Fisheries, Oxford Chemical, and Fuller Brush, before moving into vacuum cleaners by taking over Electrolux. At that point, they were selling cakes and the equipment to pick up the crumbs from the cakes, which is a far-fetched sort of synergy. But the smartest thing Sara Lee ever did was to take over Hanes. Hanes made the L'eggs stockings that caught the fancy of half the women in the country. L'eggs was a success to begin with, and Sara Lee turned it into a smashing success.

When a company takes over a string of other companies with which it has little or nothing in common, the result is known as a conglomerate. Conglomerates were popular thirty to forty years ago, then went out of style because most of them failed to live up to expectations. The managers of conglomerates found out it's not easy to run other people's businesses.

The world record for conglomeration may belong to U.S. Industries, which at one point was doing a different takeover every day. Another champion conglomerator was Charles Bluhdorn at Gulf & Western, who never saw a company he didn't want to take over. He acquired so many of them that Gulf & Western was known as Engulf and Devour. He did so many takeovers that when he died, Gulf & Western's stock went up! Shareholders believed that the new management would sell off some of Bluhdorn's acquisitions at a nice profit, which is exactly what happened. Gulf & Western became Paramount Communications—until Paramount was taken over by Viacom.

Then there was American Can, which made numerous acquisitions from mining companies to Sam Goody. This whole kaboodle was merged with Smith Barney and the Commercial Credit Company, and its name was changed to Primerica. Primerica purchased Shearson from American Express and merged it into Smith Barney. Then Primerica bought Travelers Insurance and changed the name Primerica to the Travelers Group.

Finally, there's ITT, which has had more marriages than Elizabeth Taylor. Since 1961, it has merged with or taken over no fewer than thirty-one different enterprises, while later selling off six. The takeover list includes Avis Rent-A-Car, Continental Baking, Levitt Furniture, Sheraton Hotels, Canteen Corp., Eaton Oil, Minnesota National Life, Rayonier, Thorp Finance, Hartford Insurance, and Pennsylvania Glass Sand. Along the way, ITT picked up Caesar's World and Madison Square Garden.

For twenty-five years, all the takeover activity didn't do ITT much good. The stock went nowhere. In the 1990s, the company has worked itself back into shape by cutting costs and debt, and the stock price has tripled in 1994–95. ITT has announced plans to split itself into three parts, with Caesar's World and Madison Square Garden included in one of the parts.

Extinct Companies

Companies die every year. Some die young. They try to go too far too fast on borrowed money they can't pay back, and they crash. Some die in middle age because their products turn out to be defective, or too old-fashioned, and people stop buying. Maybe they're in the wrong business, or the right business at the wrong time, or worst of all, the wrong business at the wrong time. Big companies can die right along with smaller and younger companies. American Cotton Oil, Laclede Gas, American Spirits, Baldwin Locomotive, Victor Talking Machine, and Wright Aeronautical were once big enough and important enough to be included in the Dow Jones Industrial Average, but they're gone now, and who remembers them? The same goes for Studebaker, Nash, and Hudson Motors, Remington Typewriter, and Central Leather.

There's one way a company can cease to exist without actually dying. It can be swallowed up by some other company in a takeover. And often, a company can avoid dying a quick death by seeking protection in a bankruptcy court.

Bankruptcy court is the place where companies go when they can't pay their bills, and they need time to work things out. So they file for Chapter 11, a form of bankruptcy that allows them to stay in business and gradually pay off their debts. The court appoints a trustee to oversee this effort and make sure everyone involved is treated fairly.

If it's a terminal case and the company has no hope of restoring itself to profitability, it may file for Chapter 7. That's when the doors are closed, the employees sent home, and the desks, lamps, and word processors are carted off to be sold.

Often in these bankruptcies, the various groups that have a stake in the company (workers, vendors, suppliers, investors) fight with each other over who gets what. These warring factions hire expensive lawyers to argue their cases. The lawyers are well-paid, but rarely do the creditors get back everything they're owed. There are no funerals for bankrupt companies, but there can be a lot of sorrow and grief, especially among workers, who lose their jobs, and bondholders and stockholders, who lose money on their investments.

Companies are so important to the health and prosperity of the country that it's too bad there isn't a memorial someplace to the ones that have passed away. Or perhaps the state historic preservation departments should put up plaques on the sites where these extinct companies once did business. There ought to be a book that tells the story of interesting companies that have disappeared from the economic landscape, and describes how they lived, how they died, and how they fit into the evolution of capitalism.

The Economic Climate

Companies live in a climate—the economic climate. They depend on the outside world for survival, just as plants and humans do. They need a steady supply of capital, also known as the money supply. They need buyers for whatever it is they make, and suppliers for whatever materials they make it from. They need a government that lets them do their job without taxing them to death or pestering them to death with regulations.

When investors talk about the economic climate, they don't mean sunny or cloudy, winter or summer. They mean the outside forces that companies must contend with, which help determine whether they make money or lose money, and ultimately, whether they thrive or wither away.

At one time, when 80 percent of the population owned farms or worked on farms, the economic climate had everything to do with weather. If a drought burned up the crops, or they drowned in the rain, farmers couldn't make money. And when the farmers had no money, the local general store wasn't doing any business, and neither were the suppliers to the general store. But when the weather was favorable, farms produced a record harvest that put cash in farmers' pockets. The farmers spent the money at the general store, which put cash in the store owner's pockets. The store owners would restock the shelves, which put cash in the suppliers' pockets. And so on.

No wonder the weather—and not the stock market—was the favorite topic at lunch counters and on street corners. Weather was so important to people's livelihood that a book of homespun predictions, *The Farmer's Almanac*, was a perennial bestseller. You don't see any weather books on the best-seller lists today. But books about Wall Street make those lists quite often.

Today, with less than 1 percent of the population involved in farming, the weather has lost much of its influence. In the business world, people pay less attention to the weather report and more attention to the reports on interest rates, consumer spending, and so forth, that come out of Washington and New York. These are the man-made factors that affect the economic climate.

In the economic climate, there are three basic conditions: hot, cold, and warm. A hot climate makes investors nervous, and a cold climate depresses them. What they're always hoping for is the warm climate, also known as the Goldilocks climate, when everything is just right. But it's hard to maintain the Goldilocks climate. Most of the time, the economy is moving toward one extreme or another: from hot to cold and back again.

Let's take the hot climate first. Business is booming, and people are crowding into stores, buying new cars, new couches, new VCRs, new everythings. Merchandise is flying off the shelves, stores hire more clerks to handle the rush, and factories are working overtime to make more products. When the economy reaches the high-heat phase, factories are making so many products that merchandise is piling up at every level: in the stores, in the warehouses, and in the factories themselves. Store owners are keeping more goods on hand, so they won't be caught short.

Jobs are easy to find, for anybody who's halfway qualified, and the help-wanted ads in the newspapers go on for several pages. There's no better time for teenagers and recent college grads to enter the workforce than in the middle of a hot economy.

It sounds like the perfect situation: Businesses of all kinds are ringing up big profits; the unemployment lines are getting shorter; and people feel prosperous, confident, and secure in their jobs. That's why they're buying everything in sight. But in the world of finance, a hot economy is regarded as a bad thing. It upsets the professional investors on Wall Street. If you pay attention to the business news, you'll see headlines that read: "Economy Strong, Nation Prosperous, Stock Market Drops 100 Points."

The main worry is that a hot economy and too much prosperity will lead to inflation—the technical term for prices going up. Demand for goods and services is high, which leads to a shortage of raw materials, and possibly a shortage of workers. Whenever there's a shortage of anything, the prices tend to go up. Car manufacturers are paying more for steel, aluminum, and so forth, so they raise the prices of cars. When employees begin to feel the pinch of higher prices, they demand higher wages.

One price hike leads to another, as businesses and workers take turns trying to match the latest increase. Companies are paying more for electricity, raw materials, and workers. Workers take home bigger paychecks but they lose the advantage because everything they buy is more expensive than it used to be. Landlords are raising rents to cover their increased costs. Pretty soon, inflation is out of control and prices are rising at 5 percent, 10 percent, or in extreme cases, upwards of 20 percent a year. From 1979 to 1981, we had double-digit annual inflation in the United States.

With new stores being built and factories expanding all over the place, a lot of companies are borrowing money to pay for their construction projects. Meanwhile, a lot of consumers are borrowing money on their credit cards to pay for all the stuff they've been buying. The result is more demand for loans at the bank.

Seeing the crowds of people lining up for loans, banks and finance companies follow in the footsteps of the automakers and all the other businesses. They, too, raise their prices—by charging a higher rate of interest for their loans.

Soon, you've got the price of money rising in lockstep with prices in general—the only prices that go down are stock prices and bond prices. Investors bail out of stocks because they worry that companies can't grow their earnings fast enough to keep up with inflation. During the inflation of the late 1970s and early 1980s, stock and bond prices took a big fall.

A hot economy can't stay hot forever. Eventually, there's a break in the heat, brought about by the high cost of money. With higher interest rates on home loans, car loans, credit-card loans, you name it, fewer people can afford to buy houses, cars, and so forth. So they stay where they are and put off buying the new house. Or they keep their old clunkers and put off buying a new car.

Suddenly, there's a slump in the car business, and Detroit has trouble selling its huge inventory of the latest models. The automakers are giving rebates, and car prices begin to fall a bit. Thousands of auto workers are laid off, and the unemployment lines get longer. People out of work can't afford to buy things, so they cut back on their spending.

Instead of taking the annual trip to Disney World, they stay home and watch the Disney Channel on TV. This puts a damper on the motel business in Orlando. Instead of buying a new fall wardrobe, they make do with last year's wardrobe. This puts a damper on the clothes business. Stores are losing customers and the unsold merchandise is piling up on the shelves.

Prices are dropping left and right as businesses at all levels try to put the ring back in their cash registers. There are more layoffs, more new faces on the unemployment lines, more empty stores, and more families cutting back on spending. The economy has gone from hot to cold in a matter of months. In fact, if things get any chillier, the entire country is in danger of falling into the economic deep freeze, also known as a recession.

A review of all the recessions since World War II appears on page 195. You can see that they last an average of eleven months, and cause an average of 1.62 million people to lose their jobs.

In a recession, business goes from bad to terrible. Companies that sell soft drinks, hamburgers, medicines—things that people either can't do without or can easily afford—can sail through a recession unscathed. Companies that sell big-ticket items such as cars, refrigerators, and houses have serious problems in recessions. They can lose millions, or even billions, of dollars, and unless they have enough money in the bank to tide them over, they face the prospect of going bankrupt.

Many investors have learned to "recession-proof" their portfolios. They buy stocks only in McDonald's, Coca-Cola, or Johnson & Johnson, and other such "consumer growth" companies that tend to do well in cold climates. They ignore the likes of General Motors, Reynolds Metals, or U.S. Home Corp. These are examples of "cyclical" companies that suffer in cold climates. Cyclical companies either sell expensive products, make parts for expensive products, or produce the raw materials used in expensive products. In recessions, consumers stop buying expensive products.

The perfect situation for companies and their investors is the Goldilocks climate: not too hot and not too cold. But whenever we get into a Goldilocks climate, it doesn't seem to last. Most of the time, the economy is either heating up or cooling down, although the signals are so confusing that it's often hard to tell which way we're headed.

The government can't control a lot of things, especially the weather, but it has a big effect on the economic climate. Of all the jobs the federal government does, from fighting wars to fighting poverty, it may be that its most important job is keeping the

Nonfarm Payroll Employment Changes During **Recessions**

Recession	Duration	Jobs Lost	Percent Change
1948:11–1949:10	11 months	−2.26 million	−5.0%
1953:07–1954:05	10 months	−1.53 million	−3.0%
1957:08–1958:04	8 months	−2.11 million	−4.0%
1960:04–1961:02	10 months	−1.25 million	−2.3%
1969:12–1970:11	11 months	−0.83 million	−1.2%
1973:11–1975:03	16 months	−1.41 million	−1.8%
1980:01–1980:07	6 months	−1.05 million	−1.2%
1981:07–1982:11	16 months	−2.76 million	−3.0%
1990:07–1991:03	8 months	−1.35 million	−1.2%
AVERAGE:	11 months	−1.62 million	−2.5%

Sources: U.S. Department of Labor, Bureau of Labor Statistics (BLS); National Bureau of Economic Research (NBER).

Nonfarm Payroll Employment Changes During **Expansions**

Expansion	Duration	Jobs Gained	Percent Change
1946:01–1948:11	34 months	+ 5.35 million	+13.5%
1949:10–1953:07	45 months	+ 7.58 million	+17.7%
1954:05–1957:08	39 months	+ 4.06 million	+ 8.3%
1958:04–1960:04	24 months	+ 3.83 million	+ 7.5%
1961:02–1969:12	106 months	+17.75 million	+33.2%
1970:11–1973:11	36 months	+ 7.54 million	+10.7%
1975:03–1980:01	58 months	+14.31 million	+18.7%
1980:07–1981:07	12 months	+ 1.73 million	+ 1.9%
1982:11–1990:07	92 months	+21.05 million	+23.7%
1991:03–1995:06	51 months	+ 8.13 million	+ 7.5%
AVERAGE:	50 months	+ 9.13 million	+15.0%
through 1990:07:	50 months	+ 9.24 million	+14.3%

Sources: U.S. Department of Labor, Bureau of Labor Statistics (BLS); National Bureau of Economic Research (NBER).

economy from getting too hot or too cold. If it weren't for the government, we might have had another Great Depression by now.

The federal government is much bigger than it was sixty years ago, during the last Great Depression. Back then, it didn't have much economic clout. There was no welfare, no social security, no housing department, none of the hundreds of departments we have today. In 1935, the entire federal budget was $6.4 billion, about one-tenth of the total U.S. economy. Today, it's $1.5 trillion, and nearly one-quarter of the total economy.

We recently crossed an important divide: As of 1992, more people worked in local, state, and federal governments than in manufacturing. This so-called public sector pays so many salaries and pumps so much money into the economy that it keeps the economy out of the deep freeze. Whether business is bad or good, millions of government employees, social security recipients, and welfare recipients still have money to spend. And when people get laid off, they get unemployment compensation for several months while they look for another job.

The dark side of this story is that the government has gotten out of whack, with huge budget deficits that soak up investment capital and keep the economy from growing as fast it as once did. Too much of a good thing has become a bad thing.

The agency in charge of climate control is the Federal Reserve System, also known as the Fed. It has a special way of heating things up and cooling things down—not by blowing on them, but by adding and subtracting money. Given its huge importance, it's amazing how few people know what the Fed is all about.

In a survey from several years ago, some people said the Federal Reserve was a national park, while others thought it was a brand of whiskey. In fact, it's the central banking system that controls the money supply. Whenever the economy is cooling off too much, the Fed does two things. It lowers the interest rates that banks must pay when they borrow money from the government. This causes the banks to lower the interest rates they charge to their customers, so people can afford to take out more loans and buy more cars and more houses. The economy begins to heat up.

The Fed also pumps money directly into the banks, so they have more to lend. This pumping of money also causes interest rates to go down. And in certain situations, the government can spend more money and stimulate the economy the same way you do every time you spend money at a store.

If the economy is too hot, the Fed can take the opposite approach: raising interest rates and draining money from the banks. This causes the supply of money to shrink, and interest rates go higher. When this happens, bank loans become too expensive for many consumers, who stop buying cars and houses. The economy starts to cool off. Businesses lose business, workers lose their jobs, and store owners get lonely and slash prices to attract customers.

Then at some point, when the economy is thoroughly chilled, the Fed steps in and heats it up again. The process goes on endlessly, and Wall Street is always worried about it.

In the last fifty years, we've had nine recessions, so in your lifetime, you're likely to be subjected to a dozen or more. Each time it happens, you'll hear from the reporters and the TV commentators that the country is falling apart and that owning stocks is too risky. The thing to remember is that we've wiggled out of every recession since the one that turned into the Great Depression. The table on page 195 shows that the average recession lasts eleven months and 1.62 million jobs are lost, while the average recovery lasts fifty months and 9.24 million jobs are created.

The seasoned investor realizes that stock prices may drop in anticipation of a recession, or because Wall Street is worried about inflation, but there's no sense in trying to anticipate either predicament, because the economic climate is unpredictable. You have to have faith that inflation will cool down eventually, and that recessions will thaw out.

The Bulls and the Bears

In a normal day of trading, many stocks will go up in price, while others will go down. But occasionally there's a stampede when the prices of thousands of stocks are running in the same direction, like bulls at Pamplona. If the stampede is uphill, we call it a "bull market."

When the bulls are having their run, sometimes nine out of ten stocks are hitting new highs every week. People are rushing around buying as many shares as they can afford. They talk to their brokers more often than they talk to their best friends. Nobody wants to miss out on a good thing.

As long as the good thing lasts, millions of shareholders go to bed happy, and wake up happy. They sing in the shower, whistle while they work, help old ladies across the street, and count their blessings every night as they put themselves to sleep reviewing the gains in their portfolios.

But a bull market doesn't last forever. Sooner or later, the stampede will turn downhill. Stock prices will drop, with nine out of ten stocks hitting new lows every week. People who were anxious to buy on the way up will become more anxious to sell on the way down, on the theory that any stock sold today will fetch a better price than it would fetch tomorrow.

When stock prices fall 10 percent from their most recent peak, it's called a "correction." We've had fifty-three corrections in this century, or one every two years, on average. When stock prices fall 25 percent or more, it's called a "bear market." Of the fifty-three corrections, fifteen have turned into bear markets. That's one every six years, on average.

Nobody knows who coined the term "bear market," but having their name linked to financial losses is unfair to bears. There are no bears within fifty miles of Wall Street, unless you count the bears in the New York zoos, and bears do not dive off peaks the way stocks do in a bear market. You can make a better case for calling a bear market a lemming market, in honor of the investors who sell their stocks because everybody else is selling.

The Papa Bear market began in 1929, as we've already discussed. In the Momma Bear market of 1973–74, the average stock was down 50 percent. There was another bear in 1982, followed by the Crash of 1987, when the Dow dropped over one thousand points in four months, and 508 of those points in a single day. There was the Saddam Hussein bear of 1990, when investors worried about the Gulf War. But these recent bears were easier to handle than the big bears of 1929 and 1973–74.

An extended bear market can test everybody's patience and unsettle the most experienced investors. No matter how good you are at picking stocks, your stocks will go down, and just when you think the bottom has been reached, they will go down some more. If you own stock mutual funds, you won't do much better, because the mutual funds will go down as well. Their fate is tied to the fate of the stocks they own.

People who bought stocks at the high point in 1929 (this was a small group, fortunately) had to wait twenty-five years to break even on the prices. Imagine your stocks being in the red for a quarter-century! From the high point in 1969 before the crash of 1973–74, it took twelve years to break even. Perhaps we'll never see another bear market as severe as the one in 1929—that one was prolonged by the Depression. But we can't ignore the possibility of another bear of the 1973–74 variety, when stock prices are down long enough for a generation of children to get through elementary, junior high, and high school.

Investors can't avoid corrections and bear markets any more than northerners can avoid snowstorms. In fifty years of owning stocks, you can expect twenty-five corrections, of which eight or nine will turn into bears.

It would be nice to be able to get a warning signal, so you could sell your stocks and your mutual funds just before a bear market and then scoop them up later on the cheap. The trouble is, nobody has figured out a way to predict bear markets. The record on that is no better than the record on predicting recessions. Once in a while, somebody calls a bear and becomes a celebrity overnight—a stock analyst named Elaine Garzarelli was celebrated for predicting the Crash of 1987. But you never hear of somebody predicting two bear markets in a row. What you do hear is a chorus of "experts" claiming to see bears that never show up.

Since we're all accustomed to taking action to protect ourselves from snowstorms and hurricanes, it's natural that we would try to take action to protect ourselves from bear markets, even though this is one case in which being prepared like a Boy Scout does more harm than good. Far more money has been lost by investors trying to anticipate corrections than has been lost in all the corrections combined.

One of the worst mistakes you can make is to switch into and out of stocks or stock mutual funds, hoping to avoid the upcoming correction. It's also a mistake to sit on your cash and wait for the upcoming correction before you invest in stocks. In trying to time the market to sidestep the bears, people often miss out on the chance to run with the bulls.

A review of the S&P 500 going back to 1954 shows how expensive it is to be out of stocks during the short stretches when they make their biggest jumps. If you kept all your money in stocks throughout these four decades, your annual return on investment was 11.5 percent. Yet if you were out of stocks for the forty most profitable months during these forty years, your return on investment dropped to 2.7 percent.

We explained this earlier, but it is worth repeating. Here's another telling statistic. Starting in 1970, if you were unlucky and invested two thousand dollars at the peak day of the market in each successive year, your annual return was 8.5 percent. If you timed the market perfectly and invested your two thousand dollars at the low point in the market in each successive year, your annual return was 10.1 percent. So the difference between great timing and lousy timing is 1.6 percent.

Of course, you'd like to be lucky and make that extra 1.1 percent, but you'll do just fine with lousy timing, as long as you stay invested in stocks. Buy shares in good companies and hold on to them through thick and thin.

There's an easy solution to the problem of bear markets. Set up a schedule of buying stocks or stock mutual funds so you're putting in a small amount of money every month, or four months, or six months. This will remove you from the drama of the bulls and bears.

FOUR

The Invisible Hands

Who's Rich and How They Got That Way

Every year, *Forbes* magazine prints a list of the four hundred richest humans in the United States. This issue is as popular with the business crowd as the *Sports Illustrated* swimsuit issue is with the sports crowd. It makes for interesting reading, because it tells you who these people are and what made them so rich, and also how the country has changed over the years.

When *Forbes* first published its list in 1982, the number-one spot was held by Donald K. Ludwig, the shipping tycoon, followed by J. Paul Getty, who got his money the old-fashioned way: inheritance. Five of the top ten were in the Hunt family that drilled Texas full of holes and hit a lot of gushers, which reminds us of the saying attributed to billionaire J. Paul Getty, that the way to get ahead in the world: Rise early, work hard, strike oil.

This original list from fourteen years ago is crawling with Rockefellers and du Ponts, a Frick, a Whitney, a Mellon or two—all great family fortunes that stretch back to the nineteenth century. The word "inheritance" appears in the biographical blurbs no fewer than sixty-five times, and in addition to the sixty-five heirs there are at least twelve sons and daughters who hold positions of influence in family enterprises: a Mars from Mars candy bars, a Disney, a Busch of the beer Busches, a Johnson of Johnson & Johnson.

There weren't as many old-money fortunes on the 1993 list as there were in the 1980s, which leads to a couple of conclusions about wealth in America. First, it's not easy to hold on to money, even among billionaires. Inheritance taxes put a big dent in any large fortune that's handed down from one generation to the next. Unless the heirs are careful and invest wisely, they can lose their millions as fast as their ancestors made them.

Second, America is still the land of opportunity where smart young people like Bill Gates of Microsoft can end up on the *Forbes* list ahead of the Rockefellers, Mellons, Gettys, and Carnegies.

Just ahead of Gates on the 1993 list is Warren Buffett, who made his $10 billion doing what you're interested in doing (or you wouldn't have gotten this far in the book)—picking stocks. Buffett is the first stockpicker in history to reach the top.

Buffett follows a simple strategy: no tricks, no gimmicks, no playing the market, just buying shares in good companies and holding on to them until it gets very boring. The results are far from boring: $10,000 invested with Buffett when he began his career forty years ago would be worth $80 million today. Most of the gains come from stocks in companies you've heard of and could buy for yourself, such as Coca-Cola, Gillette, and the Washington Post. If you ever begin to doubt that owning stocks is a smart thing to do, take another look at Buffett's record.

If you count the du Ponts as one person, only forty-three of the four hundred people on the 1993 Forbes list got there through inheritance. We're seeing fewer sons and daughters of yesterday's tycoons and more Horatio Algers, who came out of modest backgrounds and rose to the top on pluck, luck, and a great idea. Harry Helmsley, husband of Leona and owner of multiple hotels, began his business career as a clerk in the mailroom of a real-estate office; David Geffen, the music magnate, worked in the mailroom of the William Morris agency; Ray Kroc, the man who put

McDonald's on the map, was a traveling salesman for milk-mixing machines; Sam Walton, founder of Wal-Mart, started out as a trainee at J. C. Penney; H. Ross Perot was an IBM salesman; and Curtis Leroy Carlson, the trading-stamp king and the son of a Swedish immigrant grocer, subcontracted his paper route to his brothers for a small profit, sold soap for Procter & Gamble, making $110 a month, then started the Gold Bond Trading Stamp Company with a fifty-dollar loan.

A surprising number of dropouts have made it into the top four hundred, beginning with Gates, the Microsoft whiz kid who left Harvard to tinker with software and invented the operating brain that is installed in most of the world's personal computers.

Then there are Kirk Kerkorian, son of an Armenian immigrant fruit farmer, and a junior-high-school dropout; Les Wexner, founder of the Limited stores, a law school dropout; Geffen, the record producer mentioned above, a college dropout; Paul Allen, cofounder of Microsoft with Gates, a dropout from Washington State; Ted Turner of Turner Broadcasting, booted from Brown but later went back to graduate; Lawrence J. Ellison of Oracle computers, a University of Illinois dropout; David Howard Murdock, who made his fortune in real estate and corporate takeovers, a traveling salesman's son and a high-school dropout; John Richard Simplot, who sold McDonald's the potatoes for their French fries, left home and quit school after the eighth grade to take a job sorting potatoes and raising hogs; Harry Wayne Huizenga, yet another college dropout, who started a trash hauling business with a beat-up old truck and by the age of thirty-one had built it into the world's largest trash disposal company, Waste Management, before he turned his attention to a Dallas video store, which he built into Blockbuster Video.

Don't drop out of school because these people did. When they got started in business, it was still possible to get a decent job without a college education—today it's nearly impossible. Also, every one of them had mastered the basic skills they needed to succeed in business. They didn't drop out to avoid work, they dropped out to start a company or pursue an interest.

There's no end to the ways you can make a billion these days: auto parts, the single-handled faucet, the yellow pages, coffee creamer, plastic cups, retread tires, plastics from industrial waste, Slim-Fast, Ping Golf Clubs, high-risk auto insurance, duty-free shops, Carnival Cruises, pizza franchises (Domino's and Little Caesar), and rental car agencies (Enterprise). There's even a lawyer on the list, who made his bundle from "sore back cases."

Several of these billion-dollar ideas were hatched in basements, garages, and small-town storefronts, and grown on shoe-string budgets. Hewlett-Packard, the computer giant, came out of $538 worth of electronic parts in David Packard's garage; Wal-Mart came out of a five-and-dime store in Newport, Arkansas, which lost its lease and later was reopened in Bentonville; Amway Corp. started in a basement where Richard Marvin De Vos and Jay Van Andel made biodegradable soap with a formula they bought from a Detroit chemist.

Only thirty-one in this well-heeled group made their fortunes in real estate, and eighteen from oil, so Getty's statement no longer rings as true as it once did. A couple of these multi-millionaires (Charles Schwab, for one) got there by starting brokerage firms and mutual fund companies; another thirty or so have prospered in the cable and media industry, and at least twenty are involved in electronics and computers.

The biggest change between 1982 and the present is the size of the four hundred biggest fortunes. Back then, you could make the list with $100 million. Now it takes at least $300 million just to bring up the rear. On the top end, there are twenty-five people whose net worth exceeds $2 billion, whereas in 1982, there were only five.

It may be that, as F. Scott Fitzgerald once wrote, the rich "are different from you and me," but you couldn't prove it by the *Forbes* list. It turns out there are all kinds of rich people: short, fat, tall, skinny, good-looking, homely, high IQ, not-so-high IQ, big spenders, penny-pinchers, tight-fisted, and generous. It's amazing how many people keep up their frugal old habits after they've made it big. Sam Walton, the Wal-Mart billionaire, who died a couple of years ago, could have bought a fleet of limousines out of his pocket change, but instead, he continued to drive around in a beat-up Chevy with dog teeth marks on the steering wheel. He could have moved to Paris, London, Rome, and other places where they film episodes of *Lifestyles of the Rich and Famous*, but he stayed with his wife in his two-bedroom house in their hometown of Bentonville, Arkansas.

Warren Buffett is another person who hasn't let financial success come between him and his hometown of Omaha, Nebraska, and who still enjoys the simple pleasures of a good book and a bridge game. Gordon Earle Moore, a founder of Fairchild Semiconductor and a cofounder of Intel, arrives at the office in his old pickup every day. There are many such stories of self-made millionaires and billionaires living modestly, avoiding publicity, and working long hours even though they can pay the bills without lifting a finger. "Lives quietly" and "avoids press" are phrases that appear frequently in the descriptions of the Forbes four hundred.

These people are still doing whatever it was that led to their successes. There is a good lesson in this. Find something you enjoy doing and give it everything you've got, and the money will take care of itself. Eventually, you reach the point where you can afford to spend the rest of your life at the side of a swimming pool with a drink in your hand, but you probably won't. You'll be having too much fun at the office to stop working.

How Coke Got Started

God didn't look down one day and say, "Let there be Coca-Cola." The Creator had nothing to do with this, unless you figure He had Coke in mind when he created Dr. John Styth Pemberton. Pemberton went to Atlanta from Columbus, Georgia, in 1869 and went into the patent medicine business as soon as he was old enough to wow an audience.

This was before we had truth in advertising and a Food and

Drug Administration to watch over products that people ate or drank. So there was nothing to stop Pemberton from mixing a bunch of ingredients (the main one being alcohol) in the family bathtub, scooping the potion into bottles, and selling it as a miracle cure, which is what patent medicine was all about.

Pemberton's product line included Indian Queen Hair Dye, Gingerine, Triplex Liver Pills, and an exotic concoction made of sugar, water, extract of coca leaf, kola nut, and caffeine. The label said it was a "brain tonic and a cure for all nervous afflictions," and in his sales pitches, Pemberton claimed it could cure headaches, hysteria, and melancholy, and put the customer in a very fine mood. This was the original Coca-Cola.

Pemberton spent $73.96 on advertising in the first year, but he sold only fifty dollars' worth of Coke syrup, so consumers weren't exactly buying his story. Five years later, they still weren't buying it, and Pemberton was tired of trying to convince them. So he sold the recipe, the equipment, the coca leaves, and the kola nuts to an Atlanta druggist, Asa Candler. Candler paid twenty-three hundred dollars for the whole shebang.

Candler was a religious man who preferred telling the truth to stretching it the way Pemberton had. He took the coca leaves out of the recipe, so by 1905, Coca-Cola was entirely cocaine-free. It's a good thing he did, because otherwise people could have gone to jail for sipping Coke after cocaine became illegal in 1914. The revamped Coke recipe is the best-kept secret of the century, still guarded in the vaults of the Trust Company of Georgia.

He also changed the label, leaving out the part about Coke being a "brain tonic," a "cure for nervous afflictions," and other dubious claims. In 1916, he invented the curvy bottle that most of the world's population can identify right away as a Coke.

In Candler's factory, the kola nuts, sugar, water, caffeine— plus a few secret ingredients of his own—were boiled in giant kettles and stirred with giant wooden paddles until they thickened into a syrup. The syrup was sent out to drugstores, where druggists added soda water for the fizz and served Cokes to people sitting at the counters. Drinking Coke got so popular that druggists had to hire helpers, called "soda jerks," to pour the syrup and apply the fizz. That's how thousands of teenagers across the country got their spending money—working after school pouring Cokes.

In 1916, Congress slapped a new tax on businesses, and Candler was furious. To avoid paying higher taxes on his Coke profits, he sold the company for $25 million to an Atlanta banker, Ernest Woodruff. His son, Robert, became Coca-Cola's president.

Soon after they bought the company, the Woodruffs went public with it. In 1919, they sold 1 million shares for forty dollars apiece. This was a stock a lot of people wished they didn't own, especially after the cost of syrup went through the roof. Angry bottlers protested the price hikes and threatened to cancel their contracts with the company. Lawsuits were filed. Coke's sales went down, and the company wobbled on the edge of bankruptcy.

Thanks to Robert Woodruff's serious cost-cutting, Coke managed to survive long enough to reach the Great Depression. This was a terrible time for most companies, but a good time for Coke. Even though people had very little money to spend, and went without new shoes, new clothes, and so on, they kept buying Cokes.

Here's a useful piece of advice for investors: Act like a bloodhound and ignore everything except the evidence that shows up in front of your nose. The economy in the 1930s couldn't have been worse, but since Coke was very profitable, the stock price rose from $20 in 1932 to $160 in 1937. Imagine making eight times your money when everyone around you was predicting the end of the world.

Robert Woodruff ran Coke for thirty years, dodging reporters, trying to keep his name out of the papers. He had several houses and at least one big ranch, but other than that, he spent modestly for a multimillionaire. Apparently, he never read books and rarely listened to music or looked at a painting, unless it had a duck or a deer in it. He gave parties, but only because he had to.

Just as Coke had benefited from one calamity, the Great Depression, it benefited from another calamity, World War II. People around the world saw the GIs drinking Coke, and they decided to imitate their heroes by doing the same. The GIs were the most effective unpaid sponsors in the history of commercial advertising.

It was after the war that Coke became the first truly multinational company. Coke's snazzy red billboards were seen on walls and buildings on six continents—sometimes, they were used to cover holes in the buildings. Coke became a symbol of the American way of life, which is why the communists in Russia hated it. (In the 1970s, the Russian leaders signed a contract with Pepsi!) Our missiles were aimed at the Russians, and their missiles were aimed at us, and they worried about the fallout from a soft drink. Even in France, the Communist party tried to ban Coke.

To get the full benefit from owning Coke stock, you had to be patient for two decades, until 1958, when the price took another flying leap. Five thousand dollars' worth of Coke shares in 1958 was worth nearly $100,000 by 1972. There aren't many chances in life to turn $5,000 into $100,000 in fourteen years, unless you win the lottery or do something illegal.

In the crash of 1972, Coke suffered along with all the other stocks, dropping a quick 63 percent and not gaining it back for three years, until 1985. But once again, patience was rewarded when the stock price took another flying leap and Coke turned $5,000 into $50,000 from 1984 to 1994.

In a fight between communism and Coca-Cola, Coke won hands down, because while the communists have gone out of business, Coke is still going strong. As it turns out, its biggest threat didn't come from the Russians. It came from Pepsi.

To think that Coke could have bought Pepsi for next to nothing in the 1930s, when Pepsi wobbled on the edge of bankruptcy. But it didn't happen, and Pepsi came back to haunt Coke fifty years later. In 1984, Pepsi was outselling Coke in the U.S. market, and the brains at Coke headquarters were forced to launch a counterattack. In the heat of battle, they invented diet Coke, which changed the soft-drink industry and took millions of excess pounds off the waistlines of the human race. Without the pressure of Pepsi's competition, Coke might never have thought of diet Coke.

The Woodruff era ended in the mid-1950s, when Robert Woodruff went into retirement, when he passed the time giving away his money. He donated hundreds of millions to medicine, the arts, and Emory University, and he gave the land on which the Center for Disease Control and Prevention was built in Atlanta. He opened his wallet to the Atlanta Art Center Alliance, even though he never liked going to museums and symphonies. Many of his gifts were anonymous, but people figured out Woodruff was responsible—who else in Atlanta was that rich and that big-hearted? They started calling him "Mr. Anonymous."

Roberto Goizueta took over the reins at Coke in 1981, and serves as chairman to this day. He and Don Keough, Coke's former president, made a fabulous team. They have pushed international sales to the point that people in 195 countries are drinking Cokes the way they once drank water. Given the sorry condition of the world's water supply, they may be better off drinking Cokes than drinking water.

Goizueta is a story in himself. He comes from a wealthy farming family in Cuba that lost its property in the Castro revolution. He worked for Coke in Cuba, then transferred to a Coke office in the Bahamas after Castro took power. From there, he moved to Coke headquarters in Atlanta, where he worked his way up the corporate ladder.

There's no end in sight for Coke's popularity worldwide, but it's taken Wall Street a long time to catch on to this. Some "experts" haven't caught on yet.

How Wrigley's Got Started

William Wrigley, Jr., left Philadelphia for Chicago in 1891 to become a salesman for his father's soap company. Besides soap, the company also made baking powder, and to sell the baking powder they gave away free cookbooks as a prize. The baking powder got so popular they decided to forget about the soap.

At some point, they stopped giving away cookbooks and offered chewing gum as a prize. The chewing gum got so popular they dropped the baking powder and began to sell gum.

Wrigley's spearmint made its debut in 1893, but like Coke, it wasn't an instant hit. However, by 1910, it was America's favorite brand. In 1915, to boost sales even further, Wrigley sent a free sample to every person listed in all the phone books in the United States.

Campbell's Soup

Dr. John T. Dorrance, a chemistry buff, turned down offers of a professorship at four different universities to take a job at a soup company owned by his uncle, Arthur Dorrance, and by Joseph Campbell. Once installed there, Dr. Dorrance invented a process for making condensed soup, then bought out his uncle to become sole owner of the business. This was a mistake on his uncle's part, because Campbell's continued to grow its earnings and became the $11.4 billion company it is today.

An enthusiastic stockpicker in his spare time, Dr. Dorrance took his broker's advice and sold all his stocks before the Crash of 1929. This was the best advice ever given by a broker, before or since.

Levi's

Levi Strauss was an immigrant from a part of Germany known as Bavaria. He made pants out of tent canvas and sold them to the prospectors who came to California to get rich in the Gold Rush of 1849. While most of the prospectors went home empty-handed, Strauss got rich on his blue jeans. He took out a patent on the denim version in 1873.

Strauss's company was private until 1971, when it sold shares to the public, then bought back the shares and in 1985 went private again.

Levi's, Campbell's soup, Wrigley's gum, and Coca-Cola got started one hundred or more years ago, when life wasn't as complicated as it is today and there weren't so many lawyers getting in the way of progress. But that doesn't mean you can't start a great business from scratch in the modern era. Ben and Jerry, Bill Gates, and Bernard Marcus have done it with ice cream, software, and hardware stores.

How Ben & Jerry's Got Started

Ben Cohen and Jerry Greenfield met in seventh-grade gym class on Long Island, and a few years later, they became hippies. Ben dropped out of college, then drove a taxi, flipped hamburgers, mopped floors, guarded a racetrack, and took up pottery. He once lived in a cabin in the Adirondacks with a woodstove and no plumbing. He had a big beard and a belly to match.

Meanwhile, Jerry went to Oberlin College in Ohio, where in addition to his regular studies he learned parlor tricks and how to run carnival games. He applied to medical school, got rejected, then took a job stuffing beef hearts into test tubes. He was skinnier than Ben, and he adopted the grunge look long before it was fashionable.

The two of them crossed paths again in Saratoga Springs, New York, and decided since they had nothing better to do, why not start an ice cream restaurant? Jerry spent five dollars for a mail-order course on how to make the ice cream. With six thousand dollars they'd saved, plus two thousand dollars they borrowed from Ben's father, they patched the roof of an old gas station in

Burlington, Vermont, threw a coat of paint on the walls, and renamed it the Scoop Shop. That was 1978.

The people who came to the Scoop Shop couldn't get enough of Ben and Jerry's scoops. Their ice cream was rich and creamy, and full of big chunks of fruit, or chocolate, or whatever they put into it. It was high-fat and high-cholesterol, but in 1978, people didn't care about cholesterol, so they could eat large quantities of Ben & Jerry's without feeling guilty.

Soon enough, Ben and Jerry were selling so much ice cream they outgrew the gas station. They decided to build an ice cream factory. They could have gone to venture capitalists to get the money, but instead, they went straight to the stock market. In 1984, they sold 73,500 shares of stock at $10.50 apiece and raised roughly three quarters of a million dollars. This was peanuts as far as big business went, but that's all they needed for the factory.

To make sure the company was locally owned, they made it a rule that only residents of Vermont could buy shares in the initial offering. Vermont is not a wealthy state to begin with, so many investors bought one share apiece—this was all they could afford. Ten years later, the stock was worth ten times the original price.

Ben & Jerry's is one of the most interesting public companies on record. The bosses came to work in tee shirts and bib overalls and never wore suits—they didn't own any suits. They named one of their flavors Cherry Garcia, in honor of Jerry Garcia, the rock star of the Grateful Dead. At the annual meetings, Ben would lie down with a brick on his belly and let Jerry smash the brick with a sledgehammer.

You couldn't tell the executives from the mop-up crew. The parking lot was full of dented Volkswagens. The higher-ups were paid low salaries by normal standards—the idea was that everybody deserved to make a living, but nobody deserved to make a killing. The narrow salary gap made for friendlier relations between labor and management, and better parties on the weekends.

Ben and Jerry piped rock and roll into the plant, to inspire the staff to dance around and do its best. They showed free outdoor movies in Burlington during the summer. They bought so much milk from local farmers that they revived the entire Vermont dairy industry. They even paid extra for the milk, to help out the farmers. And 7.5 percent of the annual profits went to charity.

Where else but in America could two hippies invest five dollars in a mail-order course and end up as the third-largest ice cream manufacturers in the country? A couple of years ago, the company had its midlife crisis: People had discovered cholesterol, and they stopped eating so much of the rich, creamy ice cream that was Ben & Jerry's claim to fame.

The company has changed with the times, and now it puts out a line of yogurt and low-fat substitutes for the creamy stuff their customers once craved.

In 1994, Ben stepped down as chief executive officer, although he was never as much a chief executive as he was a chief ice cream taster. The company had a contest to find Ben's replacement. To win the job, you had to send in something interesting, besides the usual résumé. The man who got the job wrote a poem.

Microsoft

Bill Gates is William Henry Gates III, born in 1955. He grew up in the suburbs of Bellevue, Washington, and attended the nearby Lakeside School. Lakeside had a computer lab, which was very unusual in the 1960s, and Gates took full advantage of it.

Gates was entranced, captivated, smitten with computers. He spent as much time as possible in the lab with his friend and sidekick Paul Allen, who was a couple of years ahead of him in school. Computers got to be such an obsession with Gates that his parents issued an order: Give them up for a while. Reluctantly, Gates complied, but this absence only made his heart grow fonder.

Soon enough, Gates and Allen were up to their old tricks, experimenting with the primitive hardware and software that existed then. There were no instruction manuals or *DOS for Dummies* books to guide them—Gates and Allen invented DOS. They were the pioneers of software, while hundreds of miles to the south, the two Steves, Jobs and Wozniak, were creating the Apple.

Scientists and engineers in fancy research labs couldn't accomplish what these young "hackers" in blue jeans and tee shirts accomplished by themselves. Before they left high school, Gates and Allen had become experts in the exciting new field of computer programming.

Gates went on to Harvard, thinking he would become a lawyer, while Allen got a job with a small computer company in New Mexico, called MITS. Dividing his time between the classroom, the poker table, and the computer room, Gates was soon bored with college life. When he couldn't stand it any longer, he dropped out of Harvard to join his old friend in New Mexico. The two of them had already invented a new computer language called BASIC.

MITS had hired Allen to create a version of BASIC for a computer chip made by Intel. But BASIC made such a big splash that several other computer makers wanted to use it as the operating system for their machines. This led to a nasty lawsuit over who had the rights to BASIC: Gates and Allen, or MITS? The courts ruled in favor of the inventors, because they'd developed BASIC before they got to MITS. Now, they were free to sell the language and keep the profits for themselves.

Gates started his own company, Microsoft, even before he escaped the clutches of MITS. After the lawsuit was resolved, he put all his energy into Microsoft. The company was informal and disorganized, and the employees worked crazy hours. Computers were scattered around the office, but the books were kept by hand. Visitors would peek into the boss's office and ask: "Who's that kid sitting at Mr. Gates's desk?" That kid was Gates himself. He was twenty-five, and he looked even younger.

One triumph led to another, and in 1980, this tiny company found itself in serious negotiations with the computer giant IBM. IBM had developed a new line of personal computers, and it needed a software system to go with it. Gates went to a meeting, impressed the IBM executives, and got the assignment of a lifetime. Working day and night and in secrecy, under contract with IBM, Gates and his cohorts created MS-DOS.

People have tried and failed to create a universal language for humans, but Microsoft has come close to doing it for computers—MS-DOS is currently spoken by 75 percent of the personal computers on the planet.

If IBM had been smart enough to demand some of the rights to MS-DOS, its shares would be selling for a much higher price. Instead, IBM let Microsoft retain all the rights, which is why Microsoft has become a billion-dollar company in its own right. The moral to this story is: If you are about to make somebody very rich, insist on a piece of the action.

Home Depot

Home Depot got its start when three executives at the Handy Dan Home Center stores got the boot. Convinced they could do a better job than the people who fired them, this trio of rejects decided to open their own version of Handy Dan. Handy Dan has disappeared from the scene, but Home Depot is everywhere.

This decision was only a prelude to serious business for the organizers of Home Depot. They convinced a venture capital group to put up the money to build the first super hardware store, in Atlanta. The grand opening was a flop. The ad promised a free dollar to every person who walked through the door. The crowd was so small that at the end of the day, there was a pile of cash left over. At that point, people wouldn't go to Home Depot even if you paid them.

But it wasn't long before customers were flocking to Home

Depot, attracted by the huge selection of merchandise, the low prices, and the well-trained clerks who could answer questions about everything from floorboards to floodlights. It was such a popular store that it continued to ring up sales in a recession, when most retailers were hurting. In fact, when the recession forced J. C. Penney out of four shopping centers around Atlanta, Home Depot took over the leases and opened four more stores.

Once they saw they had a winner, the organizers planned a rapid expansion. They went to the stock market to raise the money. In 1981, Home Depot sold its first shares to the public, at twelve dollars apiece. Today those same shares (adjusted for splits) are worth $3,308 apiece!

By 1984, Home Depot had nineteen stores. In 1985, the company stumbled a bit when profits fell. It had made the common mistake of trying to expand too fast. In 1986, it sold more stock and used the proceeds to pay some of its debts. Three years later, it became the largest home-repair chain in the country. In 1995, Home Depot had more than 365 stores and sold more than $14 billion worth of hardware.

It's Not Over Yet

In spite of everything you hear about the United States getting weak in the knees and long in the tooth and old in the hat and losing its place in the world, we are leading the world in new ideas. We're number one in music, television, and movies; the low-cost producers in forest products, paper, aluminum, and chemicals. Wall Street is still the financial capital for stocks, and we're gaining back our prominence in banking, as the Japanese banks are beset with problems.

Believe it or not, our railroads are so good at moving cargo that other countries are studying how we do it. Our freight system is the envy of freight haulers everywhere. (Our passenger system leaves a lot to be desired.)

We're tops in cellular phones, electronic test equipment, pharmaceuticals, telecommunications, and farm equipment. We excel at genetic engineering, semiconductors, and medical advances. After years of decline, our share of the export market is rising. That means that consumers in other countries are buying more of what we make.

We ship steel to Seoul, transistors to Tokyo, cars to Cologne, Spandex to Siena, and bike parts to Bombay. Men on six continents shave their whiskers with Gillette. The skies are filled with Boeing's aircraft. Japan is supposed to be the master of electronics—memory chips, TVs, and fax machines—but the Japanese can't keep up with the brainstorms coming out of such U.S. companies as Intel, Micron Technology, Microsoft, and Compaq Computer.

We're number one in personal computers. In software, work stations, laser printers, computer networks, and microprocessors, we dominate the field.

Many of our most fantastic innovations emerge from small companies. We lead the world in small companies as well. We've already seen how a bunch of kids at Microsoft and Apple Computer changed the computer industry forever. Twenty years later, there is a bunch of kids in software labs giving a repeat performance.

It wasn't long ago that we were scolded by our own newspapers and news magazines for being fat, lazy, and overpaid. We have a free press and the press likes to focus on warts and not halos, because warts sell more papers than halos do.

So we heard over and over that the Japanese people worked harder than we did and the German people worked harder than we did, and while we were sitting around channel surfing or goofing off in school or playing with Frisbees (another great American invention), these other countries would be passing us by.

It was inevitable, the doomsayers said, that America would become a land of do-nothings and make-nothings, except maybe we'd still be smart enough to make those little paper umbrellas they stick into cocktails.

The auto industry was the most obvious trouble spot. Before the 1960s, we were first in war, first in peace, and first in cars, and Detroit was the car lover's Mecca. But after that, our auto companies got sloppy and let the factories run down. Through their powerful unions, the workers demanded higher and higher wages. At this point, the Japanese and the Germans attacked Detroit with their spiffy, well-made, low-priced cars. Millions of U.S. consumers preferred these foreign models to the humdrum, poorly made, overpriced American cars.

Journalists and academics wrote articles and books about the decline and fall of U.S. autos, which they saw as a symptom of the decline and fall of the American way of life. The most influential of these books was David Halberstam's *The Reckoning*.

You could read Halberstam's work and weep for the future of Ford, of General Motors, of Chrysler, and of America, but the year it was published, 1986, was also the year that Chrysler began its comeback from near bankruptcy and Ford started on a huge rebound, while Nissan and the Japanese automakers were starting to flop. The U.S. losers have become winners again.

Investors who did their homework and saw this happening got very wealthy buying Ford, Chrysler, and General Motors stock. If they bought at the right time, they made fifteen times their money in Chrysler, ten times in Ford, and three times in General Motors.

This wasn't a one-year improvement, or five years, it was a gigantic long-term trend. Just as it took years for Detroit to lose its place at the top of the auto industry, it took years for the comeback. This comeback totally surprised a lot of people, but that's because we weren't getting the real story. We were hearing the old news, about how the auto industry was controlled by the Japanese. But it wasn't the Japanese who invented the minivan; it was Chrysler. It wasn't the Japanese who put a new generation of snazzy, low-cost automobiles on the road; it was Ford, Chrysler, and General Motors. It wasn't Nissan that redesigned the Jeep; it was Chrysler. It wasn't the Toyota that became the best-selling car in Europe, it was the Ford Fiesta.

Here at home, the Japanese have been losing their share of the U.S. market, as the U.S. auto companies are winning it back.

We've fixed up our factories and made them more efficient. Our wages have come down, and that has lowered our production costs, so we can sell our goods at lower prices and undercut the foreign competition.

Over the last two decades that we've been feeling bad about ourselves, the U.S. labor force has become the most productive in the world. Today, the American industrial worker produces $49,600 worth of goods every year, $5,000 more than the average German and $10,000 more than the average Japanese. We're putting in more hours and taking fewer vacations than the average German worker, who gets five weeks of paid leave every year.

In fact, the U.S. labor force has been so busy and so productive that a professor at Harvard, Juliet Schor, has written a book called *The Overworked American.* The press did such a good job convincing us we've been goofing off, especially in comparison to the industrious Japanese, that it's a surprise to discover we've been working too hard.

That's not to say we don't have our problems. In the last two decades, our economic growth overall has lagged behind the growth rates of prior decades, and wages in the lowest-paying jobs haven't risen much, if at all. We've got high crime and high unemployment in the inner cities, where as many as half the children never finish high school. Without an education, these people can't possibly compete for all the wonderful jobs that have been created by computers and advanced technology.

As bad as our problems may be, they don't add up to the pessimism that infects us. We got a similar dose of pessimism in the late 1940s, after the war was over and 10 million to 20 million Americans lost their war-related jobs in the military or the defense industries. More than a third of the workforce had to find work elsewhere, a crisis that far exceeded any layoff crisis we face today, and yet today's headlines would make you think we're in worse shape now than what we were in after World War II.

In fact, the 1950s was a good decade for the economy and a

great one for stocks—second only to the 1980s in this century. So people's pessimism and their low expectations for the future turned out to be misplaced, just as they're turning out to be misplaced in the first half of the 1990s.

Heroes

In school, we debate whether Hamlet is a hero or a wimp, or whether King Lear was stupid or a victim of a greedy daughter, or Napoleon was a great general or a land-grabbing tyrant. But we never debate whether Sam Walton is a villain or a hero. Sam Walton got rich by starting Wal-Mart: Was this a good thing or a bad thing? What about Michael Eisner at Disney? Is Eisner a rich pig or a corporate savior?

Joe Montana, who played football, is a national celebrity who is nearly deified for his great contribution to society. No doubt he has contributed. But how does Montana stack up as a hero against Sam Walton or Lee Iacocca at Chrysler? Who, for instance, has created more jobs?

Iacocca never brought an NFL team back from a two-touchdown deficit in the fourth quarter, the way Joe Montana did. But he brought back Chrysler, which was about to go out of business during the crucial quarters in 1981–82. The game was on the line—imagine what would have happened if Iacocca had failed.

Not only would Chrysler's more than 115,948 workers have been sent home for good, but the tire makers, aluminum and steel suppliers, auto glass suppliers, seat leather suppliers, and so forth, would have been forced to lay off workers in the wake of Chrysler's demise. By saving Chrysler, Iacocca may have saved more than three hundred thousand paychecks. How many paychecks did Joe Montana save?

By putting fans in the seats, Montana indirectly kept some ticket sellers and hot-dog vendors in business, and there's nothing wrong with that. But the jobs Iacocca saved weren't of the hot-dog vendor variety. Many of them were high-skilled positions, paying twenty dollars an hour. Over three hundred thousand well-paid workers can thank Iacocca for their vacations, for their second homes, and for helping to put their kids through college.

Is Jack Welch, the head of General Electric, a more important person than Elton John? Is Dr. Roy Vagelos, who helped Merck develop many innovative drugs to combat diseases, a more important person than Jodie Foster, Princess Diana, or Shaquille O'Neal? If it came to a vote, we'd vote for Welch and Vagelos. And yet the baker in the Dunkin Donut commercials is better known than most of the people on our list.

You'll notice we often name two heroes—usually the person who got the company started and the person or persons who kept it going. These are the Invisible Hands of the 1990s, and we're sure they would have impressed Adam Smith back in 1776. Their counterparts in other countries are carrying out capitalist missions around the globe.

We regret to report a shortage of women and minorities in the ranks of our heroes. Only one woman makes the list—Doris Fisher, cofounder of The Gap. We can only hope that as more young people are attracted to careers in business, women and minorities will get their chance to run public companies.

Perhaps after reading this book (it's a family assignment) the three Lynch daughters, Mary, Annie, and Beth, and the two Rothchild daughters, Berns and Sascha, will be inspired to join the corporate ranks.

The corporate leaders of America aren't just a gang of moneygrubbers whose main purpose in life is to ride on Learjets to the golf courses of the world. Fred Smith didn't start Federal Express, also known as FedEx, because he needed the money; Smith was already rich. He did it for the challenge, to create a mail system that works better than the post office. Because Smith succeeded, the post office has shaped up considerably. Now, in addition to delivering mail in the rain, hail, sleet, and snow, the postal service can even deliver it overnight.

Because they end up with big bucks, the people who run companies are often made out to be villains, lumped together with bank robbers and con artists. You'd think they wrote themselves $10-million paychecks and left town with the loot, when in fact, their money doesn't come from their paychecks. This is a major point that is overlooked by the jeering section.

In most cases, the big corporate fortunes come from owning the company's stock. The higher up you are on the corporate ladder, the more likely it is that you will be paid in shares instead of cash. Executives are also given "options," which enable them to buy more shares at a specific price.

But all of this works to the executives' benefit only if the company does well and the stock price goes up. If the company does poorly and the price goes down, these people stand to lose money and may be worse off than if they earned a huge salary.

Being paid in stock puts a company's leadership on the same side of the table as the shareholders. When they make big bucks on the stock, other investors also are profiting from the shares they own. It's a win/win situation.

So instead of booing when Michael Eisner makes $50 million on his Disney shares, we ought to be cheering him on, because it means that Disney is thriving under his leadership, the stock price is rising (up elevenfold in ten years), and investors large and small are reaping the benefits.

That said, we'd be willing to bet that Eisner isn't just doing it for the money. Like most of his colleagues at the CEO level, he's already got plenty, yet he still goes to work every day. Why does he bother? He enjoys the challenge of outsmarting the competition. Business demands savvy, strength, and cunning. There may be monotony on the assembly line, but not in the boardroom or the offices upstairs.

In teaching the post office a lesson, Fred Smith created jobs. All the corporate heroes honored in this chapter have created jobs, not that we've been hearing much about job creation. Lately, we've only been hearing about job losses.

From the news reports of the last couple of years, you'd think there weren't any jobs left in America. Every time you pick up a paper, you see another headline about a big corporate layoff. A reporter doesn't have to dig very far to find one of these stories, because the largest five hundred companies in the United States reduced their workforce by 3 million workers in the 1980s, and they're on a pace to do the same in the 1990s.

A layoff is always painful to the person who loses the job, but that doesn't make layoffs a national crisis. In the larger scheme of things, these layoffs are healthy.

Companies aren't Scrooges who wring their hands in glee and shout "Bah Humbug" as they shove loyal employees out the door. In many cases, the layoffs are done by attrition: A person who is about to retire isn't replaced. But the layoffs have a purpose: to make companies more competitive and better able to survive in the future.

Imagine the catastrophe we'd be facing if those five hundred big companies had kept the 3 million workers they dismissed in the 1980s. Eventually, the bloated payrolls would have destroyed these companies. They couldn't possibly have been able to compete against their more efficient rivals, which could operate at lower cost and drive them out of business. So instead of the 3 million jobs lost in the big companies, we might have lost 10 million, or 15 million, and the country would have been thrown into another Depression.

That brings us to the twenty-five large companies listed on page 228. There are at least three kinds: companies that have kept growing for decades (Walgreen, McDonald's, and Raytheon, for instance); companies that had lost their way before the hero arrived to turn them around; and companies that were doing OK but then got a second wind and accomplished amazing things, given that they were getting old and people thought their best years were behind them.

Chrysler is one of the turnarounds, along with Colgate, Allied Signal, Caterpillar, Fannie Mae (Federal National Mortgage), and Citicorp, so we've got several different kinds of companies represented here. Then in the "second-wind" category, we've got Coca-

Cola, which has done the improbable and accelerated its growth rate along with Gillette, Motorola, and Merck.

There are two heroes of the Fannie Mae story, David Maxwell and Jim Johnson. Fannie Mae, formally known as the Federal National Mortgage Association, is the country's number-one owner and packager of home mortgages. When David Maxwell came along, Fannie Mae was an unstable enterprise—one year in the black, the next in the red, flirting with insolvency. Maxwell straightened Fannie Mae out and put it squarely in the black.

Johnson took over in 1991. Under his direction, Fannie Mae has more than doubled its earnings and made future earnings less volatile and more dependable. While Fannie Mae employs only three thousand people, a tiny payroll for such a big company, it affects millions of homeowners directly and indirectly through its ownership of one out of five mortgages in America.

The fate of large numbers of jobs depends on Fannie Mae's ability to finance mortgage loans. If this company were poorly managed and got into trouble, we might see a collapse of the new housing market as well as the resale market. Home builders, carpet layers, real-estate agents, insurance agents, bankers, appliance stores, hardware stores, and home-furnishings stores would suffer as a result.

Hewlett-Packard was an old-line technology company that made testing equipment and measuring equipment for the electronics industry. As you can see on the table on page 242, in 1975, it had $981 million in sales; twenty years later, it approaches $30 billion in sales. The testing and measuring part of the company accounts for only 11 percent of the revenues. Seventy-eight percent comes from printers and computers. Hewlett-Packard didn't make printers fifteen years ago, but it has quietly become the Goliath in the business, selling an estimated $9 billion to $10 billion worth of printers and related products every year. The printers have given Hewlett-Packard a quality brand name that helps it sell computers. In now ranks sixth in personal computer sales worldwide.

Hewlett-Packard has grown to nearly half the size of IBM, but in 1975, it was fifteen times smaller. It grew and prospered because the employees were encouraged to invent new products and to develop new ideas. The hero who aided and abetted this innovation is CEO John Young.

This drive to make companies more competitive can be traced back to 1982. We'd just come through the worst recession since World War II—a tough stretch. The auto industry was hopeless, we had high unemployment, and Americans from coast to coast sensed that the country was losing it.

In this general crisis, corporate leaders made a momentous decision. They decided to change the basic way they approached business. Before 1982, they had stumbled through each economic cycle, adding workers during periods of prosperity, then laying them off during recessions. When business was bad, they cut back in stages, first eliminating the overtime, then giving older workers early retirement, and so forth.

Since 1982, companies of all kinds have dedicated themselves to becoming more efficient overall. On Wall Street, this is known as restructuring, rightsizing, downsizing, or getting leaner and meaner. Whatever you call it, it means reducing costs and boosting productivity, not just to survive recessions, but to become more profitable and more competitive as a matter of course.

Take a company like Johnson & Johnson, with a record of thirty years of nearly uninterrupted increased earnings—under the old system, it wouldn't have occurred to Johnson & Johnson to make rightsizing a priority. But under the new system, even a healthy company like Johnson & Johnson realized it had to take steps to maintain its edge, while continuing to develop new products.

That's why we've seen this surge in corporate profitability in the last fifteen years, which has produced a surge in stock prices that tops any other period in history. We're a much wealthier nation than we were in 1982, and much of this prosperity has to do with the change in the way companies do business, including laying off workers to become more competitive. No one has noticed this out in medialand. They still think our corporate leaders are busy playing golf.

Companies are no longer resting on their laurels. They might have record earnings this year, but they are worried about what happens ten years out. They don't want to go the way of Pan Am, Eastern, and Braniff—three airlines that lost their edge and went out of business. Directly or indirectly, tens of thousands of workers lost their jobs when these airlines disappeared.

Being more competitive isn't just a matter of handing out the pink slips and turning off some lights to save money. Let's say a company invests $100 million to build a new plant, where the same workforce from the old plant can increase the output by 15 percent.

This extra 15 percent can help a lot of people. The company can give its employees a 5 percent raise, making the workers happy; it can lower prices by 5 percent, making the customers happy; and it can increase its profits, making the shareholders happy. Of course, this 15 percent could be divided up differently. But the point is there are multiple benefits when a company becomes more competitive.

There's another way to increase productivity: making better products with fewer mistakes. Fewer mistakes mean fewer complaints from customers, fewer phone calls to apologize for those mistakes, fewer replacement items that have to be shipped out, fewer repairs of defective merchandise. A company that cuts down on its defects from 5 percent to 0.5 percent can save huge amounts of time and money that otherwise would be expended on cleaning up messes and handing irate customers.

In the table beginning on page 236, you'll find the list of heroes that have turned small companies into big companies. It's another side of the job story that rarely gets told. You've heard about the 3 million jobs lost from the big companies in the 1980s—and more of the same in the 1990s—but have you heard about the 21 million jobs created by small and medium-sized companies in the 1980s? There haven't been many headlines about that.

Nobody has an exact count of the jobs created by small companies, but we do know that 2.1 million new businesses opened their doors in the 1980s. Some are bigger than others, some have succeeded and some have failed, but if we assume that on average, each small business employs ten people, that's 21 million new jobs. That's seven times more jobs than were lost in the well-publicized big layoffs.

Among these 2.1 million businesses was a small group of high achievers that eventually went public. Twenty-five of the most successful have made it to our heroes list. It's amazing how far they've come in a short time. In 1985, the twenty-five added together had sales of $30.8 million, less than half of what Exxon sold by itself. IBM's earnings in 1985 were four times the combined earnings of all twenty-five.

Back then, these twenty-five companies provided jobs for 358,000 workers, while the large companies on our list provided jobs for more than 2.6 million workers.

Look what's happened in ten years. While the large companies on our list have lost more than 420,000 jobs over that period, our small companies have turned into giants. In 1995, their combined sales will be $225 billion, and they employ nearly 1.4 million workers, adding 1 million jobs to the workforce.

In 1975, Disney qualified as a small company; today, it is huge. Walt Disney is the superhero of the Disney story; Michael Eisner is the hero. Disney's great organization had begun to nod off a bit when Eisner prodded it awake. In the old days, Disney would reissue the classic animated films, but until Eisner came along, the company had stopping making new ones. Under Eisner's regime, the company brought out *The Lion King*, *Aladdin*, and *Beauty and the Beast*, among others; became a major producer of feature films; revitalized the existing theme parks and opened new ones; triumphed in the music business with soundtracks that were as popular as its movies; and launched a merchandising campaign that put Disney souvenirs in stores around the world.

Toys R Us was a medium-sized enterprise in 1985, but today it has more sales than Gillette or Colgate and 20,000 more

Corporate Heroes

Company Name	Corporate Heroes	Commentary
Allied Signal	Lawrence A. Bossidy, Chairman & CEO	*Turned Around.* Bossidy eliminated losing businesses. More than doubled profits and strengthened profit lines.
American Express	Harvey Golub, Chairman & CEO; Jeffrey E. Stiefler, President (until 9/95); Jonathan S. Linen, Kenneth I. Chenault, George L. Farr, Vice Chairman	*Turning Around.* Led by Golub, this team healed wounds with merchants, cut costs, sold Shearson-Lehman, restored growth potential in the card business. Grew IDS and other financial services, and expanded to become number-one travel agent.
Boeing	Frank Shrontz, Chairman & CEO Philip M. Condit, President	*Turning Around.* Initiated cultural change, increased focus on efficiency and shareowners' interests. Promoted team-based leadership. Developed the Boeing 777.
Caterpillar	Donald V. Fites, Chairman & CEO	*Turned Around.* Implemented six-year worldwide plant modernization plan. Reorganized company; increased market share worldwide; slashed product introduction time.
Chrysler	Lee A. Iacocca, Chairman & CEO, 1978–1992 Robert J. Eaton, Chairman & CEO, 1993–	*Turned Around Twice.* Revived the company and assembled team that saved it from bankruptcy. Cut costs by outsourcing components; launched minivan and bought AMC to get Jeep.
Citicorp	John S. Reed, Chairman	*Invested Heavily* in domestic consumer franchise despite operating problems. Fixed real-estate problems. Cut costs. Improved services. Stayed in international markets while most other banks didn't.
Coca-Cola	Roberto C. Goizueta, Chairman & CEO Donald R. Keough, retired President and COO	*Sped Up Growth Rate.* Woke up sleepy bottlers in over 190 countries. Keough assisted Goizueta in strategy development and carried out global plan.

Company Name	Corporate Heroes	Commentary
Colgate-Palmolive	Reuben Mark, Chairman & CEO	*Turned Around* and expanded market share by: consolidating plants, lowering costs and expanding overseas where they could dominate market.
Deere	Robert A. Hanson, Chairman	*Turned Around.* Improved farm equipment products and promoted growth of non-agricultural businesses.
Emerson Electric	Charles F. Knight, Chairman & CEO	*Kept Growing* earnings decade after decade. Implemented a stringent sales- and profit-planning process.
Exxon	Lawrence G. Rawl, Chairman, 1987–1993 Lee R. Raymond, Chairman & CEO, 1993–	*Turned Around.* Kept focus on costs; pruned or eliminated marginal operations; grew business through strategic selection of worldwide opportunities.
Federal National Mortgage Association	David O. Maxwell, CEO, 1981–1991 James A. Johnson, CEO & Chairman, 1991–	*Turned Around.* Innovative problem-solver; eliminated government culture. Johnson solidified financial strength; extended benefits to low-income, minority, and underserved populations; enhanced technology changes; worked with Congress to institute change.
General Electric	John (Jack) F. Welch, Jr., Chairman & CEO	*Kept Growing*—no small task for such an enormous company. Encouraged creative risk-taking; restored productivity to many old, plodding businesses and got rid of underperformers. Made great acquisitions.
Gillette	Colman M. Mockler, Jr. (deceased), Chairman & CEO, 1975–1991 Alfred M. Zeien, Chairman & CEO, 1991–	*Sped Up Growth Rate.* Redirected company back to basics; cut costs; company fought off takeover attempt with ingenuity: shareholders ended up with a 10-bagger because company said "no" to raider—bought back stock. Zeien emphasized top-line growth, geographic expansion; new product development.
Goodyear Tire & Rubber	Stanley C. Gault, Chairman & CEO	*Turned Around.* Reduced debt; contained costs; introduced global product sourcing, new channels of distribution.

Company Name	Corporate Heroes	Commentary
Hewlett-Packard	David Packard and William R. Hewlett, Founders John A. Young, Pres & CEO, 1977–1992 Lewis E. Platt, Pres, Chairman & CEO Richard A. Hackborn, Exec VP	*Sped Up Growth Rate.* Hewlett and Packard defined company culture built on teamwork, management by objective, consensus building. Entering new lines, including printers, computers, and related products, so that the original businesses represent less than 20 percent of sales.
International Business Machines (IBM)	Thomas J. Watson, Jr., former Chairman & CEO (deceased) Louis V. Gerstner, Jr., Chairman & CEO, 1993–	*Turning Around.* Watson "bet the company" when he invested in System 360. Was first to allow users to upgrade computers as information needs grew. Gerstner first top executive from outside; restructuring IBM into market-sensitive, cost-competitive company.
ITT	Rand V. Araskog, President, Chairman & CEO, 1971–	*Turned Around.* Sold underperforming assets; cut costs; split company into 3 units to realize value of individual pieces.
Johnson & Johnson	James E. Burke, Chairman & CEO, 1976–1989 Ralph S. Larsen, Chairman & CEO, 1989–	*Sped Up Growth Rate.* Willing to spend on healthcare R&D; got operating costs in line. Consolidated autonomous businesses without sacrificing entrepreneurial spirit.
McDonald's	Ray A. Kroc (deceased), Founder James R. Cantalupo, President & CEO, McDonald's International	*Kept Growing.* Kroc responsible for early domestic growth; franchise strategy; began international focus. Cantalupo accelerated the pace of international development.
Merck	P. Roy Vagelos, M.D., Chairman, President & CEO, 1986–1994	*Sped Up Growth Rate.* Headed research operation when key blockbuster drugs were developed.

Company Name	Corporate Heroes	Commentary
Motorola	Robert W. Galvin, joined company in 1940. Named president, 1956. Chairman of Exec Committee, 1990– George M.C. Fisher, President & CEO, 1988–1990; Chairman & CEO, 1990–1993 Gary L. Tooker, Vice Chairman & CEO, 1993– Christopher B. Galvin, President & COO, 1993–	*Kept Growing.* Galvin's father founded company in 1928; established family culture. R. Galvin led semiconductor business, then developed cellular and mobile communications. Fisher fought Japanese competition; got into paging business in Japan. Tooker and C. Galvin responsible for building sales. Improving products and lowering costs drives this company.
Raytheon	Thomas L. Phillips, CEO, 1968–1991; Chairman 1975–1991 Dennis J. Picard, Chairman & CEO, 1991–	*Kept Growing* despite defense cutbacks, broadened product base, streamlined management; focused on quality; led movement to apply defense expertise to commercial applications, markets.
Walgreen	Charles R. Walgreen III, Chairman	*Kept Growing.* Repositioned Walgreen as drugstore operator; disposed of non-core businesses and focused on expansion strategy.
Xerox	David T. Kearns, CEO & Chairman, 1985–1991 Paul A. Allaire, Chairman & CEO, 1990/91–	*Turned Around.* Kearns inherited problem of brand name/market share erosion; initiated quality focus to combat Japanese competition. Allaire expanded quality program, sold non-core businesses, lowered costs to make company competitive.

employees than Goodyear Tire. Wal-Mart was the biggest of the small companies in 1985, but today it is bigger than every one of the big companies on our list, except Exxon.

Amgen didn't exist in 1975, and in 1985 it had less than 200 employees. Today, it manufactures two billion-dollar pharmaceuticals, Neupogen and Epogen. These are important drugs that help patients worldwide and could help Amgen earn more than $300 million in 1995. The heroes there are George B. Rathmann and Gordon Binder.

Then there's Ross Perot's creation, Electronic Data Systems, bought by General Motors in 1984. Perot used to work for IBM. He tried to talk IBM into helping companies solve their information-processing problems, but IBM wasn't particularly interested. So Perot went off on his own and started EDS. It had $100 million in sales in 1975, $3.4 billion in 1985, and in 1995, it will reach $10 billion in sales. Perot has been out of EDS since 1986, but the company has grown dramatically since he left. It's been a fantastic acquisition for GM.

This shows you the importance of a hero. For at least a couple of decades, IBM didn't have heroic leadership. This dominant company was caught flatfooted. It lost the information services business to Perot's EDS, the software business to Microsoft, and the microprocessor business to Intel. It lost its number-one ranking in personal computer sales to Compaq and a big chunk of its mainframe memory business to EMC. All five of these successful competitors to IBM are on our list of small companies that have made it big.

Bill McGowan and Bert Roberts are the heroes at MCI. They dared to compete with AT&T in the long-distance market while people laughed at them for doing it. For ten years, MCI lost money, but it has survived and it has succeeded. Because of MCI's competition, we all pay less for long-distance calls.

Ken Iverson is the hero at Nucor, a steel company in a hopeless industry. Iverson doesn't waste money on trifles, so he put Nucor headquarters in a strip mall in Darlington, South Carolina. (It remained there for years.) Nucor started out as a buyer of steel, but soon learned to make its own high-quality steel from scrap, something U.S. Steel never figured out how to do. By the year 2000 Nucor will produce as much steel as U.S. Steel. It will have caught up to the first billion-dollar company in U.S. history.

Tom Stemberg is the hero at Staples. He once wrote a business plan for an office superstore. Nobody paid much attention to it except Stemberg himself. He put it into practice with the first superstore in Brighton, Massachusetts. That was just about ten years ago. Today, office superstores are on the verge of becoming a $10-billion industry, and at the current growth rate, they will be a $20-billion industry by the year 2000.

A pair of brothers makes the heroes list. They left home in opposite directions. Jim Burke went the large-company route and ended up in the chairman's chair at Johnson & Johnson, while Dan Burke went the small-company route and joined a tiny communications outfit that became the hugely successful Capital Cities/ABC, which recently agreed to a merger with Disney.

The nation's prosperity depends on small companies getting bigger and big companies getting more competitive. If, while our twenty-five small companies were coming along, the twenty-five old-timers on our list had fallen apart, the net result would have been zero job growth, or possibly a huge loss in jobs.

Imagine the disaster if dozens of the Fortune 500 companies had gone bankrupt instead of downsizing and rightsizing. In that case, we might have lost 15 million jobs in the last decade, and today we'd have 20 percent unemployment in spite of the 21 million jobs created by small companies nationwide.

Don't think it couldn't have happened. It could have happened if companies had decided to keep every last worker and throw productivity out the window, and to hang on until foreign rivals put them out of business. It could have happened if our heroes hadn't come along to inspire their colleagues to a maximum effort.

In the United States, we're fortunate to have such an excellent mix of small companies on the rise and large companies doing well. You won't find this mix in Europe, which suffers from a shortage of small companies. We have so many success stories to choose from that our list could have run several pages.

It was difficult to narrow our list to twenty-five. Many other heroes at other great companies were left out. We could easily have picked 250 small companies that hit the big time in the last twenty years, along with one hundred large companies that kept going or turned themselves around.

We also could have packed our list with all-stars of software, computing, and electronics (Cisco, Sun Microsystems, and Micron Technology) and the performance of our twenty-five small companies would look even better. But we tried to get a sampling from different industries to show that companies of all kinds can grow fast in America. We've included a toy company, a payroll processor, an airline, even a company that makes the "carbon black" that's used to strengthen tires. That's Cabot. Cabot went through a difficult period, but turned itself around. It's the only turnaround among the twenty-five.

The heroes list gives you one more example of how you can make money investing in big companies or in small companies, but if you specialize in small companies, you could do amazingly well. Among our big companies there are three ten-baggers in which investors could have made ten times their money—Fannie Mae, Gillette, and Coca-Cola. In the 1985–95 period, among the small companies, there are six ten-baggers, three twenty-five-baggers, and three forty- to fifty-baggers. You've got Amgen up from $1.36 to $84, Oracle up from $0.83 to $42, and Compaq up from $1.69 to $50. Those are impressive moves.

You can see why you don't need to be right all the time to make money in stocks. Let's say you own ten small companies and three of them go from $40 million in sales to zero, and their stocks go from $20 a share to zero. These losses will be more than offset by one big winner that goes from $40 million in sales to $800 million, sending its stock price soaring from $20 a share to $400 a share.

The dynamic process of new companies' going public continues at a heady pace. From 1993 through mid-1995, more than seventeen hundred new stocks have made their debut. Investors have risked $100 billion on these fledglings. Some will be flops, but among these seventeen hundred you will find the next Amgen, the next Staples, the next Home Depot.

Corporate Heroes

Company Name	Corporate Heroes	Commentary
Amgen	George B. Rathmann, Ph.D., CEO through 1988, Chairman through 1991, currently Chairman Emeritus Gordon Binder, CEO since 1988, Chairman, 1991–	*Pioneer in Commercialization* of recombinant technology and genetic engineering. Binder, former Ford Motors CFO, took conservative approach to avoid financial loss before products were approved.
Automatic Data Processing	Henry Taub, Founder; Frank R. Lautenberg; Josh S. Weston, CEO & Chairman Arthur F. Weinbach, Pres & COO	*Thirty Years of Double-digit Earnings* growth every quarter, despite recessions: amazing in a mundane business. ADP showed how outsourcing payroll would reduce costs and improve service.
Cabletron Systems	Craig Benson, Cofounder, Chairman, COO, Treasurer since 1989 S. Robert "Bob" Levine, Cofounder, President & CEO	*From a Two-man Company* started in a garage, Benson and Levine built Cabletron Systems into the leading hub manufacturer for local-area networks with direct-sales strategy, emphasizing account control, superior customer service, and broad range of products at low cost.
Cabot Corporation	Samuel W. Bodman, Chairman & CEO, 1988–	*Turned Around* company adrift. Divested businesses and focused on core specialty chemicals and original carbon black operation.
Capital Cities/ABC	Thomas S. Murphy, Chairman & CEO Daniel B. Burke, retired President and CEO, President and COO, 1972–1990	*Joined Small Albany, NY, UHF TV Station* and AM radio station in 1954. Oversaw expansion into publishing, programming for cable TV, and 8 TV and 19 radio stations. Extremely cost conscious. Murphy and Burke helped build enormous empire through development and acquisition program, including ABC purchase in 1986.

Company Name	Corporate Heroes	Commentary
Circuit City Stores	Samuel S. Wurtzel, Founder Alan L. Wurtzel, current Vice Chairman, President & CEO, 1972–1986 Richard L. Sharp, President & CEO, Chairman since 1994	*Sam Wurtzel Founded Wards Company*, the original name of Circuit City Stores. Son Alan joined business and started the superstore concept. Sharp responsible for ten years of outstanding growth in a competitive business. Broad product line and low prices win.
Compaq Computer	Joseph R. Canion, Founder, CEO, 1982–1991 Benjamin M. Rosen, Chairman Eckhard Pfeiffer, CEO	*Went Head-to-Head With IBM;* saw the PC market as compatible with Intel and Microsoft, not IBM. Rosen guided the company to becoming world's low-cost producer in the PC market. Pfeiffer kept Compaq a low-cost producer with new high-quality products.
Walt Disney	Walt Disney and Roy O. Disney, Founders Michael D. Eisner, CEO & Chairman, 1984–	*Founded Company and Provided the Creative Vision;* launched Disneyland, Disney World and Epcot Center. With Frank Wells, revitalized Disney's theme park profitability. With Roy Disney Jr. and former studio head Jeffrey Katzenberg, accelerated feature animation development, generated unprecedented box-office revenues and ancillary profits.
EDS	H. Ross Perot, Founder & CEO, 1975–1986 Les Alberthal, CEO, 1986–	*Attacked Markets with More Passion than Vision,* had right timing and worked hard. Visionary who has inspired employees to act responsibly. EDS has achieved greatest success under his leadership.
EMC	Richard J. Egan, Cofounder & CEO, 1979–1992 Roger Marino, Cofounder, 1979, left company in 1990 Michael C. Ruettgers, President & CEO, 1992–	*Egan and Marino Built Young, Aggressive Sales Force.* Ruettgers obsessed with quality and operational discipline, entered client/server market, helped company overtake IBM in mainframe storage market, becoming the first company to unseat IBM in a core market.

Company Name	Corporate Heroes	Commentary
Federal Express	Frederick W. Smith, Founder, Chairman, President & CEO since 1983	*Visionary Leader*, he recognized the need for express small-package delivery system. Built operations on information technology that promoted reliability, established hub and spoke network to provide service to more remote areas.
The Gap	Doris F. and Donald G. Fisher, Founders Millard S. Drexler, President, 1987–, CEO, 1995–	*Founded the Company*, creating the concept of casual apparel with denim as core apparel base. Drexler transformed company into a premier specialty retailer, realizing biggest growth in the late 1980s.
Home Depot	Bernard Marcus, Founder, Chairman & CEO Arthur M. Blank, Founder, President & COO	*Marcus and Blank Created the First Warehouse Home Center* retail chain, based on high volume, low cost, and service excellence. Creative management has been successful.
Intel	Gordon E. Moore, Ph.D., Founder & Chairman, 1979– Robert N. Noyce, Ph.D., Founder & Chairman, 1975–1979 (deceased) Andrew S. Grove, Ph.D., President, 1979–, CEO, 1987–	*Intel Created the Microprocessor* under leadership of Moore and Noyce. Company has doubled microprocessor performance every 12 months for the past few years. Noyce was first to commercialize the DRAM memory-chip business. Grove made Intel world's undisputed leader in microprocessors.
MCI	William G. McGowan, Founder, Chairman & CEO, 1968–1992 (deceased) Bert C. Roberts, Jr., Chairman & CEO, 1992–	*Built Nationwide Telecommunications Network*; battled AT&T in every telecommunications market. Roberts's vision led to MCI's alliance with British Telecommunications; positioned MCI for global electronic leadership.

Company Name	Corporate Heroes	Commentary
Microsoft	William H. Gates, Cofounder, Chairman & CEO Paul Allen, Cofounder, Executive Vice President, 1981–1983; Director Steven A. Ballmer, Sr. VP, 1984–1989	*Set the Technical Direction* for company. Regarded as product visionary. Allen and Gates created first computer language program for personal computer. Ballmer built sales and marketing machine.
Nucor	F. Kenneth Iverson, Chairman, CEO & Director John D. Correnti, President, COO & Director	*Rewards Employees for Generating Return on Assets* and awards production bonuses; company avoids corporate overhead. "Success is 70% culture and 30% new technology." Correnti encourages risk-taking, which has led to reduced costs.
Oracle Corporation	Lawrence J. Ellison, Founder, President & CEO since 5/77, Chairman 4/90– Jeffrey O. Henley, EVP & CFO Raymond J. Lane, EVP & President of Worldwide Operations	*Ran the Company until 1990;* continues as technology visionary. Henley credited with financial turnaround after company stumbled in 1990. Lane took Oracle from under $1 billion to over $3 billion in sales in four years.
Shaw Industries	Robert Shaw, President, CEO & Director since 1967; Chairman since 5/10/95 W. Norris Little, Senior VP of Operations since 1977; Director, 1979– William C. Lusk, Jr., Treasurer since 1971, Senior VP since 1977 & Director since 1973	*Changed Carpet Industry* through consolidation and by focusing on lowering manufacturing costs. Tough competitor, willing to sacrifice short-term earnings for long-term success. Little helped improve manufacturing cost structure. Lusk critical in developing Shaw's systems and in financing acquisitions.
Southwest Airlines	Herbert D. Kelleher, Founder, Chairman since 1967; also President & CEO since 1982	*Visionary Whose Affable Style Motivates* employees. Customer service and lowest prices are crucial.

Company Name	Corporate Heroes	Commentary
Staples	Tom Stemberg, Founder, CEO since 1985 & Chairman since 1988	*Founded Office-Supply Superstore* using supermarket background, where he championed use of generic labels and warehouse format. Entrepreneurial management style.
Tele-communications, Inc.	John C. Malone, Ph.D., President & CEO since 1973	*Used Sophisticated Financing* to leverage existing small cable ownership to buy additional cable systems. Industry believer, willing to take risks, who became #1 in only ten years and has increased dominance in last ten.
Thermo Electron	George N. Hatsopoulos, Ph.D., Founder, Chairman, CEO & President since 1956 John H. Hatsopoulos, joined in 1956, CFO & EVP since 1988 Arvin H. Smith, President & CEO of Thermo Instrument Systems Inc. since 1986, EVP Thermo Electron since 1991	*A Unique "Way-out" Technical Company* with eleven public "spin-outs," a concept they pioneered for providing capital and motivation. In addition they have made brilliant fill-in acquisitions, then turned them around. Smith is a phenomenal operations and manufacturing guy who helps the two brothers.
Toys R Us	Charles Lazarus, Chairman since 1987 & CEO 1987–1994	*Lazarus Envisioned the Superstore Concept for Toys.* Toys R Us became one of the first U.S. department store "category killers"; Lazarus then took the concept international.
Wal-Mart	Sam Walton, Founder (deceased) March 1918–April 1992; started company in 1962	*Worked at J.C. Penney;* took discount retail concept into small towns; strong customer focus; used distribution centers to keep costs low.

Lots of very good moves!

Sales and profits doubled

400,000 jobs lost. However, downsizing kept companies competitive and allowed them to stay in business.

Large Companies	No. of Employees (000's)			Sales (Mils)			Net Income (Mils)			Stock Price		
	FY'75	FY'85	Q1 '95	FY'75	FY'85	12 Mos Jul-95	FY'75	FY'85	Jul-95	1975	1985	7/31/95
Allied Signal, Inc	33.4	143.8	87.5	2,331.1	9,115.0	13,250.0	116.2	(279.0)	788.0	11.69	21.22	46.75
American Express	32.3	70.5	72.4	2,490.2	12,944.0	14,683.0	165.0	810.0	1,413.0	9.13	22.42	38.50
Boeing Co	72.6	104.0	115.0	3,718.9	13,636.0	20,616.0	76.3	566.0	745.0	1.64	20.19	67.00
Caterpillar Inc	78.3	53.6	54.0	4,963.7	6,725.0	14,955.0	398.7	198.0	1,063.0	22.05	17.64	70.38
Chrysler Corp	217.6	114.2	121.0	11,598.4	21,255.5	51,051.0	(259.5)	1,635.2	3,367.0	4.85	16.54	48.75
Citicorp	44.6	81.3	82.6	4,780.5	21,597.0	28,110.0	349.9	998.0	3,642.0	16.20	22.59	62.50
Coca-Cola Co	31.1	38.5	33.0	2,872.8	7,903.9	16,674.0	239.3	722.3	2,671.0	3.31	5.92	65.63
Colgate-Palmolive Co	42.0	40.6	32.8	2,860.5	4,523.6	7,798.2	119.0	109.4	587.1	14.23	13.49	70.00
Deere & Co	53.8	40.5	34.3	2,955.2	4,060.6	9,789.2	179.1	30.5	702.8	21.79	28.83	89.88
Emerson Electric Co	34.0	61.9	73.9	1,250.3	4,649.2	9,279.9	96.2	401.1	846.7	11.69	24.35	70.75
Exxon Corp	137.0	146.0	86.0	44,865.0	86,673.0	102,927.0	2,503.0	4,870.0	5,600.0	10.53	26.07	72.50
Federal Natl Mortage	1.5*	1.9	3.2	2,475.6	10,342.0	17,756.9	115.0	37.0	2,072.7	5.23	6.62	93.63
General Electric Co	375.0	304.0	216.0	13,399.1	28,285.0	62,082.0	580.8	2,336.0	5,030.0	5.76	15.56	59.00
Gillette Co	33.5	31.4	32.8	1,406.9	2,400.0	6,245.1	80.0	159.9	730.4	1.87	3.85	43.75
Goodyear Tire & Rubber Co	149.2	131.7	90.3	5,452.5	9,585.1	12,621.9	161.6	412.4	584.3	9.42	14.16	43.38
Hewlett-Packard Co	30.2	84.0	98.4	981.2	6,505.0	27,787.0	83.6	489.0	2,002.0	6.09	17.39	77.88
Intl Business Machines Corp	288.6	405.5	219.8	14,436.5	50,056.0	66,414.0	1,989.9	6,555.0	3,918.0	51.50	131.94	108.88
ITT Corp	349.0	232.0	110.0	11,367.5	11,871.1	24,949.0	396.2	293.5	1,048.0	21.04	33.54	120.00
Johnson & Johnson	53.8	74.9	81.5	2,224.7	6,421.3	16,540.0	183.8	613.7	2,116.0	7.45	11.34	71.75
McDonald's Corp	71.0	148.0	183.0	926.4	3,694.7	8,686.1	86.9	433.0	1,261.7	2.45	7.32	38.63
Merck & Co	26.8	30.9	47.5	1,489.7	3,547.5	15,272.8	228.8	539.9	3,079.2	4.15	6.22	51.63
Motorola Inc	47.0	90.2	132.0	1,311.8	5,443.0	23,563.0	41.1	72.0	1,634.0	3.87	8.65	76.50
Raytheon Co	52.7	73.0	60.2	2,245.4	6,408.5	10,085.5	71.0	375.9	763.8	5.65	24.31	82.63
Walgreen Co	29.0	37.2	61.9	1,079.1	3,161.9	9,831.0	9.8	94.2	305.7	0.38	6.53	25.88
Xerox Corp	93.5	102.4	87.6	4,053.8	8,732.1	17,321.0	244.3	475.3	812.0	63.84	50.54	119.38
Total	2,376.0	2,642.1	2,216.7	147,538.7	349,536.1	608,288.6	8,257.8	22,948.4	46,783.4			

*Estimate
Source: Factset, First Call, Moody's Industrial Manual   Created by: FMR Equity Research Infocenter—Julian Lin

Small Companies	No. of Employees (000's)			Sales (Mils)			Net Income (Mils)			Stock Price		
	FY'75	FY'85	Q1 '95	FY'75	FY'85	12 Mos Jul-95	FY'75	FY'85	12 mos Jul-95	1975	1985	7/31/95
Amgen Inc		0.2	3.5		21.1	1,723.3		0.5	334.8		1.36	85.13
Automatic Data Processing	5.4	18.5	22.0	154.7	1,030.0	2,758.8	13.8	87.9	379.3	3.28	12.46	64.00
Cabletron Systems		0.4	4.9		3.9	870.8		0.2	174.1		4.78¹	52.88
Cabot Corp	5.6	7.7	5.4	411.8	1,407.5	1,755.8	14.1	71.3	120.7	1.63	13.33	56.38
Capital Cities/ABC Inc	2.9	8.9	20.2	174.4	1,020.9	6,581.1	25.4	142.2	721.5	1.91	20.68	116.25
Circuit City Stores Inc	0.6	4.6	31.4	61.2	705.5	5,925.9	1.4	22.0	172.8	0.02	3.07	37.00
Compaq Computer Corp		1.9	14.4		503.9	11,547.0		26.6	870.0		1.69	50.63
Disney (Walt) Company	14.5	30.0	65.0	520.0	2,015.4	11,276.5	61.7	173.5	1,291.3	2.68	5.48	58.63
EMC		0.2	3.4		33.4	1,531.0		7.5	279.8		1.70²	22.88
Federal Express Corp		34.0	101.0		2,606.2	9,187.3		131.8	291.0		44.61	67.50
Gap Inc		11.0	55.0		647.3	3,820.0		27.7	306.9		2.13	34.88
EDS	3.7	40.0	69.9	119.4	3,406.4	10,519.2	14.6	189.8	847.0	0.54	9.36	44.00
Home Depot Inc		5.4	67.3		700.7	13,173.5		8.2	622.5		1.41	44.00
Intel Corp	4.6	21.3	32.6	136.8	1,365.0	12,418.0	16.3	1.6	2,560.0	0.93	4.58	65.00
MCI Communications	0.5	12.4	40.7	28.4	2,542.3	13,678.0	(27.8)	113.3	830.0	0.30	4.78	24.00
Microsoft Corp		1.0	15.3		140.4	5,609.0		24.1	1,447.0		1.93³	90.50
Nucor Corp	2.3	3.9	5.9	121.5	758.5	3,167.6	7.6	58.5	259.1	0.44	6.93	53.50
Oracle Corp		0.6	12.1		55.4	2,617.1		5.9	374.3		0.83³	41.88
Shaw Industries Inc	1.6	4.3	24.2	86.8	519.5	2,714.6	3.5	25.9	128.2	0.27	1.48	16.75
Southwest Airlines	0.4	5.3	18.8	22.8	679.7	2,593.5	3.4	47.3	149.3	0.10	5.71	28.75
Staples Inc		0.2	14.6		8.8	2,271.4		(1.9)	44.5		3.99⁴	22.50
Tele-Comm (TCI)	1.1	4.7	32.0	40.6	577.3	5,400.0	(0.16)	10.12	(22.00)	0.05	4.11	20.00
Thermo Electron Corp	1.3	3.2	10.2	56.2	265.7	1,713.4	1.3	9.6	110.4	0.98	5.45	42.75
Toys R Us Inc		45.2	111.0		1,976.1	8,776.6		119.8	512.6		10.26	28.00
Wal-Mart Stores	7.5	104.0	622.0	340.3	8,451.5	85,247.8	11.5	327.5	2,735.5	0.09	3.20	26.63
Total	368.7	1,400.7		31,442.2	226,877.3		1,630.9	15,540.9				

Handwritten annotations:

Small companies added more than 1 million jobs

Sales rose 7-fold

Huge Profit gains

Huge stock gains

APPENDIX ONE

Stockpicking Tools

It wasn't long ago that amateur stockpickers had a hard time following the fundamentals of the companies whose stocks they owned. Analysts at the brokerage houses were scurrying around, finding out everything they could, but this information rarely reached the client. If a brokerage house changed its recommendation from "buy" to "sell," the small-time customer was the last to know.

If you asked for it, your broker might send you an analyst's report on a company, but these reports were often several months out of date. Amateur investors had to rely on the quarterly and annual reports put out by companies themselves. They also made frequent trips to the local library, where they pored over a publication called *Value Line*. *Value Line* gives a one-page rundown on hundreds of companies and is packed with useful information—it's an excellent resource even today. Make use of it if you can—if you've got a stockbroker, you can probably get the *Value Line* reports from him or her.

In the old days, your research was limited to *Value Line*; Standard & Poor's reports, which are similar to *Value Line*, but with less opinion; the occasional analyst's report from the brokerage house; and the material that arrived directly from companies.

Computers have changed all this. There's been an explosion in financial data that's available on computers. Every day, some new information service makes its debut—and many of these services are free.

Computers have made the stockbroker into a much more valuable resource. Instead of mailing you an out-of-date analyst's report or a page from *Value Line*, a broker can now pass along all the up-to-date information that shows up on his monitor: the latest word from the analysts, news flashes, the latest earnings estimates for thousands of companies.

If you have a home computer, you can get all this data on your own, without a stockbroker. This is another area where kids have an advantage over grownups: they already know how to use a modem and tap into on-line services, such as America Online, Prodigy, or CompuServe.

On-line services can give you an instant readout on stock prices at any time of the day or night, so you don't have to wait for tomorrow's newspaper to find out what happened to your stocks. But tracking the prices is the least of it. You can also get company reports, industry reports, news releases, and screens.

Screens are a wonderful invention—a computer dating service for stocks. You tell the computer what you're looking for—a company with no debt, for instance; or a company with no debt and lots of cash whose earnings are growing at 20 percent a year; or a company that's losing money, has no debt and lots of cash, and sells for less than three dollars a share. In seconds, the computer spits out a list of names of companies that fit these descriptions. Before we had computers, it would have been impossible to search the universe of thousands of companies to find the few that meet our requirements. Now, it's easy.

You can set up a screen for almost anything: companies that have raised their dividends for twenty years in a row, companies that have increased their earnings twenty years in a row, companies where the dividend yield exceeds 6 percent a year, and so forth. It's a whole new way to approach stocks. Instead of looking for good investments in the mall, you can look for them on-line.

Along with the explosion in on-line services, there's been a surprising turnabout in investor relations. Companies have always tried to communicate with their largest investors, but now they are reaching out to the smallest investors as well. You can get annual reports and quarterly reports on certain companies free, on-line.

You can call an 800 number to get the latest update on a company's progress, in a tape-recorded message, sometimes straight from the CEO. If you read *The Wall Street Journal*, you can't miss the "club" symbol in the listings on the stock pages. Wherever that symbol appears, it means the company will mail or fax you its reports for free.

You can also get more and better information on the thousands of mutual funds in existence today. The funds themselves are making an effort to simplify their reports and prospectuses so people can better understand what their strategy is, how risky they are, and how well they've performed.

Magazines such as *Forbes* and *Money* and financial newspapers such as *The Wall Street Journal* publish detailed reviews of mutual funds, where you can learn about different types of funds and their various risks, and which funds in each category have done the best and the worst.

In addition, two great research organizations, Morningstar and Lipper, track mutual fund performance. Morningstar puts out a mutual-fund guide that does for funds what *Value Line* does for stocks—there's a page on each fund that tells the complete story.

Brokers keep copies of *Morningstar* in their offices. Before you buy a fund, check to see what *Morningstar* says about it.

The Lipper Standings are reprinted twice a year in *Barron's* magazine and four times a year in *The Wall Street Journal*. There, you'll find out which funds have done the best in different categories.

Following is a list of some of the services available to any and all investors, most of them free. Take advantage of as many as you can!

Resources

STOCK SCREENS: ON THE PRODIGY ONLINE SERVICE

In Prodigy's Strategic Investor section you can search, browse, print, or download data on some six thousand stocks that interest you, as well as analyze their income statements, balance sheets, and key ratios. You can screen for companies by industry, yield, five-year EPS growth, and p/e ratio.

Bloomberg
800-256-6623

Listen to interviews with economists, market strategists, and company CEOs, and get updates on financial news. Will fax information, including price charts, Bloomberg research reports, telephone numbers, and addresses for any company traded on a major exchange worldwide. All free.

Investor In Touch
617-441-2770
Fax: 617-441-2760
http://www.money.com/ssnhome.html
or by e-mail send to: info@money.com

Available in the World Wide Web. Free access to Nelson's Directory of over fifteen thousand public companies worldwide. Provides company address, phone number, and fax, and access to SEC filings and headline press releases. Access to technical graphs on almost all U.S.-traded stocks.

IRIN
800-474-7702
On Internet browser http://www.irin.com

Access to annual reports and SEC documents on-line, free. Available on the Internet or an on-line service with access to the Internet, such as CompuServe, America Online and Prodigy. You can view the documents exactly as they appear in printed form.

FINANCIAL FAX (product of the *Los Angeles Times*)
818-597-2990 or 800-521-2475 x8202

Fax service that provides a personalized one-page financial report on the performance of stocks you want to track. It's thirteen to fifteen dollars a month for a daily fax. Weeky service also available.

Stocks On Call
Available through PR Newswire
800-578-7888
Instant access to full-text news releases of roughly four thousand public companies faxed to you free.

Morningstar OnDemand
800-876-5005
Mutual fund information by fax or mail. Data comes from *Morningstar Mutual Funds*, a directory of 363 closed-end funds and 1,500 open-end funds. Five dollars per fund page.

InvestQuest, Inc.
614-844-3860
3535 Fishinger Boulevard
Suite 140
Columbus, OH 43026
Internet address: invest.quest.columbus.oh.us
World Wide Web address:
http://invest.quest.columbus.oh.us
Fax-on-Demand available twenty-four hours every day. Search for companies by trading symbol, or alphabetically using phone keypad. Get financial statements, news and earnings releases, product information, market research, industry comparables. Listen to messages from CEO and CFO.

No Internet access or fax? Here are books or resources available at many libraries and stockbrokers' offices. Some are too expensive for you to buy on your own.

Value Line Investment Survey
800-833-0046
Value Line Publishing, Inc.
220 East 42nd Street
New York, NY 10017-5891
Classifies 3,500 stocks by industry, updated quarterly. Historical information for each stock is provided on one page of data in the form of a technical chart and table, supplemented by an updated editorial by a Value Line analyst, who ranks each stock for its timeliness. Also provides the names, addresses, and phone numbers

of key officers. Each section begins with a Value Line analyst's industry summary and outlook.

Nelson's Directory of *Investment Research*
800-333-6357
One Gateway Plaza
Port Chester, NY 10573

Volume I profiles over 6,800 U.S. publicly traded companies, and Volume II profiles over eighty-six hundred international public companies. Provides the names and phone numbers of Wall Street analysts covering the company. Describes companies' core line of business and lists their address, phone and fax numbers, name and title of their key executives, and a five-year operations summary. Identifies over five hundred research firms, their key executives, analysts, and the industries they cover. Indexes companies by industry, by location, and alphabetically.

Nelson's Catalog of *Institutional Research Reports*
800-333-6357
One Gateway Plaza
Port Chester, NY 10573

Catalogues virtually every research report published anywhere in the world. Published ten times a year.

Investment Company Institute's Directory of Mutual Funds
202-326-5800
Investment Company Institute
1401 H Street, NW
Suite 1200
Washington, DC 20005-2148

An introduction to mutual-fund investing including a directory of more than 4,500 funds organized by investment objective. For each fund the directory provides the name, address, phone number, the year it began, investment advisors, assets, fees, assets under management, and where shares can be bought. Also provides a glossary of terms.

Investment Company Institute's Mutual Fund Fact Book
202-326-5800
Investment Company Institute
1401 H Street, NW
Suite 1200
Washington, DC 20005-2148
A yearly publication tracking trends and statistics observed in the mutual-fund industry. Has text as well as charts and graphs. Also provides a glossary of terms.

Morningstar Mutual Funds
800-876-5005
225 West Wacker Drive #400
Chicago, IL 60606
Tracks and rates 363 closed-end funds and 1,500 open-end funds for risk. A page dedicated to each fund combines an editorial by a Morningstar analyst with historical technical charts and tables of pertinent financial data. Some information is available on-line through America Online or Prodigy.

The Wall Street Journal—Quarterly Mutual Fund Review
Discusses happenings in the mutual-fund industry at the end of each quarter. Provides phone numbers, minimum investment requirements, sales charges, and performance data on funds.

Wall Street Journal's Annual Reports Service
800-654-CLUB (800-654-2582)
For companies in *The Wall Street Journal* Money & Investing section, with a club symbol next to their names. Free annual reports and, if available, quarterly reports by mail. Dial 1-800-965-5679 to fax a request.

APPENDIX TWO

Reading the Numbers— How to Decipher a Balance Sheet

If a picture is worth a thousand words, in business, so is a number. No matter what the CEO says in the text of an annual report, the numbers in the back of the report give you the complete, unvarnished account of the company's behavior. If picking stocks becomes your hobby, do yourself a favor and take an accounting course.

To help you decipher the numbers in the meantime, we've concocted a sample of what you'll find in the typical corporate financial report. It's the five-year history of Compuspeak, an imaginary enterprise started by an imaginary character, Barclay.

Barclay is a research scientist from Silicon Valley. In his spare time, he has developed a new gadget called the Interface, which enables the user to issue verbal commands—such as "turn on," "turn off," "switch windows," or "copy to floppy"—to any personal computer. He's gotten to the point that he's producing the units in the makeshift laboratory/factory in his garage. He's taken a second mortgage on his house to pay the bills.

To get the rest of the story, we move to the balance sheet, shown on page 261. A balance sheet is a list of everything a company owns, as well as everything it owes. It's similar to a list of pluses and minuses you might make about your personality.

We call it a balance sheet because the two sides are always kept in balance, with the pluses adding up to the same result as the minuses. Normally, a balance sheet has a left side and a right side, but in our sample balance sheet, we've put one side on top of the other.

Compuspeak gets its start in life from the $100,000 Barclay borrowed from the bank against the value of his house—his second mortgage. He invests this money in his fledgling company. On day one, it shows up on the plus side of the balance sheet under Current Assets in two places: $50,000 in Cash, and $50,000 in Gross Property, Plant, & Equipment. Barclay has spent $50,000 on equipment—the machinery to make his gadgets. At this point, he has no factory, or Plant, because he's working out of his garage.

This brings us to depreciation. Depreciation results from the fact that factories, offices, machinery, computers, desks, chairs, and so forth lose their value as they get older. The Internal Revenue Service recognizes this and allows businesses to deduct the lost value of equipment and buildings as they deteriorate or become outmoded.

Raw land can't be depreciated, but the IRS has a formula for everything from tape recorders to tanning beds. Buildings usually can be "written off" over twenty to twenty-five years; machinery, typewriters, computers, and so forth have a much shorter depreciation—three to fifteen years depending on the item in question. That's because they become obsolete faster than buildings do.

On day one, you can see that there is no Less Accumulated Depreciation under Gross Property Plant & Equipment. That's because Barclay hasn't taken any depreciation.

So much for the pluses—the assets. Now we get to the bottom half, the Current Liabilities. This is what the company owes. On day one, Compuspeak doesn't owe anybody anything, because Barclay's $100,000 bank loan is personal—he took out a mortgage on his house. The company's liabilities are zero.

Below Current Liabilities, you find Equity. A company gets

equity in two ways: by selling shares of its stock or by making money from its business. On day one, Compuspeak hasn't made any money in its business—notice the Retained Earnings are zero—so its only equity is the $100,000 that Barclay invested in the company. That's the Paid-In Capital.

Below equity, you get to Liabilities & Shareholder Equity, which is the sum of Total Liabilities, Paid-In Capital, and Retained Earnings. After that, you reach Shares Outstanding. When Barclay invested the original $100,000 in his company, he issued himself 10,000 shares of stock, so each share would be worth $10, as shown in the Book Value of $10 on day one. This was an arbitrary decision on Barclay's part. He could just as easily have issued himself 1,000 shares worth $100 apiece.

No matter whether it's Barclay's company or General Motors, the balance sheet is set up the same way. You can see at a glance what the pluses are—the cash, the inventories, and so forth—and what the minuses are.

Beyond day one, we see the balance sheet going forward. Let's look at the situation at the end of year one, returning to the top of the balance sheet. Under Current Assets, you see there's only $25,000 in cash left in the company—Barclay has spent the rest to run the business and to manufacture his product, the Interface.

Then there's Accounts Receivable of $19,500. This tells us that some of Barclay's customers have bought the Interface, but they haven't gotten around to paying the bills. The $19,500 is money owed to the company it hasn't received yet—hence Accounts Receivable. It's the total amount that customers owe.

Next, we come to Inventories of $30,000. That means $30,000 worth of Interfaces are sitting in Barclay's garage waiting to be sold—along with the parts to make more Interfaces. Unsold merchandise is counted as an asset, although there's no guarantee Barclay will ever be able to sell these unsold Interfaces at the regular price.

Dropping down to Gross Property Plant & Equipment, you notice the Less Accumulated Depreciation figure of $10,000.

Barclay has "written off" $10,000 worth of machinery. He spent $50,000 to acquire this equipment, but now he's carrying it on the books at a value of $40,000. He will get a $10,000 deduction on his taxes for this depreciation. Because of the kind of machinery he has, which is quickly outmoded, the IRS allows him to write off 20 percent of the value each year. The $10,000 is 20 percent of the $50,000 expenditure that showed up earlier under Gross Property Plant & Equipment.

In the Liabilities area, we find $10,000 in Accounts Payable. If Accounts Receivable is money the people owe Barclay, Accounts Payable is money that Barclay owes. It represents all the bills he hasn't yet paid: telephone bills, electric bills, bills from his suppliers, and so forth.

Below Liabilities, on the Equity line, you see the Retained Earnings: $4,500. That's the bottom line—Barclay's profit from one year in business. The company now has equity of $104,500. This includes the $100,000 Barclay invested at the outset, plus the $4,500 the company earned in the first year.

Barclay had a choice of what to do with his profit. He could have put the $4,500 into his own pocket by paying himself a dividend. But instead, he left it in the company, so the extra money could be invested in the growth of the business. That's why we say the earnings were "retained."

Thanks to the retained earnings plus his original $100,000 outlay, Barclay's company is valued at $104,500—the Equity at the end of year one. Since Barclay issued himself 10,000 shares, each share is valued at $10.45 ($104,500 divided by 10,000). This is called the company's "equity per share" or its "book value."

Going forward into year two and beyond, the numbers show how Compuspeak has increased its business, selling more Interfaces while the accounts receivable and the inventories continue to mount. In year two, another element is introduced on the minus side: $121,000 in Bank Debt. This time, Barclay isn't borrowing the money, the company is doing the borrowing. Compuspeak needs these funds to pay for expansion: new machinery, more inventory, new workers, and so forth.

Did you notice that bank debt doesn't count as equity at the bottom of the balance sheet? When banks lend money to companies, the banks don't become owners. Neither do individuals who buy a company's bonds. Barclay still owns all 10,000 shares, and after two years of retained earnings, his equity has increased to $114,500.

Compuspeak has come a long way by the end of year five. The company has $180,000 in cash, plus other Current Assets that add up to $744,500. Just below Current Assets, in Gross Property Plant & Equipment, we discover that Barclay has increased his capital spending, because the gross value of his plant and equipment has jumped from $120,000 at the end of year two to $500,000 at the end of year five.

To have spent this much, he must have left his garage, set up a small factory someplace else, and installed fancy new machinery. As he buys more equipment, his depreciation rises accordingly.

Different kinds of companies require different levels of capital spending. Steel mills, for instance, have huge expenses: It costs a lot of money to maintain and to upgrade a steel plant. Oil wells require very little capital spending once the well is drilled and the oil is gushing out. Advertising agencies have almost no capital spending: All they need is an office and a bunch of desks.

Barclay has fewer capital improvements to pay for than the owner of a steel mill, but relative to the rest of his budget, his capital spending is a big drain on his resources. That's the nature of the high-tech hardware business he's in.

Down in the Liabilities section, we find out that Barclay has paid off the bank debt, because at the end of year five, the debt is back to zero. Where did he get the money to do this, you wonder? You'll find the answer under the Equity line. Paid-In Capital has jumped from $100,000 to $700,000. Barclay must have issued and sold some stock. Notice the change in Shares Outstanding? There used to be 10,000 shares, all owned by Barclay. Now there are 15,000 shares.

Another investor has been brought in! On the Paid-In Capital line you can follow his tracks. See the $700,000 figure? We know

Barclay put in $100,000 to begin with, so this new investor has paid $600,000 for 5,000 newly issued shares of Compuspeak stock. The new investor owns one-third of Barclay's company.

Thanks to this much-needed infusion of capital, the Equity per Share at the end of year five has jumped to $59.63. Another way of saying this is that Compuspeak now has a book value of $59.63 per share. That means Barclay's own 10,000 shares are worth $596,300. His original $100,000 investment and all his hard work are starting to pay off.

Why is the mystery investor willing to risk $600,000, paying $120 a share for Barclay's company? Because he sees how well Barclay has done so far, and he believes the growth in sales and profits will continue. That's the promise of a small company that's more than doubling in size every year.

You can track the earnings for yourself in the category marked Income per Share on the Income Statement on page 262: $0.45 after year one, $1 after year two, $6 after year five. The mystery investor has paid $120 per share for a company that is earning $6 per share, based on the earnings from year five.

Dividing the stock price ($120) by the earnings ($6), we get the price/earnings ratio: 20. The average stock on the New York Stock Exchange today has a price/earnings ratio of 15 to 16, so the mystery investor is paying slightly more for his stake in Compuspeak than investors in general are paying for publicly traded stocks. He's doing this because he knows the potential of fast-growing small companies. He knows its risky, but if all goes well, he figures there's a chance that Compuspeak will eventually go public, the stock will become a ten-, twenty-, or fifty-bagger, and he'll make many times his money.

If he had a choice, Barclay wouldn't sell a third of his beloved Compuspeak. He's doing it because he needs the money to expand the company, to cover the costs of maintaining the inventory, to carry the accounts receivable, and to pay salaries. His success has produced a cash crunch, and selling shares is the easiest way to raise cash.

By giving up a third of Compuspeak he insures its survival. He figures that owning 67 percent of a well-funded enterprise is better than owning 100 percent of a company that's strapped for cash so it can't realize its potential.

A few more years down the road, Barclay will reach the point where he needs more money. That may be a perfect time to go public. Until then, Barclay is making a big sacrifice to chase his pot of gold. He has left his "real job" to devote full time to his company, and he's taking out a minimal salary, just enough to cover basic living expenses. He's borrowed money on his house to make his initial investment in the company, so his mortgage payments are higher than before. He's too busy to take vacations and can't really afford them.

Barclay's wife is working overtime at her job so she can pay as many of the household bills as possible. The two of them are eating at home and avoiding expensive restaurants. Instead of buying a new car every four years, as they have in the past, they are keeping the old ones. Their standard of living has declined considerably, but they are both putting up with it. Barclay's wife is as bullish on Compuspeak as he is.

Let's get back to the numbers. Once again, we turn to the Income Statement. Here we get a breakdown of the operations inside the company: how much money is being made and how it's being spent. In year one, under Sales Revenue, we see that Compuspeak sold $200,000 worth of Interfaces. Meanwhile, the cash that was left in the company savings account earned $2,500 in interest. So Compuspeak's total take from its first year in business was $202,500. In the lingo of accounting, the total take is called "net revenues."

Just below Net Revenues, we find out where most of the net revenues went. This is the Costs section. Here we get a rundown on the costs of materials and manufacturing labor, and also the selling, general, and administrative costs (known as SG&A) of operating the business and promoting the product.

In year one, you'll also notice that Barclay spent $20,000 on research and development. He was trying to improve the Interface so competitors would have a hard time knocking him off.

Not all companies are saddled with as many expenses as Compuspeak is. It's something to consider before you invest in any stock: Is this a capital-intensive business? Does it require huge outlays for a sales staff and research and development? If so, a lot of money that might otherwise go into the investors' pockets will be lost to expenses.

If you invest in a sand-and-gravel-pit company, the research and development costs will be zero, because the company won't need to improve the sand and gravel to keep up with technological advances. Also, the sales costs will be low, because the company won't need to hire a sophisticated sales force to market the sand and gravel.

Likewise, in a company that owns a chain of hamburger joints, research and development will be minimal because it's hard to improve a hamburger, and the sales force can be hired for minimum wage because selling a hamburger doesn't require an advanced degree.

Being in his line of work, Barclay can't get away with a cut-rate sales force. He needs a trained staff that understands the Interface and can explain it to corporate buyers and to computer stores that stock it for retail sale.

Some of Barclay's capital expenditures and all of his research and development expenditures are what we'd call "discretionary." That means he didn't have to spend this money. He wasn't obligated to do research or to upgrade his machinery.

The head of any company has to decide how much to spend on capital improvements and on research, or whether the company can get along without these improvements. CEOs and other corporate managers have to make these judgments all the time. If they skimp on research or they don't upgrade their factory and machinery, they run the risk of being destroyed by a competitor who comes along with a better product, manufactured at a lower cost. On the other hand, if they cut capital spending and research, their earnings will go up dramatically in the short run.

In most cases, higher earnings will boost the stock price, making the shareholders happy. And with the money it didn't spend on upgrades, the company can declare a fat dividend, making the shareholders even happier. But if the company loses its edge and a competitor steals the business, this happiness will be short-lived. The company's sales will drop, its earnings will drop, and the stock price will decline. Soon, it will be too broke to pay a dividend.

By eliminating his research and his capital spending, Barclay could have taken the easy route, awarding himself a tremendous dividend. By boosting his short-term earnings, he could have made the company more profitable to attract a buyer for the rest of his shares. He could have sold out and headed for the golf course.

But like many of the heroes you read about in Chapter Four, Barclay has resisted the temptation to take money out of his company. He's keeping up his capital spending and his research, because he believes in the future of the company. Someday, when Compuspeak becomes a $100-million business, he can sell his shares and buy two golf courses and a Learjet. But he probably won't. He'll be too busy figuring out how to make Compuspeak into a $200-million business.

Below Research & Development Expense, we come across our old friend Depreciation. In year one, as we've already mentioned, Barclay was able to claim $10,000 in depreciation. This shows up as a cost, as it should. Soon enough, his equipment will be outmoded, and Barclay will have to spend $10,000 to replace it. That's why the government allows his company to deduct depreciation. The replacement cost of machinery, factories, and so forth is a business expense that someday will have to be paid.

The next stop is Earnings Before Federal & State Taxes. We see here that Compuspeak earned $7,500 in the first year, before Uncle Sam took his cut. Most of the complaining about the IRS is done by individuals who are unhappy about their income tax rates, but taxes take a sizable bite out of companies as well. Of its $7,500 in earnings, Compuspeak has to send 40 percent, or $3,000, to the government. That leaves the $4,500 in Net Income that we already saw on the balance sheet. If the company doesn't pay a dividend (Compuspeak doesn't), "net income" is the same as "retained earnings." In layman's language, that's "profit."

Compuspeak is growing very fast, and the numbers are mounting up in all categories. By the end of year five, the company is selling almost $2 million worth of Interfaces, while spending $1 million on materials and labor and $210,000 on research and development (R&D). The annual R&D budget is now more than twice what Barclay invested in the company in the first place. Compuspeak is making a profit of $90,000 a year.

The Cash Flow Statement on page 263 helps you follow the trail of the money as it moves from one place to another. The $4,500 Net Income from year one shows up again, in the Sources of Funds section, along with the $10,000 that disappeared in the Depreciation. Add in the $100,000 that Barclay spent to buy the original 10,000 shares, plus a $10,000 increase in Accounts Payable, and you've got $124,500 in Total Sources of Funds.

Use of Funds gives you more detail on expenditures: the $50,000 Barclay spent on plant and equipment; the $30,000 in inventories; the $19,500 in accounts receivable. When you subtract the cash outflow of $99,500 from the cash inflow of $124,500, you're left with $25,000. That's the $25,000 that shows up as Cash on the top line of the Balance Sheet from year one. This sort of symmetry is beautiful to an accountant.

Congratulations! You've just graduated from the shortest accounting course in history. Now that you've gotten this far, you might as well take a peek at the numbers in a real annual report. Some of them may actually begin to make sense.

Balance Sheet

(STATEMENT OF FINANCIAL CONDITION)
ASSETS

Current Assets	Day 1	End of Year 1	End of Year 2	End of Year 5
Cash	50,000	25,000	40,000	180,000
Accounts Receivable	—	19,500	49,500	254,500
Inventories	—	30,000	80,000	310,000
Total Current Assets	50,000	74,500	169,500	744,500
Gross Property Plant & Equipment	50,000	50,000	120,000	500,000
Less Accumulated Depreciation	—	10,000	34,000	250,000
Net Property Plant & Equipment	50,000	40,000	86,000	250,000
TOTAL ASSETS	100,000	114,500	255,500	994,500

LIABILITIES

Current Liabilities	Day 1	End of Year 1	End of Year 2	End of Year 5
Accounts Payable	—	10,000	20,000	100,000
Bank Debt	—	—	121,000	—
Long-Term Debt Due w/in 1 Year	—	—	—	—
Total Current Liabilities	0	10,000	141,000	100,000
Long Term Debt	—	—	—	—
TOTAL LIABILITIES	0	10,000	141,000	100,000

EQUITY

	Day 1	End of Year 1	End of Year 2	End of Year 5
Paid-In Capital	100,000	100,000	100,000	700,000
Retained Earnings	—	4,500	14,500	194,500
	100,000	104,500	114,500	894,500
LIABILITIES & SHAREHOLDER EQUITY	100,000	114,500	255,500	994,500
Shares Outstanding	10,000	10,000	10,000	15,000
Equity or Book Value per Share	10.00	10.45	11.45	59.63

Income Statement
Statement of Operations

	Year 1	Year 2	Year 5
Sales Revenue	200,000	400,000	1,900,000
Interest Income	2,500	1,000	10,000
Net Revenues	202,500	401,000	1,910,000
Costs			
Materials & Manufacturing Labor Costs	110,000	204,000	1,000,000
Selling, General, & Administrative	55,000	111,000	448,000
Research & Development Expense	20,000	40,000	210,000
Depreciation	10,000	24,000	102,000
Interest Expense	—	6,000	—
Total Costs	195,000	385,000	1,760,000
Earnings Before Federal & State Taxes	7,500	16,000	150,000
Taxes (40%)	3,000	6,000	60,000
Net Income	4,500	10,000	90,000
Shares Outstanding	10,000	10,000	15,000
Income per Share	0.45	1.00	6.00

Cash Flow Statement

SOURCES OF FUNDS	Year 1	Year 2	Year 5
Cash Flow from Operations			
Net Income	4,500	10,000	90,000
Depreciation	10,000	24,000	102,000
	14,500	34,000	192,000
Increase in Accounts Payable	10,000	10,000	50,000
Cash Flow from Financing			
Sale of Common Stock	100,000	—	—
Proceeds from Short-Term Debt	—	121,000	—
Proceeds from Long-Term Debt	—	—	—
	100,000	121,000	0
TOTAL SOURCES OF FUNDS	124,500	165,000	242,000

USE OF FUNDS			
Additions to Property, Plant & Equipment	50,000	70,000	160,000
Increase in Inventories	30,000	50,000	80,000
Increase in Accounts Receivable	19,500	30,000	60,000
Acquisitions of Businesses	—	—	—
Repayment of Short-Term Debt	—	—	—
Repayment of Long-Term Debt	—	—	—
Dividends to Stockholders	—	—	—
Total Uses	99,500	150,000	300,000
Cash Beginning of Year	0	25,000	238,000
Increase (Decrease in Cash)	25,000	15,000	(58,000)
Cash End of Year	25,000	40,000	180,000

Index